CTORY

HMS Victory

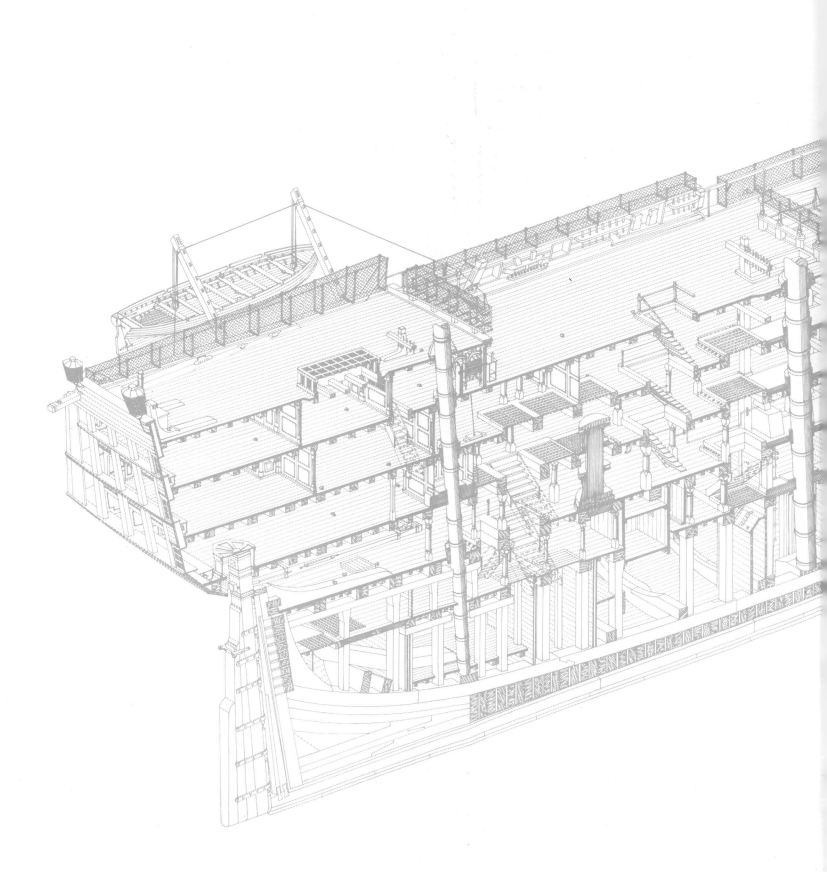

HMS VICTORY

Her Construction, Career and Restoration

Alan McGowan

Drawings by John McKay

NAVAL INSTITUTE PRESS
Annapolis, Maryland

First published in Great Britain in 1999 by
Chatham Publishing,
61 Frith Street,
London W1V 5TA

Published and distributed in the United States of
America and Canada by the Naval Institute Press,
291 Wood Road, Annapolis, Maryland 21402-5034

Library of Congress Catalog Card No. 99-75039

ISBN 1-55750-387-7

This edition is authorized for sale only in the United
States, its territories and possessions, and Canada.

Large-scale versions of the drawings found in this
book are available. Enquiries to: John McKay,
P. O. Box 752, Fort Langley, B. C., Canada V1M 2S2

Manufactured in Great Britain.

CONTENTS

Foreword

by Admiral Sir Michael Boyce KCB, OBE, ADC, *Chief of Naval Staff and First Sea Lord*

WHEN I WAS the Second Sea Lord and Commander-in-Chief Naval Home Command, I had the privilege of using HMS *Victory* as my flagship. My office overlooked this magnificent ship, and I would frequently see crowds of people, young and old, queuing to visit her. I was able to keep a close eye on the endless restoration work that is necessary to preserve her original splendour. Many times, I had the opportunity to use the Admiral's cabin to entertain the Royal Navy's guests, people from every walk of life and every corner of the world, all of whom would remember the occasion for ever, such is the enduring attraction and impact of this piece of living history.

Of course, *Victory* occupies a unique position in the affections of the Royal Navy. She is a constant reminder of a defining period in the history of our country and our Service; a period when Britain's status and prosperity as a world power depended on *Victory* and ships like her, together with the men that served in them and the strategic sea-power they represented. But to the men and women of the of the present Royal Navy she is more than a historical relic marking an important chapter in British history. She also remains as a living reminder to the sailor of today, and to the nation as a whole, of the man who lived on board her for the last two years of his life – Vice Admiral Lord Horatio Nelson.

We, in the Service, pay homage to Lord Nelson's life and death every year on 21 October, the anniversary of his last famous victory at the Battle of Trafalgar and the day of his death at the hands of a French marine sniper. At sunrise on that day, the Commander-in-Chief lays a wreath on the upper deck of *Victory* at the spot where Admiral Nelson fell mortally wounded. It is a moving ceremony which honours the man and his achievements.

And he certainly was a remarkable man. At sea from the age of twelve, he grew into a national hero who, through his remarkable victories, secured a century of maritime supremacy for Britain and who is, by common consent, regarded as the greatest naval officer of all time; and his example of leadership and courage is one upon which we are blessed to be able to draw.

But we must remember that *Victory* has an impressive record in her own right, and not just as Nelson's flagship. The first timbers of her keel were laid in 1759, launched in 1765, she saw active duty until 1812 so her career totalled some forty-seven years, a period seldom matched by any modern warship. She represents by any standards a remarkable feat of engineering, and she is testimony to the great skill and craftsmanship of the eighteenth century shipwrights who constructed her. Just walking through the decks, even the modern sailor cannot fail but be impressed by the complexity of this extraordinary fighting machine. Able to stay at sea for months on end, to cope with storm and battle damage, to support and sustain her crew of over eight hundred men, to remain capable of floating and sailing in the extreme conditions of battle and to bring to bear her devastating arsenal of one-hundred-and-four guns with maximum effect; that was *Victory*'s purpose. When one is on board, the sense of organisation, discipline, loyalty, determination, stamina and sheer courage necessary to make her the great ship she was emanates from every timber.

It would also be remiss in any foreword to a book about *Victory* to exclude her continued service – not just as the oldest warship anywhere still in commission, nor even as the Commander-in-Chief, Naval Home Command's flagship, but rather as the centrepiece of the Flagship Portsmouth initiative and our historic Portsmouth Dockyard. Together with her sister ships, the *Mary Rose* and HMS *Warrior*, *Victory* forms one of the greatest monuments to a maritime heritage anywhere in the world, one which sees well over a million visits each year and contributes enormously to the prosperity of Portsmouth and the surrounding area.

The modern Royal Navy is widely envied for its professionalism and success, attributes for which we depend hugely on our proud heritage and traditions. This naval ethos has at its very heart the legacy of Nelson and *Victory*. The two names stand side by side in history – indeed, it is a telling coincidence that the great man was born the very same year his future flagship was ordered by the Admiralty. Although anniversary events, celebrations, memorabilia and monuments all help to sustain his memory, there can be no substitute for being in the very ship in which he achieved his immortal reputation.

This book tells the story of that ship. It has been compiled with the true care and devotion of those captivated by the spirit of *Victory* and all she stands for. It is a fascinating and detailed biography of the lifetime of this historic vessel and I commend it to all.

Mike Boyce

ACKNOWLEDGEMENTS

I AM PLEASED to acknowledge the help and advice given by so many people in the production of this volume. That I am doubly indebted to nearly all of them I freely own, inasmuch as they have at various times also given valued support and encouragement to the *Victory* Advisory Technical Committee (VATC) and in particular to me as its chairman.

The origin of this book lay in a conversation with the late Lieutenant-Commander Peter Whitlock MBE, when he was a member of the VATC. Peter was a former *Mercury* boy who 'came up through the hawse-hole', retiring as the Commanding Officer of *Victory*. We spoke of Arthur Bugler's monumental work on the restoration and repair of *Victory* to which this volume owes much. It was published in 1966 but rapidly went out of print. The first thought was for a revised edition brought up to date, but for various reasons it was decided to start afresh. The result, I hope, is a work that presents *Victory* in the context of the eighteenth and early nineteenth century Navy, and an account of her restoration and repair since 1922 that is technically accurate whilst at the same time being readable and comprehensible to the layman.

Of the many busy people who have helped to make this book I must first thank Alec Barlow who had worked on *Victory* as a shipwright and who retired as Foreman of the Boat Shop. Alec did all the early work on Chapter 5, producing from the records a voluminous and highly detailed account of the repairs after 1964. This was reduced to a manageable size, together with a suggested draft for Chapter 6 by Keith Foulger, a member of the VATC and a retired Director of Naval Construction. I am

also greatly indebted to Constructor Commander Terry Eagle, former Base Naval Architect at Portsmouth, for his assistance and advice, as also for his contribution to Chapter 5 and in Aspects of Restoration. Brian Lavery, naval historian and another member of the VATC, has given sound advice, especially with regard to the excellent drawings, all of which have been produced by John McKay of Fort Langley, British Columbia. In this regard I have to thank Austin Farrar for his unhesitating agreement to provide John with copies of his cutter plans so that they might be redrawn. Dr Tony Bravery, also a member of the VATC, has been most helpful with the somewhat arcane science of the chemistry of wood and the pests and fungi that destroy it. In the early days there was assistance from Chris Giffen when he was Constructive Manager and from Brian Dolley of the Society for Nautical Research. I am indebted to David Hurst and his dockyard colleagues George Lawrence, Simon Murray and John Hayes for the provision of photographs, and to John Munday, a fellow committee member for drawing to my attention the splendid engraving by E W Cooke. Peter Goodwin, Curator HMS *Victory*, has been a mine of information and I thank him for allowing me to benefit from his painstaking research into the records of *Victory* and her contemporaries, especially during the period of her active career. His enthusiastic pursuit of detail has led to certain 'as Trafalgar' features on board that were unknown to Geoffrey Callender and his colleagues in the 1920s. I am pleased also to acknowledge the support and encouragement provided by successive Commanding Officers, in particular Lieutenant Commander Nowosielski. Early drafts of some sections were produced by typists at RNC Greenwich and Portsmouth Naval Base. Sue McGowan cheerfully accepted the task of producing the final version on disc. They all deserve my thanks.

Drafts were read by former Controller of the Navy, Admiral Sir Kenneth Eaton and John Coates, who retired as Deputy Director, Warship Design MOD, possessor of a fund of knowledge on wooden ships. Their comments and often detailed criticisms were of great value.

The Trustees of the National Maritime Museum have generously donated the use of illustrations of paintings and photographs in the Museum's collections and in this regard I wish to thank Lindsay MacFarlane, as well as the Reading Room staff and Tina Chambers of the Photographic Studio. Reproduction fees have also been waived by the Trustees of the Imperial War Museum, where Hilary Roberts and her staff in the Photographic Archive have been particularly helpful in tracking down photographic portraits. I am also indebted to the Controller of HMSO for permission to reproduce freely from Bugler's volume. I am especially grateful to the Navy Board in the person of Admiral Sir John Brigstocke, Second Sea Lord and Commander-in-Chief Naval Home Command, for permission to use the official records and photographs and to reproduce the six monthly report provided for the VATC's April meeting in 1992. Although it is evident that I have been helped by so many with the facts on which this text is based, any error that has crept in must be my responsibility. Finally, I am indebted to the Sir John Fisher Foundation for its generous contribution which has enabled me to use so many illustrations and drawings.

I am also pleased to record that no-one involved with the writing will receive any financial reward. All royalties will go to the Save the *Victory* Fund administered by the Society for Nautical Research.

INTRODUCTION

IN THE YEAR of the Battle of Trafalgar there were one hundred and sixteen ships of the line on the active list of the Royal Navy, and a roughly similar number in the navies of the rest of the world. *Victory* is the only one still in existence, having outlived all her contemporaries by more than a century. Indeed, she has also outlived her successors, with the exception of the remarkable HMS *Warrior*, all but one hundred years her junior, for these vessels continued to be the world's capital ships for fifty years after Trafalgar. None of her successors took part in a battle on the open sea; many, including *Warrior*, saw no action at all. It is appropriate that this unique specimen should have been present at Trafalgar, the last of the great sea battles under sail.

However, *Victory* is not still with us merely because she was at Trafalgar. She has been preserved principally because she was Lord Nelson's flagship. As such she was bound to play a key role in the battle, and she did, but the long one hundred years she spent stationary at buoys in Portsmouth Harbour were not at first the result of sentiment about Lord Nelson's association with her, or for the ship as a ship. On being removed from the active list she was used, as any other warship might have been, for purposes appropriate to her downgrading and increasing obsolescence. One suspects that sentiment did not enter into it until the 1860s, by which time she was one hundred years old. It is just possible that the then Superintendent of Portsmouth Dockyard, Rear Admiral Astley Cooper Key, decided that, because of her association with Lord Nelson, she should not be broken up. Instead she was 'found a job' as tender to her successor

as flagship, although there must have been a dozen other ships that might have been so used. In 1891, when she was paid off even from this most menial post, *Victory* was still not removed from the *Navy List*, no doubt with an eye to the Trafalgar Centenary looming on the horizon; she remained in the harbour, an all but dead hulk. Sentiment now began to take over, not only for the ship as a relic of Lord Nelson but also increasingly as a relic of Trafalgar and all it stood for.

However, until the work of Geoffrey Callender and others after the First World War, few people realised how fortunate it was that the ship preserved was the *Victory*. Whatever flagship Lord Nelson had chosen at Trafalgar would have been so revered: it might have been any one of the other half-dozen First Rates on the active list, but fortunately *Victory* was the ship available to carry Lord Nelson to his final command. Throughout her career, with a clean bottom – one free of marine growth – *Victory* sailed as well as any ship of the line and better than most. In his little book *HMS Victory*, first published in 1914, Geoffrey Callender averred that whenever she was available *Victory* was the first choice of any flag officer offered the command of a fleet. He was probably right, although after the Battle of St Vincent in 1797 Jervis moved his flag from *Victory* to the *Ville de Paris* as soon as she joined the Mediterranean Fleet. However, the *Ville de Paris* was newly built and straight out from Chatham Dockyard, while *Victory* had been in the Mediterranean for nearly two years. When she was surveyed in Portsmouth eight months later she was found to be in a very poor state. So the ship that is preserved at Portsmouth is not merely 'a

1

First Rate'; nor is she merely 'a First Rate that was Nelson's flagship'; she is the *nonpareil* of the sailing line-of-battle ships.

Those associated with *Victory* are often asked how much of the ship is original, although the enquirer usually means how much of the ship currently in No 2 Dock was at Trafalgar. As it happens, the questions amount to the same thing because the parts that are believed to have survived Trafalgar and the subsequent two hundred years are, with one exception, almost certainly original. The qualification is necessary because there is no document that catalogues those timbers that were not replaced or repaired. However, logic and the sometimes not very detailed accounts of what was repaired or replaced suggest that the following date from 1765: the keel, with the exception of about 18ft damaged during an air raid in 1941 and part of the keelson; the lower gun-deck, less some 270sq ft (out of more than 7000sq ft); the upper half of the sternpost; the four uppermost transoms, especially the huge wing transom at the foot of the lower counter timber, and the upper ends of twelve riders in the hold where they project several feet into the orlop. Nor should one forget the relic which, while not part of the structure of *Victory*, is most redolent of the events of the afternoon of 21 October 1805: *Victory*'s fore topsail. Although almost two hundred years old and shot through with holes, it is in remarkably good condition. When on display during the 1998 Festival of the Sea at Portsmouth it was viewed by hundreds of visitors at a time in awed silence.

Sadly, all this amounts to very little, but although we would like there to be far more, I am not certain that it matters very much. The ship underwent an enormous repair – almost a rebuild – in 1814, so that much, probably most, of what Nelson and Hardy knew of her went then. What matters is that the aura of the *Victory* of 21 October 1805 should have remained – and it has.

In 1923 Sir Philip Watts, Director of Naval Construction 1902–1912, addressed a meeting of the Institution of Naval Architects. He was at that time chairman of the SNR sub-committee to consider what steps should be taken to preserve and restore *Victory*, and in his paper he said,

> As a piece of practical wood shipbuilding, I hope that someday someone will trace out what may be called the life history of the structure of *Victory*, dealing with all matters bearing on her repairs from time to time and her exceptionally long life.

I hope that he would approve of this volume.

Alan McGowan
Beckenham
Trafalgar Day 1998

Chapter One

THE ROYAL NAVY IN THE EIGHTEENTH CENTURY

THROUGHOUT THE eighteenth century, and indeed until shortly after *Victory* had ceased her service as a line-of-battle ship, the Royal Navy was controlled by two bodies, the Board of Admiralty and the Navy Board[1]. The former executed the function of the Lord High Admiral, last effectively held by an individual in the seventeenth century, and was responsible for directing the service. Appointments to the Board were almost entirely political, but because so many naval officers were involved in politics the Board of Admiralty was rarely without some members of considerable sea experience. The Navy Board, on the other hand, consisted of professionals, and its principal officers were the Controller, the Treasurer, the Surveyor of the Navy and the Clerk of the Acts. The Controller was invariably a naval officer, usually a captain, while the Surveyor was always a former master shipwright at one of the Royal Dockyards. The Navy Board was responsible for the provision of the navy's material wants, men, ships, and therefore also dockyards.

The ships of the Royal Navy were deployed to safeguard the national interest; this meant that the principal fleet was based on the English Channel with squadrons in the Mediterranean, the West Indies, the North American coast, the East Indies and South Africa. The dispositions were increased in wartime according to the needs of the moment, but generally speaking the Mediterranean Fleet was second only in importance to the Channel Fleet.

The Navy's most important component was its battle fleet, the ships of the line, consisting of all those warships of 64 guns or more that were considered fit to take their place in the line of battle, virtually the only tactical configuration used in major actions. The most powerful warships, those of the First Rate, mounted 100 guns or more; flagships were invariably First Rates when these were available. With a full complement a First Rate carried well over eight hundred men of all ranks and because of this and their size, such ships were very expensive to build, maintain and operate. Rarely were there as many as ten First Rates, out of a total of between one hundred and fifty and one hundred and eighty ships of the line, in commission even in wartime. Second Rates carried 90–98 guns and about 740 men and were also expensive; there were rarely more than twenty in commission. The bulk of the line was made up of Third Rates of 64–84 guns, and of these by far the most numerous and the most effective were the 74-gun ships which had a complement of about six hundred. In general, the 74-gun Third Rates were the best sailers in the line. Because of their size, First and Second Rates did not normally handle so well, though *Victory* was a notable exception, which accounts for her popularity with flag officers.

The importance of the sailing qualities of a warship cannot be over-emphasised. The best point of sailing for most vessels was with the wind on the quarter. A well-handled ship of the line with a clean bottom might make about 11.5 knots; a frigate would make a little more than

---

1. The Admiralty Act of 1832 merged the Navy Board's responsibilities with those of the Admiralty Board.

12 knots[2], both speeds being the broad maxima recorded in the captains' reports required by the Admiralty. Speed depended very much on the state of the wind and sea, but more important than speed *per se* was the ability of the ship to go to windward. A clean, well-handled ship of the line could sail about six points off the wind (67.5°), but, as with speed, performance to windward fell off very quickly as the hull became foul with marine growth. For most of the time a ship of the line could probably do little better than about seven or seven-and-a-half points off the wind, roughly 79° – 84°.

The Fourth, Fifth and Sixth Rates were also normally the command of a captain. The Fourth Rate carried, 44 – 54 guns, but was of limited value as it had neither the power of a Third Rate nor the sailing qualities of the two lower rates. Fourth Rates were usually found on distant stations where, in peacetime at least, they were appropriate to the requirements while being reasonably cheap to man and maintain. The Fifth and Sixth Rates, mounting 32 – 40 guns and 24 – 28 guns respectively, sailed well and the efficient ones were prized by flag-officers for they were his scouts, the eyes of the fleet. Frigates, normally Fifth or Sixth Rates of 28 – 36 guns were popular with both officers and men because they were the ships most likely to be detached from the fleet for special duties and were therefore more often in positions to obtain prize money. These major warships were supported by a whole host of vessels that were smaller still. These were sloops, brigs, ketches and schooners – the first named might carry eighteen guns, the last two six or eight guns. Ship-rigged sloops were commanded by a master and commander, the remainder by a lieutenant.

For the men who manned all these ships, life was hard; but throughout the eighteenth century and for much of the nineteenth century, life ashore was also hard. For most of the eighteenth century the men were largely vol-

unteers. Impressment was used, especially during wartime, but the popular concept of the Press is quite at variance with the evidence except during the great wars with France at the end of the century. The powers of the Press were closely controlled, and even then the Regulating Officers received little co-operation from magistrates and other local officials. During the Seven Years War, for example, the Press was frequently refused permission to operate in a town; occasionally the officers were actually imprisoned[3].

Discipline was harsh, but it must be remembered that slovenly work by one man could endanger the ship and the life of everyone on board. For the most part floggings were not as common as is popularly supposed, although the threat was ever present. Flogging was worse in the Army, and in civilian life both men and women could be whipped at the tail of a cart for quite minor offences. Much more freely used than the cat of nine tails, which required a formal enquiry and logging by the captain, was the 'starter' – a rope's end – or the rattan wielded unofficially by the boatswain and his mates to keep the laggard up to the mark. As with the more widespread and perhaps less scrupulous use of the Press, floggings increased sharply during the Revolutionary and Napoleonic Wars, but by then the Navy was vastly larger and the problems of manning much greater. In addition, after about 1780 there was for ships' officers the spectre of mutiny and the prospect of a ruined career – or worse – as a consequence. Disaffection, such as it was, was rarely caused solely, or even principally, by the indiscriminate use of the lash.

The most common cause was the tardiness of pay, even the total lack of it. In 1780 an able seaman's pay of 29s 6d a month (ordinary seaman 23s 6d, landsman 21s 6d) was not generous, but if paid regularly would not have been unreasonable. One of the difficulties lay in the fact that service on the lower decks was not continuous. A man was engaged for a voyage or commission. During the great wars the problems of manning were such that a captain rarely let his men ashore. In any case pay might only be forthcoming when a ship reached its home port. If the administration was not efficient, either locally or at the Navy Office in London, the money was not immediately

2. A knot is a nautical mile (6080 ft) per hour.

3. N A M Rodger, *The Wooden World* (London, 1986) p169

4. Rodger p137 shows that some captains who were certain of their men gave leave, but this was much less likely in the very different conditions prevailing in the 1790s and after.

to hand; by the time it did arrive the ship might well have sailed again. With captains known to be reluctant to give shore leave and thereby to risk losing trained seamen – even if only to other warships when the money ran out – the local administration might well be dilatory in organising the pay muster. The other great cause for complaint – the lack of shore leave – also arose from the captain's unwillingness to hazard his career by the possibility of not having enough men to put to sea again[4].

Food was often, but not invariably, a cause for complaint. The rations allowed were in theory quite adequate. The problems were caused by venal victuallers who provided the supplies, and corrupt pursers who brought and issued them. Faults such as the poor quality of food, the use of dirty casks and blatant short measures all became exaggerated on a long voyage. As with the ferocity of the methods of enforcing discipline, the circumstances varied with each ship depending on the probity of the purser and that of his commanding officer.

There was no official uniform for the seaman. The clothes that he wore he had to make for himself or buy from the Purser's 'slops', the latter taking one shilling in the pound as discount for the service. The clothing on the slop list was in a sense therefore an unofficial uniform, a practical dress developed over the years. The seaman's dress was usually a checked shirt or blouse with a loose knotted kerchief at the neck, a short jacket usually blue, loose trousers – canvas for working, white duck for best if he was lucky – with a tarred canvas or, later, straw hat. On board ship he went barefoot, especially in the Mediterranean or the tropics. Ashore he liked to wear a more expensive version of his working rig with perhaps a red waistcoat, ribbons on his jacket and buckled shoes.

The ship's day was divided into watches of four hours beginning at 8pm (First Watch) until 4pm the next day,

A watercolour depicting two divisions of line of battle ships in close line-ahead on the larboard (port) tack. Fine seamanship and ship handling were required for this sort of station keeping even though the proximity of the ships in this view may be exaggerated. The smaller two-deckers were the most easily handled ships of the line, though *Victory* was considered one of the better three-deckers and was popular with flag officers. This watercoloure was painted by Daniel Tandy, a naval officer, whose sketchbook is in the National Maritime Museum. In common with many naval officers, Tandy became a competent artist because of the requirement for all young officers to include sketches – particularly landfalls – in their logs (NMM)

HMS *Revenge*, 74, in heavy weather off the Gironde on the French Atlantic coast, in 1814. The major ports of France were under continuous blockade almost throughout the war, to stifle trade and report on the movement of warships. Exposed to the full force of the Atlantic and with a hostile coastline to leeward, blockading was a dangerous task and no three-deckers were ever risked for this role. (NMM)

when the last four hours of the twenty four comprised two two-hour watches. The seamen, or the 'people', as those on the lower deck were called, were divided into two groups also called watches: the starboard watch and the larboard watch (the term 'port' instead of larboard was a mid-nineteenth century innovation). These groups were on duty in turn for each of the time watches so that the ship was always adequately manned. At any time however the cry for 'all hands' might turn up everyone – on watch or not – for a particular manoeuvre or emergency. The starboard and larboard watches were subdivided by place of work. In *Victory* for example, the numbers in each watch were roughly as follows: forecastle men thirty, foretopmen thirty-one, maintopmen thirty-

five, mizzentopmen fourteen, afterguard forty-seven, waisters eighty-five, quartermasters six, quartergunners fifteen, carpenter's crew seven, boatswain's mates four. Of these the prime seamen were the topmen. The afterguard was made up of ordinary seamen and landsmen while the waisters were largely the older or less skilled seamen who were unlikely to be nimble enough aloft. The remainder of the ship's company – a further 280 or so men – was made up of the officers and petty officers who stood watch; the day-workers, men who did not, such as the warrant officers, boatswain, purser, gunner, carpenter and cook, and the idlers – the warrant officer's mates, stewards and the like. Finally, there was the detachment of marines – some 135 officers and men on a First Rate. They were not in watches, but provided 24-hour sentries as required and at sea assisted the afterguard.

The hands were turned out of their hammocks at 4am at the beginning of the morning watch. Until 7.30am decks were scrubbed, paintwork washed down and guns cleaned; then at seven bells hammocks were taken up, and lashed into a sausage shape and stowed in the nettings on either side of the quarterdeck and waist. At eight bells–the end of the morning watch–hands went to breakfast. Dinner was at noon and supper at 5pm; at 8pm Lights Out was piped and the ship quietened for the night. Those men not in a watch might, if lucky, get seven or eight hours sleep; the watches would get just less than four hours at best. Between the pipes noted above there would be a well-ordered routine of sail, boat and gun drills for those not on watch. At week-ends the routine varied slightly; on Saturday the ship was cleaned from top to bottom ready for the captain's inspection on Sunday morning. Sunday afternoons, and usually Thursday afternoons, service permitting, were given to those not on watch. This free time the Navy still calls a 'make and mend', for that was the sailor's opportunity to wash and mend his clothes. His domestic duties done, the sailor spent what remained of this precious time yarning or, more probably, sleeping.

The most senior warrant officer was the master, who was responsible for navigation. It was his job to put the ship where the captain ordered that it should be. His importance may be gauged by the fact that although not a commissioned officer he was often paid more than anyone on board except the captain. He was responsible under the captain for all aspects of ship-handling, which because of the importance of the ship's trim also included the disposition of all stores and ballast. In a logical extension of this duty he was also responsible for the care of the stores. The boatswain was responsible for the rigging, sails, ground tackle, and all the equipment and stores necessary for rigging, mooring or anchoring the ship. A seaman of considerable experience, he worked directly to the first lieutenant. The gunner, also a warrant officer and often an experienced seaman, was responsible for the state of the guns and the supplies of powder and shot. He was required to make half-yearly returns to the Ordnance Board[5] and, on permission from the captain, to make a careful audit of all powder and shot expended. The carpenter, unlike most of his brother warrant officers, was not a seaman. A qualified shipwright, he was responsible for the care and maintenance of the hull, masts, spars and boats. He was required to

check the ship's hull daily and in action he and his mates were constantly on patrol, principally on the orlop.

Perhaps the least of the warrant officers was the surgeon: least, because his was an unsophisticated craft, given the lack of anaesthetics and the unhygienic surroundings in which he had to work. Worse still was his knowledge of medicine, although it was hardly inferior to the professional knowledge of his colleagues ashore. But of all the warrant officers, despite the rattan of the boatswain or the horrors of the surgeon's operating table, the most vilified was the purser. He was responsible for victualling the ship and in consequence was blamed for the quality and quantity of the food available, regardless of what might have been its state when shipped aboard or the length of time it had lain in the hold. In many cases, he had to buy stores at prices fixed by the Navy and sell them to the ship's company, at his own risk. He was certainly in a position frequently where he could defraud them, and not surprisingly was usually suspected of doing so. If the captain was honest and strictly oversaw the purser's activities, as he was required to do, the ship could expect fair treatment. If the purser and the captain were both venal, the crew had a thin time[6].

Below the warrant officers, whose name indicates that they were appointed by a warrant from the Board of Admiralty, as opposed to the sea officers from lieutenant upwards who all held the Sovereign's commission, were the petty officers whose appointment lay in the gift of the captain. They had immediate command over men working alongside them at specific jobs assigned. They were often the mates, or assistants, of warrant officers. The most important of these, certainly in terms of advancement, were the midshipmen and the master's mates. Two years service in either position, out of a minimum six years sea-time, was a pre–requisite to sitting

---

5. The guns and powder were supplied by the Board of Ordnance, a totally separate department independent of the Admiralty.

6. Brian Lavery, *Shipboard Life and Organisation 1731-1815* (Navy Records Society vol 138) pp551-608 gives examples of Gunner's Accounts *Victory* 1793; Purser's Accounts and Journal *Victory* 1795-98; Boatswain's Accounts Britannia 1805; and Carpenter's Accounts *Africa* 1805, illustrating many of the day-to-day responsibilities of these warrant officers.

the examination for lieutenant. There was no other way to wardroom rank, and although a few young men had a much easier passage than others, the regulations were immutable in the letter if occasionally not in the spirit.

The officers were mostly drawn from the ranks of the middle-class and younger sons of the nobility. The first step up the rungs of the naval ladder was to be appointed midshipman. This could be gained by one of two ways: by the patronage of a captain or by service as a volunteer – listed officially as an officer's servant – until the captain was satisfied that the right standard of seamanship had been reached to qualify for service as a midshipman. Even acceptance as a volunteer of course involved a considerable degree of patronage.

The gundeck of the *Bellerophon* showing the 32-pounder guns – the British fleet's main armament – run out. Each gun weighed in the region of three tons and required a crew of twelve men. The spaciousness depicted in this watercolour is misleading for some 250 men would have lived on this deck. (NMM)

Some officers received their commission as lieutenant after many years spent on the lower deck, rising gradually by ability to warrant officer or master's mate. Others qualified to sit the lieutenant's examination by learning their seamanship in the merchant service and then being accepted into the Navy as a petty officer[7]. Generally speaking, midshipmen were teenage boys whose family connections had secured them their opportunity. It was not uncommon however for a child of ten or twelve to be appointed. The very young midshipmen lived in the gunroom – at the after end of the lower gundeck on a ship of the line – where they were supervised by the gunner. The older midshipmen berthed on the orlop. With the exception of navigation, the practice of which required a knowledge of mathematics, their naval education was severely practical: they learned by doing. A midshipman worked alongside seamen but with the added responsibility of seeing that they were efficient. He might be responsible for the working of particular sails or a boat or

a number of guns. At the age of twenty years, with six years' sea experience, a midshipman could sit the examination for lieutenant, the first real hurdle in his professional career. As a lieutenant his responsibilities increased. He might be the most junior of five or six in a ship of the line, increasing in seniority as experience and opportunity permitted. He would stand watch, when he would be immediately responsible for the handling of the ship; he might, in action, be responsible for one of the gundecks, command a cutting-out expedition with a number of the ship's boats, or he might be given command of a small prize to be sailed to the nearest friendly port. When senior, he might have command of a small despatch vessel – brig or schooner perhaps – but it was usually as a successful first lieutenant of a rated ship, where he would be responsible to the captain for the running of the ship in all respects, that he would be considered for promotion to captain. After three successful years in that rank he would probably be made a post-captain, the second and most important hurdle. Once made 'post', whether employed or not, he would be certain to reach flag rank provided he outlived those ahead of him in seniority in the *Navy List*. In 1746 the rank of Commander (known as Master and Commander until 1794) was introduced to provide for those circumstances where the mission or the ship carried more responsibility than could reasonably be demanded of a lieutenant yet did not warrant the rank of captain. The 24-gun ship-rigged sloops – the largest of their class – were normally a commander's appointment. Rated ships, other than sloops, also carried a Master. The captain of any vessel in the Royal Navy was, as he still is, entirely responsible for his ship and his ship's company, regardless of the size of the vessel or his actual rank. Admiralty Regulations and Instructions left little to chance. He was enjoined, in some detail, to make sure that his officers of all ranks, from first lieutenant to warrant officers, carried out their duties effectively. He was to see that all accounts were properly kept and duly rendered, and he was required most especially to see that his ship's company was kept clean and healthy. Ships of the line and frigates would always have had a post-captain in command.

It has been seen that patronage could, and usually did, play an important part in the promotion and employment of an officer[8]. Once he had reached post rank, however, and particularly flag rank, patronage was superseded by politics unless the patron was very highly placed indeed. There were influential political admirals in both the Whig and the Tory parties and although patronage, both personal and political, can be over-emphasised as a means of advancement in the eighteenth-century Navy, more than one career was ruined, and a similar number made, because of the officer's political connections. There were three grades of Admiral, in ascending order Rear-Admiral, Vice-Admiral and Admiral, but with so many each rank was also sub-divided into three. The most junior at each level wore the blue ensign at his masthead, the most senior the red ensign with the white ensign at the intermediate level. Admirals were known therefore by these distinctions and so described. At Trafalgar, for example, the Commander–in–Chief, Lord Nelson, was a Vice Admiral of the White; Collingwood, his second-in-command was a Vice-Admiral of the Blue, the Earl of Northesk, Rear-Admiral of the White. Successful officers were often promoted by two intermediate colour ranks, but rarely, if ever, was a major rank – Rear-Admiral or Vice-Admiral – so avoided.

From the standpoint of the twentieth century there was much wrong with the system of promotion in the Navy of the eighteenth century. In practice however it generally worked, pehaps because with long periods spent at sea and with the Seven Years' War and the twenty years of war at the end of the century there were so many very able officers that although A might be preferred to B for social or political reasons, the difference the choice made to the service was merely one of degree. Those in command were rarely utterly incompetent, however unsatisfactory the system might appear to us.

---

7. Captain James Cook was one such, having learned his seamanship in the coal trade; entered the Navy as an able seaman 1755, rising rapidly to master's mate, master 1759, lieutenant 1768, commander 1771, captain 1775.

8. The whole question of patronage, ability and the system generally is dealt with by Michael Lewis, The Navy of Britain (London, 1948), pp250-285 and N A M Rodger *op cit* pp252-302, the latter comprehensively.

Chapter Two

BUILDING HMS VICTORY AND HER MAINTENANCE 1758–1805

WITH THE PROSPECT of a long war ahead, in December 1758 a bill was passed in Parliament for the building of twelve ships of the line including one First Rate. A few days later the Commissioner at Chatham Dockyard was ordered to commence work on this new ship as soon as a suitable dock could be made ready. The Navy Board, responsible for the design and construction of all vessels ordered by the Admiralty, decided that the new ship should be built on the lines of the *Royal George*. The design was the work of Sir Thomas Slade, Surveyor of the Navy, and the minutes of the Navy Board for 6 June 1759 record:

Sheer draught proposed for building a First Rate ship of 100 guns at H.M. Yard at Chatham pursuant to an order from the Rt. Hon. Lords Commissioners of the Admiralty of 13th December last and of the dimensions undermentioned viz.,

Length on the gun deck 186ft.
Length of the keel for tonnage 151ft. 3⅝in.
Breadth moulded 50ft. 6in.
Breadth extreme 51ft. 10in.
To carry on the lower deck 30 guns of 42 pounds
To carry on the middle deck 28 guns of 24 pounds
To carry on the upper deck 30 guns of 12 pounds
To carry on the after deck 10 guns of 6 pounds
To carry on the forecastle 2 guns of 6 pounds

signed at the Admiralty Office by J Cleveland on the 15 June 1759. Three weeks later 'The Principal Officers

and Commissioners of His Majesty's Navy'–who constituted the Navy Board–despatched the following letter to the officers of Chatham Dockyard:

Pursuant to the order from the Rt Hon the Lords Commissioners of the Admiralty dated 13th December 1758 and 14th of the last month, these are to direct and require you to cause to be set up and built at your yard a new ship of 100 guns agreeable to the draught herewith sent to you and of the dimensions set down on the other side hereof, and you are forthwith to prepare and send us in due form an estimate of the charge of building and fitting for sea the said ship, and providing her with masts, yards, sails, rigging and store to an eight months' proportion. For which this shall be your warrant. Dated at the Navy Office the 7th July 1759.

The instruction was signed by Richard Hall, Thomas Slade, G Adams and Thomas Brett[1].

The new First Rate was begun on 23 July 1759 in the yard's second dock which had been completed in 1623[2]. Naturally, for so important a vessel, the man immediately responsible for her construction was the Master Shipwright of the Yard, one John Lock, who on his death in 1762 was succeeded by Edward Allin.

Victory–the name had been set aside for the ship in October 1760–was not floated up until 7 May 1765, so it is evident that her building was fairly leisurely. The reason for this is almost certainly that, with the battle of Quiberon Bay in 1759, the Year of Victories, a mere five months after the great ship's keel had been laid, the

Sir Thomas Slade (*fl*1703-1771). Portrait by an unknown artist. Slade was joint Surveyor of the Navy 1755-1770. (Greenwich Hospital Collection in the NMM)

French navy had ceased to be a potent force in the war. In such circumstances there was nothing to be gained by hurrying the construction of an expensive warship that was unlikely to be completed before the end of the war. Indeed, there were doubtless those who considered her completion an ill-timed and unnecessary expense. The six years of *Victory*'s, building however, brought her the inestimable advantage that her structural timbers had had time to season in frame, that is, in their position during building and before being enclosed, a fact that had considerable bearing on her longevity.

Victory was built of oak in the manner that had nearly two centuries of tradition behind it and which was to continue as long as wooden ships were built. The first stage was to build what one might call the skeleton, the backbone of which was the keel and its supporting keelson. These connected the stem at the bow with the huge timber that formed the sternpost. In the case of *Victory* the sternpost had to be worked from a single piece of oak 34ft long and measuring 25in square for at least half its length. The closely-spaced frames formed the ribs of the skeleton and delineated the shape of the hull. A frame was made up of double timbers of the appropriate shape, beginning with the floor-timbers and their adjoining first futtocks up to the top-timbers at the bulwarks, the scarphs being staggered to avoid creating weak areas.

The whole was locked together by the inner and outer planking, which varied in thickness according to its position and use. Some strakes were given names that indicated their purpose. Internally there was first the ceiling[3] and then clamps, waterways and spirketting. Externally there were the garboard strakes, bottom planking, diminishing planks and wales[4]. This structure was held rigid by transverse deck beams which stretched between port and starboard frames at the appropriate level, by pillars supporting the beams and by the decks themselves. Three methods of fastening were used: treenails, oak or beech pegs up to 2in in diameter and 3ft long; wrought-iron bolts, some of which in a First Rate could be 12ft long, driven through holes drilled with a hand auger; and wrought-iron spikes. The entire structure was stiffened by the process of caulking, the skilful insertion of lengths of oakum into the seams of both hull and deck planking. The caulked seams were then payed (covered) with pitch to make them watertight.

This greatly simplified description of the building process makes it sound straightforward, but of course it

1. Arthur Bugler, *Victory* pp8-9.

2. Alan McGowan, *The Jacobean Commissions of Enquiry 1608 and 1618*, NRS vol 116.

3. This may originally have been 'sealing' as the planks cover the frames on the inside. However the term, some 350 years old as spelt, has a certain logic in that it lies upon, and therefore above, the floors.

4. With the exception of the top four strakes where the thickness decreased to 2½in, the lightest planking was 4in thick. The wales are heavier bands of planking to strengthen the hull, especially at its extreme breadth (the main wale) and where it is subject to stress, *eg* that from the shrouds (the chain wale). The heaviest planking in the main wale of a First Rate was 10in thick.

was not. The provision of the timber alone presented a huge problem. It has been computed that an average oak tree felled for ship timber produced about one load, which made roughly two-thirds of a ton of shipping. *Victory* therefore, at 2,162 tons required something in the region of three thousand trees.

Felled timber had to be drawn to the nearest port or waterway by relays of teams consisting of a dozen or more oxen or horses, depending upon the conditions. Distances covered were rarely more than 30 miles, but by the mid-eighteenth century all the forests most easily worked had been depleted if not exhausted. A century earlier, the Justices of the Peace in Hampshire had protested at the demand that they should provide six hundred teams for the carriage of two hundred loads of timber from Alice Holt Forest to the nearest waterway.

Admiral of the Fleet Richard, 1st Earl Howe (1726-1799), painted by J S Copley. *Victory* was 'Black Dick' Howe's flagship from April to November 1782. (Caird Collection in the NMM)

This was probably the River Wey some ten or twelve miles northeast, to the northeast of Godalming[5]. Alice Holt was one of the few remaining royal forests providing ship timber at the time of *Victory*'s building, and the physical problems of moving huge logs weighing more than a ton had not changed.

By 1759 not all the oak was home grown, and a large proportion of the oak planking would have come from the Baltic. The other major shipbuilding timber used for structural members was elm, which is tough with a cross grain that holds fastenings well. The large size of the tree provides long lengths of great timber (*ie* large in section) and plank. Although elm deteriorates rapidly when exposed alternately to air and moisture, it is extremely durable when kept wet and not allowed to dry. For this reason elm was frequently used for the keel, thus saving the lengths of large section oak timber for use elsewhere, and for the garboard strakes – the lowest runs of planking – which were always below the waterline. *Victory*'s original keel, of which much still remains in place, consisted of seven lengths with each of the six scarphs 5ft long. The keel timbers were 21in wide throughout its length, but from being square amidships the keel reduced slightly in width towards the sternpost.

Upon the completion of her hull in the summer of 1765, and with the war long since over, *Victory*, rigged with her lower masts only, was put 'in Ordinary', that is, kept with minimal rigging and manned only by her standing warrant officers – boatswain, gunner, carpenter, purser and cook – supported by a number of shipkeepers. It is not clear from the records when *Victory* was rigged. Money was granted for her masts, spars and rigging in 1765. There was no need for design work as the masting and rigging of each vessel was standard according to her size and class. There is no evidence as to what happened to *Victory* next, but probably the masts, spars and cordage were made up, fitted and then struck and laid aside in a storehouse, for *Victory*'s sailing trials did not take place until 1769.

The standard rig for all rated ships in the Royal Navy was ship rig, *ie* with square sails on all three masts. A square sail is one that receives the wind on the after side, with its centre roughly above the centre line of the ship. A fore and aft sail may receive the wind on either side depending upon which tack the ship is on, *ie* whether the wind is to port or to starboard. Square sails are set on yards which, although capable of being braced to some degree to either side, are fastened to the mast with their centre above the centre line of the ship. The exact positioning of the masts on the ship's centreline was crucial to achieve the right balance. On a ship-rigged warship each mast had two extensions: topmast and topgallant mast. Each mast and extension had a yard on which its sail was spread. The lowest sails were called courses; above them and somewhat larger in area were the topsails. The topgallant masts carried two yards, for the topgallant sails and the royals. Two small square sails, the spritsail and the spritsail topsail, could be set below the bowsprit. With the exception of the royals and the spritsails, all the square sails could be enlarged in light airs by studding sails spread to booms extended from the adjacent yards. The fore-and-aft sails at the bow consisted of two jibsails, a fore staysail and a fore topmast staysail. All four were triangular and, as the name implies, were set on stays. Between the masts, other staysails could be set and at the stern was the spanker or driver, a large fore-and-aft sail set on a gaff and boom.

Broadly speaking, the square sails provided the power, and the fore-and-aft sails the ability to go to windward; the headsails and the spanker, particularly the former, gave the ship manoeuvrability by providing the force to move the bows and stern either way when required.

The deflection caused by movement of the rudder was important of course, but the rudder would have been of little use if the ship was not well balanced. This was achieved by the correct positioning of the masts to suit the hull shape, and by the trim of the ship and the skilled use of the appropriate sails according to the requirements of the moment.

When she was floated up in 1765 the *Victory* had a list to starboard. A slight list either way was not uncommon because of the variable density of timber and usually the problem was solved quite easily by ballasting the ship appropriately. Such was the case with *Victory*, and with an

additional 38 tons of ballast she successfully completed the sailing trials which were the last in a series of inspections held to satisfy the Navy Board that the ship was adequate to be taken into service. For the trials she was rigged and approximately stored as she would be when in commission.

One disturbing fact that became apparent was that when fully rigged and stored and in sailing trim, *Victory*'s lower deck gunports were only 4ft 6in above the waterline, 9in lower than Slade, her designer, had planned. The reason is not clear, but it was probably due to unforeseen extra weight because the density of timber, even from the same species of tree, is not constant. In any case the fault was not discovered – and perhaps could not have been discovered – until it was far too late to make the necessary changes. While it is true that use of the lower-deck guns were restricted in heavy weather, it is fortunately also the case that there is no evidence of its having made the ship seriously less effective in any action of importance.

There is no detailed record of the trials, and it seems probable that they were classed as merely satisfactory. In commission later, however, *Victory* proved to be an excellent sailer, particularly so for a First Rate. The reason lies in a combination of three factors: design, trim and handling. The design was the responsibility of the Surveyor of the Navy, Sir Thomas Slade, and referred principally to the underwater shape and the positioning of the masts, the length and proportion of which were set by established regulations. The trim, *ie* how the ship sat in the water and the stiffness of the ship under sail, while determined by the design, could also be greatly affected by the overall weight distribution of the men and material on board. A First Rate normally drew between 15in and 24in more by the stern than by the bow. Once the ship was in commission this trim was achieved by the sailing master according to the captain's requirements.

Experienced officers found that certain measures

---

5. National Maritime Museum CAD/A13 folio 108b; also Alan McGowan, *The Naval Miscellany* V NRS 125 p9. The '600 teams' presumably means 600 team hauls.

worked well to improve the performance of a ship and applied them accordingly, even when they ran counter to accepted standard practice or even contravened Establishment regulations. If the captain of a 74-gun ship found that he could improve her sailing qualities by redistributing the weight of two guns by placing them in the hold as ballast, he is likely to have so ordered it. As for the reaction of his superiors, it was far more important that he should get his ship into action promptly with only 72 guns than arrive ten minutes too late bearing her full complement of 74.

Until the nineteenth century, all ships were built with bio-degradable material—wood—and rigged with rope made from hemp, and canvas made from flax. In the nature of things therefore, any vessel, no matter the care taken in her building, began to deteriorate from the moment she was launched. The decline was accelerated by wind and waves and by the seepage of rainwater into the timber, a process aided by the thousands of joints in her structure each of which moved slightly with the motion of the ship. There was yet a further hazard. English oak was the prime shipbuilding timber because of its solid durability, but it was susceptible to the gribble and the ship-worm. The gribble is the common name for *Limnoria*, a small crustacean of about ⅛in in length. Although its burrows are not deep they can so weaken the surface of the timber that it becomes easily eroded. The ship-worm, the *Teredo Navalis*, on the other hand, is 3–4in long and perhaps ³⁄₁₀in in diameter. Widespread infestation by the *Teredo* can be a direct threat to the strength of planking or even timbers. And in tropical waters both creatures can be very much larger.

For nearly two centuries the Navy Board had sought ways of keeping ship bottoms free from weed that inhibited sailing qualities, and attacks from the gribble and ship-worm. The results had been ineffective. Any preparation which inhibited weed did not last long enough to be worth the time and cost. The attempts to counter

Limnoria and *Toredo Navalis* had largely consisted of a sacrificial fir sheathing. Unfortunately it proved impossible to gauge accurately how long the sheathing would last before the worm reached the hull beyond, and the sheathing itself frequently reduced the sailing qualities of the vessel.

Soon after the end of the Seven Years' War in 1763, the frigate *Alarm* had spent two years in the West Indies with a coppered bottom, but although she had remained free of weed and attack from the worm, the corrosion of the iron bolts as a result of the galvanic action between them and the copper caused serious doubts about its safe use. During the next ten years experiments were made in the means of protecting the bolts, successfully enough for the Navy Board, rather optimistically perhaps, to order the coppering of all vessels. In 1780 alone some forty six major warships were coppered, including *Victory* during her refit. In fact the problem of safe coppering was not completely solved for another six years, when the Navy Board required the dockyards to replace all iron fastenings in the vicinity of copper sheathing with others made of an alloy that did not react to it[6].

One hazard not mentioned above is the incipient rot that is to be found in large timber that is inadequately seasoned. While this is in theory avoidable, it is not always the case in practice, for rot is often quite difficult to detect. In addition there was always the danger that, pressed to complete a ship or finish a repair because of the needs of the service, especially in wartime, short cuts might be taken using timber of uncertain quality. With all these problems it is not surprising that wooden ships needed frequent attention, and where possible the design included features intended to reduce the cost of repair in the event of damage. For example, in order to protect the keel proper in the event of grounding, a false keel 6in thick was fitted immediately below it. Moreover, the false keel was fastened from the outside so that it could be replaced cheaply and easily. Steps such as this however, had only limited application.

Dockyard repairs were classed as small, middling or large dependent upon the total cost, which included not only that required for repair of the defects but also the

6. R J B Knight, 'The Introduction of Copper Sheathing 1779-1786', *The Mariner's Mirror* vol 59 pp299-309, gives an excellent account of the problem and its solution.

cost of all other work deemed necessary. This could range from major modifications resulting from a change in design – usually introduced only when the vessel already required major work on her – to minor changes in dockyard practice such as, in 1771, painting the bottom of ships' boats with white lead instead of using a resin or tar compound. Understandably the repairs themselves frequently grew in size as outer coverings of timber were removed and the true extent of the damage became apparent.

The dockyard term for dismantling was 'ripping down', an unfortunate expression seeming to imply a destructive tearing-apart of the hull structure. In fact, 'taking to pieces', the term used by the Navy Board to describe shipbreaking, was far more accurate. It was just that, a careful taking to pieces so that re-usable timber might not be wasted. Metal clench bolts were backed out after the clench had been cut away with a cold chisel, and could often be re-used as a shorter fastening. If the bolts could only be released by cutting with a special saw, for example through the join between two timbers, the remains of the copper or iron fastenings were removed and kept as valuable scrap. Timbers were only split out when the wood was clearly of no further use or when there was no other way of removing it. Beam ends, frequently damp but totally enclosed by other timbers, were a common source of rot. When discovered, the decayed end was cut back to sound timber and either a new piece was scarphed in or the shortened beam was used elsewhere. If it could not be used in the same ship, then it was laid aside in the dockyard for use in another. Recovered timber of this sort was especially valuable because it not only saved the cost of new timber of equivalent size, but was better than new timber because it had become thoroughly seasoned.

The shrinking of inboard timbers as they dried out caused fastenings to become loose, which the continual movement of the ship while afloat made still worse. The loosened joints allowed the ingress of damp and, with so many of the joints covered on at least three sides, the lack of air soon resulted in rot. In certain places the joints could be hardened up with wedges and stopped up or

payed to keep out further moisture. Too often the fastenings had to be released, the faying surfaces refinished and new fastenings put in. The moment the ship floated out, the deterioration cycle began again, and although the ship's carpenter inspected the hull daily while at sea, he could deal effectively only with minor problems. Masts, spars and rigging also always came under close scrutiny and received attention whenever the vessel was docked for repairs. The condition of these items was monitored carefully by the boatswain and his mates, who carried out a steady programme of maintenance and repair while the ship was in commission. However, the

Rear Admiral John Jervis, 1st Earl St Vincent (1735-1823), painted by Sir William Beechey. Jervis hoisted his flag in *Victory* in December 1795 and hauled it down in February 1797 after the Battle of Cape St Vincent (NMM)

masts, spars, rigging and sails bore the brunt of the wear and tear. As with the hull timbers, nothing was discarded that could be used elsewhere. Damaged spars were reduced in size and remade for other purposes, worn but serviceable sails and rigging were laid aside where appropriate for use on smaller vessels or vessels on harbour service, which were not likely to be exposed to the rigours of a full gale for days on end.

With all these hazards to her well being, irrespective of any injury that might be inflicted by an enemy, it is evident that a wooden ship, even one as well-built as *Victory*, needed daily maintenance and continual repair. In 1771, six years after floating up and only two years after her sailing trials whence she had been returned to Ordinary in the Medway, it was discovered that defective planking below the waterline was causing a serious leak. At 10in per hour when moored, the water intake was only surpassed by the 12in per hour while on tow to Gibraltar after Trafalgar. As a result a proposal to put her into commission because of the worsening political situation had to be shelved. The repair took six months, by which time the crisis had passed and *Victory* was again returned to the Ordinary. Four years later a virtually identical problem arose which required another six months in Chatham Dockyard. The cause is not recorded, but Bugler is probably correct when he says that it was most likely to have been the effects of either gribble or *Teredo*, as in each case she had lain for years on the Medway moorings that were known to be infested[7].

The entry of France into the War of American Independence in February 1778 led to *Victory*'s first commission, which lasted from March of that year until November 1782 when she paid off at Portsmouth. The five or six weeks in the dockyards in 1778 were spent preparing her for service with minor repairs to hull, spars and rigging and loading her with stores and ordnance. She was also brought up to date in minor details such as

the fitting of sash ports abaft the forward bulkheads of the quarters for the admiral and the captain, the fitting of deadeyes that could be removed relatively easily, and the painting of boats which has already been noted. These modifications had been authorised in 1771 but would not have been carried out until preparations for commissioning made them necessary.

Once a ship came out of the Ordinary, she took on board her guns, which had been removed to reduce the strain on her timbers. Throughout *Victory*'s active career there was only one major weapon at sea: the smooth-bore muzzle-loading gun. This came in varying sizes from the largest, the 42-pounder, to the 6-pounder, the smallest used as a main armament for any vessel in the Royal Navy. Naturally, within this range the smaller the ship, the smaller the gun; but most vessels carried at least two sizes, the heavier on the lowest gundeck with lighter guns mounted higher in the ship on the quarterdeck or forecastle.

Thus *Victory*, a First Rate, nominally of 100-guns although at Trafalgar she carried 104 guns, disposed her armament as follows:

Lower deck	30	32-pounders
Middle deck	28	24-pounders
Upper deck	30	12-pounders
Quarterdeck	12	12-pounders
Forecastle deck	2	12-pounders
	2	68-pounder carronades

Each type of gun was known by the weight of the solid shot it used, for instance 32lbs. The 32-pounder was the heaviest of those commonly used in the Royal Navy, although the 42-pounder had been introduced in the middle of the eighteenth century. Indeed, we have seen that it was specified for the *Victory* at her fitting out in 1759 as it was at subsequent refits. Certain officers preferred the lighter 32-pounder, which had the advantage of carrying less weight and having a faster rate of fire with little loss of penetrating power. To depart from the establishment laid down for a ship's main armament however required a captain – or more probably a flag-offi-

---

7. Bugler p15.

8. Each member of a gun's crew was given a number according to his duties. The number one was the gun captain. The slow match was a loosely laid length of rope steeped in saltpetre solution which burned at about one inch an hour.

cer – of considerable reputation and influence. Admiral Keppel, the first to hoist his flag in *Victory*, was one such. Lord Nelson was another, but to show how much this was a matter of personal opinion, it should be noted that flag officers of great ability such as Howe, Hood and Jervis all preferred the heavier gun.

The 32-pounder weighed approximately 3 tons and normally had a crew of thirteen men, one of whom, the powder-man, was usually a boy whose job it was to keep the gun supplied with cartridges and shot from the magazine and shot lockers. The establishment allowed for crews for one broadside only, which on a First Rate amounted to some four hundred and fifty men, rather more than half the total complement. In the fairly rare actions when both broadsides were needed it is probable that a crew served two guns adjacent on the same broadside. The number of men per gun was based roughly on a ratio of one man per 500lbs but this excluded the weight of the massively-built wooden carriage which could add another 100lbs per man. A full crew serving two guns successively would certainly achieve a faster rate of fire than a half-crew on each gun.

The gun was trained laterally by the use of handspikes under the carriage and vertically by adjusting the position of the quoin, a heavy wooden wedge inserted between the breech and the rear axle tree. The gun was fired by the number one jerking the lanyard which operated the flint lock, causing a spark to ignite the powder. In case the flint lock failed the match tub nearby contained a length of slow match[8].

Sections of five or six guns were under the charge of midshipmen, with a lieutenant commanding the whole deck who had his instructions as to the particular type of shot to be used. Most commonly it was the solid ball, approximately 6in in diameter for a 32-pounder. The gun might be double-shotted at close range or loaded with anti-personnel case-shot, which burst upon impact releasing its deadly cargo of small iron balls. Alternatively chain or bar shot – heavy balls or discs connected by chain or solid bars – might be used to cut rigging and so disable the enemy by bringing down a mast.

The extreme range was something approaching 2500 yards; at close range, say 400 yards, a 32-pound solid shot could penetrate 3ft of timber. In some actions, notably at St Vincent (1797) and Trafalgar (1805), ships were laid alongside each other barely feet apart.

Victory's first engagement – the indecisive battle off Cape Ushant in July 1778 – was followed by three weeks in the dockyard at Plymouth, largely for repair to topsides and to masts and rigging. The ship quickly returned to the Channel Fleet until in April 1779 she was given a refit at Portsmouth, during which her name was painted in large letters on the stern and the 42-pounder guns restored to the lower gundeck. After a further twelve months with the Channel Fleet she was again brought into Portsmouth for refit. On this occasion, however, there was rather more to it than the repairs of wear and tear and the introduction of minor modifications.

At the conclusion of her 1780 refit, *Victory* returned to the Channel Fleet and in the course of the next two years had brief spells successively as flagship, private ship and then flagship again for five different flag officers. The last of these, Admiral Lord Howe, joined *Victory* on 20 April 1782 following his appointment to the command of the Channel Fleet, but the ship wore Lord Howe's flag hardly any longer than that of his immediate predecessors. Following the relief of Gibraltar and the action against the French and Spanish fleets off Cape Spartel later in the year, *Victory* returned to Portsmouth, where Howe struck his flag on 14 November. *Victory* had suffered some damage to her hull and rigging in the action which Howe doubtless viewed with mixed feelings: although the outcome had been successful, the launch towed astern of the flagship had been destroyed. Unfortunately the launch had contained the furniture from his sleeping and dining cabins and no doubt that from the quarters of the flag captain as well, for in clearing for action all such effects were removed to facilitate the working of the guns and to reduce the danger of fire.

Victory was paid off for refit, to be returned to Ordinary on its completion, a new government being determined to end the war. Despite previous refits the cumulative effects of the years at sea as well as the damage inflicted by the enemy, were becoming evident. *Victory* was laid up in Ordinary in March 1783, but brought up to date to comply with the regulations introduced since her previous period in the dockyard. Thus her quarterdeck and forecastle 6-pounders were exchanged for 12-pounder guns and the shot racks were moved from the sides of the deck to the centreline. The introduction of copper sheathing had necessitated an order in May 1780 that all anchor stocks must from then on be rounded, as the square corners were liable to damage the copper whilst the anchors were being worked. However, it seems probable that this minor but important modification was carried out by the ship's carpenter and his mates. During this refit, *Victory* had her sides painted for the first time. The order abandoning the old practice of paying them had been issued in 1780, but too late to be applied to the ship at that year's refit.

From 1783 until 1787 *Victory* remained in Ordinary, receiving attention only from her shipkeepers and an annual inspection followed by the minimal repair from the dockyard. The brief crisis over the Netherlands in 1787 saw a number of ships, including *Victory*, made ready for active service, but the danger was short-lived and by the end of the year most of the vessels had been returned to the reserve. The affair brought some benefit to *Victory* because it had highlighted her somewhat parlous state. One wonders how long she could have been kept at sea had the crisis demanded it, for in April 1788 she had the first of her three great repairs in Portsmouth Dockyard and one which cost £37,523 17s 1d[9]. It is evident that the repairs necessary required a considerable amount of the structure to be opened up, as it was decided to alter the position of all three masts. Beginning with the foremast, they were moved aft by 2ft, 1ft and 6in respectively.

So drastic a change would have been made only as a result of experience, and presumably came about following recommendations from former captains, perhaps even from Lord Howe himself. The increased trim by

---

9. It is virtually impossible to relate such costs in the late eighteenth century to today's values with any accuracy. However, a multiple of say 200 gives some idea.

the stern and, one may surmise, greater weatherliness improved the ship's sailing qualities, and although there seems to be no direct evidence, it may be that *Victory*'s reputation as an excellent sailer in all weathers dates from this time. *Victory* had already proved to be a ship which was popular with flag officers as discerning as Keppel, Kempenfelt and Howe, and her best years were yet to come.

As usual there were a number of modifications to be made so that *Victory* would conform to the latest regulations. By an order of September 1783, the 'people's' accommodation, that is the lower deck, middle deck and the forecastle, was whitewashed and the cabins painted. Cabins, it should be noted, with the exception of those for the admiral and his flag captain, usually consisted of canvas screens that could be quickly struck to give the gun crew room and to reduce the risk of fire. Following the completion of the large repair *Victory* once more returned to Ordinary. Two years later, however, another crisis in Europe caused her to be brought forward for active service. Originally *Victory* was to have again worn the flag of Admiral Lord Howe as C-in-C Channel Fleet, but he changed to the newly built First Rate, *Queen Charlotte*. *Victory* was the flagship of Lord Hood until 1791. The following year it was decided to send her to the Mediterranean and after the inevitable refit she sailed from Portsmouth in June 1793 wearing the flag once again of Samuel Hood. An exhausting eighteen months ensued which saw the capture of Bastia and San Fiorenzo and the ruin of the French fleet. *Victory* returned to Portsmouth in December 1794 and the now ailing admiral, nearly 70 years of age, struck his flag.

Victory was repaired and again brought up to date. In August 1794 the use of the flying jib-boom had been authorised and it is probable that this new spar was fitted to the ship for the first time. Chain-stoppers for the anchors had also been approved a year earlier, and this was the refit at which they would have been issued.

Although Lord Hood was ready to hoist his flag in *Victory* again as soon as she was fit to return to sea, he was superseded, and in July 1795 she left England for the Mediterranean, this time as the flagship of Rear Admiral

John Man. *Victory* suffered fairly extensive damage to spars and rigging during the battle with the French fleet off Hyères, but these were dealt with, largely by the ship's company no doubt, in Gibraltar. For a very brief period, *Victory* wore the flag of Vice-Admiral Robert Linzee before receiving on 3 December one of the most distinguished of British sea officers, Admiral Sir John Jervis.

One of the most important tasks facing Jervis was the blockade of Toulon, a thankless and boring job carried out for almost the whole of 1796. That it was successful for nearly a year says much for the organisation and procedures he established. The wear and tear on the ships

Victory, wearing the flag of Sir John Jervis at the Battle of Cape St Vincent in 1797, raking the stern of *Salvador del Mondo*. Not only was the stern the most vulnerable point of a wooden warship, but it could also be attacked with the least return fire.

in such a service was largely on the rigging, but this was the area of maintenance and repair that could most easily be dealt with by the ship from her own resources. The withdrawal of the fleet from the blockade at the end of November may have relieved the pressure on the French in Toulon, but it also permitted Jervis to be in a position where he could intercept the Spanish fleet off Cape St Vincent. The battle, which was fought on 14 February 1797 between fifteen British and twenty-seven Spanish warships, made Nelson a national hero. Four enemy ships were captured, including two First Rates. As so often in the battles with continental fleets, damage to the British ships was almost entirely confined to the upper deck and rigging. Consequently the ships were able to deal with the repairs themselves in the shelter of Lagos Bay, Portugal, where the Spanish prisoners were landed.

Shortly afterwards the fleet was joined by the new First Rate *Ville de Paris*, to which Jervis immediately transferred his flag. *Victory* became a private ship and in September she was ordered home. The survey carried out in October of that year showed that her list of defects was considerable, including the fact that the fastenings in a large number of her structural timbers had become loose. Her return to the Mediterranean was considered impractical and she was paid off at Chatham at the end of 1797.

Victory was refitted as a hospital ship for prisoners of war and moored in the River Medway, but after only a few weeks the Admiralty ordered that she should be completely converted to a prison hulk. The Navy Board pointed out that such a drastic alteration would mean that *Victory* could never be a fighting ship again, whereupon the Admiralty seems to have reconsidered. It is unlikely that the reprieve had anything to do with sentiment. Rather, it is more probable that on reflection the Admiralty Board realised that funds would be more easily obtained for repair than for the provision of a new First Rate. At all events the decision was set aside for the time being.

---

10. The Commander-in-Chief of the Channel Fleet was Admiral Sir William Cornwallis.

In 1800, the Navy Board ordered that *Victory* should have a middling repair, to be completed by the end of the year. After a few months in the dockyard it became evident that the £25,500 set aside for the work was woefully inadequate. Not only had her condition proved far worse on opening her up than had been estimated, but also it had become apparent that it would be absurd to spend so much on repairing her for sea service without including major new features that had been introduced since her launch. The revised costs, in excess of £70,000, were eventually accepted, no doubt with a great deal of soul-searching and with not a few hard words exchanged between the parties most concerned.

The great repair, as it became, was finally completed in April 1803. The most noticeable new feature, and one which had undoubtedly added appreciably to the increased costs, was the closed stern. When built, *Victory* had stern galleries with access from the quarters of the captain and the admiral on their respective decks. In the intervening years the design had been changed and the stern windows glazed flush, with shutters to protect them in bad weather. This new arrangement not only gave the respective cabins more usable room, but it also restricted the damage likely to be caused by a heavy following sea. At the same time the forward and main chainwales were raised above the upper-deck gunports. Again, this was no mere fashion, for it avoided the possibility of the rigging interfering with the use of the adjacent guns.

An order of June 1795 was particularly relevant to *Victory*. This required that high coamings be fitted to the lower-deck hatches of two- and three-decked ships. The idea was to prevent water taken on board through open gunports in heavy weather from getting down into the hold where it could damage provisions. It will be remembered that *Victory*'s lower-deck gunports were nearer the waterline than had been planned. In theory, any water shipped on the lower deck found its way outboard again through the lead lined scuppers, but the movement of the ship in heavy weather would first have sent it washing across the deck. At the bow, the enormous original figurehead which comprised four huge figures representing Europe, Asia, Africa and America was replaced by a smaller one showing two figures similar to that in position today. The effective broadside was increased slightly, two of the four gunports in the transom being blanked off and two additional ports being cut for the lower deck, which now had sixteen on each side.

In the magazine, all metalwork had now to be in copper to avoid the possibility of anything striking a spark. In addition, felt slippers were provided and had to be worn by everyone working in the magazine. Finally, in connection with ordnance, the 42-pounder lower-deck guns were removed again and the 32-pounders re-instated.

Sick berths were introduced by an order of August 1801 and took the form earlier prescribed for cabins: canvas screens stiffened by either a wooden frame or a bolt-rope. The order moving the cabins and stores for the boatswain and the carpenter from the forecastle to the orlop had come at the end of 1791. It is not clear whether it was executed at an earlier refit or whether it, too, had to wait for the great repair at Chatham in 1803.

The few changes in rigging practice that had been introduced since *Victory*'s first commission had been included in her periodic refits. Two new changes were brought in at this repair. The fighting tops were to be constructed of fir rather than oak in order to save weight, and they were to be fitted in two halves to make replacement easier. Finally, the rope woldings on the masts were replaced by iron bands.

The peace brought by the Treaty of Amiens in March 1802 soon showed itself to be fragile, and within the year the worsening relationship with France caused the Admiralty to press the Navy Board for *Victory* to be made ready for sea as soon as possible. She was undocked in April and arrived in Portsmouth on 14 May. War was declared four days later and on 20 May *Victory* sailed for the Mediterranean, the flagship of Lord Nelson, arriving at Malta 9 July 1803.

From July of that year until early in 1805 *Victory* led the watch on the French base at Toulon, remaining out of sight just over the horizon, ceaselessly patrolling in all weathers. In January 1805, whilst his main fleet was taking on water in the Maddalena Islands off north-eastern Sardinia, his frigates reported to Lord Nelson that the French fleet – known to have embarked several thousand troops – had sailed, apparently heading to the south of Sardinia. Nelson sailed within three hours and there followed the fruitless search to the eastward as far as Alexandria and then to the West Indies and back to Gibraltar. Some indication of the continous sea-time and the consequent wear and tear upon the flagship may be gauged in that when Lord Nelson went ashore at Gibraltar on 16 July 1805, it was the first time that he had been out of his ship in only ten days short of two years. *Victory* remained in Gibraltar for only five days. Searching again, Nelson fell in with the Channel Fleet[10] on 15 August and *Victory* was ordered home to Portsmouth where she arrived four days later.

For more than two years *Victory* had been maintained almost entirely by the efforts of her crew. This remarkable tribute to the determination of Lord Nelson to keep his ships at sea, the resourcefulness of *Victory*'s crew and the quality of the workmanship in the great repair of 1803 was emphasised by the fact that only minor dockyard repairs were necessary. In little more than three weeks she was fit to sail again.

There seems to be no record of the minor defects to *Victory*'s hull but it may be assumed that they were the common faults: displaced caulking and started planks. The rigging was overhauled as no doubt were all the masts and spars, but there was no major replacement. Her armament differed slightly from when she had last left Portsmouth. The broadsides remained unchanged but in addition to the two 12-pounders on the forecastle, she now carried two enormous 68-pounder carronades.

Chapter Three

TRAFALGAR TO A PERMANENT DRYDOCK
1805–1922

LORD NELSON RESUMED command of the Mediterranean squadron when *Victory* rejoined that fleet off Cadiz on 28 September. On 21 October 1805 was fought the Battle of Trafalgar. Nelson and *Victory* were already famous in their own time, but it was Trafalgar that ensured their fame ever after. The details of the action are not relevant here, but with reference to the considerable damage the ship suffered it should be noted first that for nearly ten minutes *Victory* was fired on by the four or five ships in the centre of the French line, although it is true that the guns were chiefly aimed at her rigging to dismast her as she slowly approached in the light winds. This early period saw *Victory* lose her mizzen topmast and all her studdingsails and their booms. Secondly, for nearly an hour *Victory* had the French 74 *Redoubtable* only feet away on her starboard side, each ship pounding the other. The resulting damage required *Victory*, as also *Temeraire* and *Belleisle*, to be towed to Gibraltar. On 4 November *Victory* left Gibraltar under jury rig but the damage done was so serious that she again had to be taken in tow, reaching Portsmouth on 4 December. No doubt to honour both Lord Nelson and the now forty-year-old *Victory*, it was decided that he should be brought to London by his flagship. Further urgent repairs were quickly carried out and the ship sailed for the Thames on 11 December. Heavy gales delayed her, however, and it was not until 22 December she arrived at Sheerness. Lord Nelson's body was transferred to the commissioner's yacht for the passage to Greenwich, to lie in state in the Painted Hall. *Victory* paid off at Chatham on 15 January 1806 for an extensive survey prior to a major repair and refit.

There is no official report on the damage sustained by *Victory*, but at Appendix B in A M Broadley and R G Bartelot, *Nelson's Hardy* there is quoted a statement written by R F Roberts who was a midshipman on board the ship at Trafalgar.

Defects to HMS *Victory* 5 December, 1805. Thos M Hardy Esq, Captain.

The hull is much damaged by shot in a number of different places, particularly in the wales, strings and spirketting, and some between wind and water, several beams, knees and riders, shot through and broke; the starboard cathead shot away; the rails and timbers of the head and stem cut by shot; several of the ports damaged and port timbers cut off; the channels and chain-plate damaged by shot and the falling of the mizzen mast; the principal part of the bulkheads, half-ports and portsashes thrown overboard in clearing ship for action.

The ship makes in bad weather 12 inches water an hour[1].

That the ship suffered widespread damage to her rigging and spars is evident in that she could not be fitted with even a jury-rig that would serve in any but the lightest winds, although with the amount of water she was mak-

---

1. A M Broadley and R G Bartelot, *Nelson's Hardy* p286.

ing *Victory* would have been sluggish enough in the water under any sail. In fact, analysis of the Roberts account suggests that there wasn't a single mast or spar on board that had not been destroyed or severely damaged in the action or had required to be cannibalised in order to form a weak jury-rig. This includes the very large and strong lower sections of the fore and main masts.

The structural damage listed by Roberts shows that the hull suffered nearly as badly, although its ravages were not perhaps so widespread. It is reasonable to assume that most of the damage was on the starboard side, which had been closest to *Redoubtable*. It is worth repeating here the size of some of the timbers 'shot-through'. The wales were 8 or 10in thick; spirketting – the two strakes inboard between the waterway and the gunport sills – was 6in thick; strings could refer either to the stringers or beam shelves on which the beam ends are lodged, strakes 9in thick and 17in deep, or to the top-mast plank on the ceiling inboard, in which case it would be 5in thick; the riders were heavy strengthening timbers inboard varying in section from 17ins x 16ins to

15ins square. Much of this timber was just below or barely above the waterline ('between wind and water') and that severe damage was caused to timber of this size illustrates the battering taken by *Victory*.

The comments of Bugler are pertinent with regard to the amount of water she was taking on board. Although Roberts doesn't indicate where the soundings were taken, it was standard practice to measure at the well and it is reasonable to assume that the soundings quoted were taken there. Bugler says,

The extent of the leakage cannot be assessed accurately from this figure alone because the first 12ins of water would have had considerably less volume than the second and third 12in layers . . . . The ship's trim must be considered. but it does appear from measure-

This print, after Nicholas Pocock, depicts the French and Spanish line being broken at Trafalgar. The British fleet, coming from the right in the print, attacked in two columns on a port tack in a light breeze with *Victory* leading the weather column. (NMM)

ment and calculation that the first 12ins would have contained about 30 tons of water, the second 12ins about 70 tons and the third over 90 tons. Thus after the battle a sounding of 3ft (for example) in the well would indicate an estimated 190 tons and the *Victory* would have had this to pump in addition to what was leaking in while the pumping was in progress[2].

Victory's pumps had an estimated capacity of 120 tons per hour, but this assumes that the pumps were undamaged – an unlikely case after such a battle. A hundred tons of water slopping about would also strain the weakened hull even further, as well as greatly reducing her mobility.

Victory was docked on 6 March 1806, her hull repaired and coppered, fitted with new masts and spars, and then re-rigged. She was floated up again on 3 May, almost exactly forty-one years after her original 'launching' in the same dock.

Changes were again made in her armament. Of the quarterdeck armament of twelve 12-pounders, eight were removed to make way for eight 32-pounder carronades fitted with the new slide carriages. The two forecastle 12-pounders were also replaced by 32-pounder carronades. The 68-pounder carronades were removed and not replaced.

The dockyard at Chatham had done well to complete this major refit in two months, but *Victory* was not recommissioned. Instead she swung at her mooring in the Medway until March 1807, at which time she was again taken into the yard to remedy defects that had caused her to leak badly[3]. An Admiralty Order of 26 January that year required that all ships entered for repair were to have the mizzen mast stepped on the lower deck –

Victory, under tow and jury-rigged on her way to Gibralter in the gale that blew up during the night after the battle of Trafalgar. The fore topsail, which is still extant today, has been lowered along with the topmast. (NMM)

'The *Victory* coming up the Channel with the body of Nelson'. This atmospheric pen and ink and watercolour by Turner shows *Victory* re-rigged and on her way to Sheerness at the end of 1805. (Tate Gallery, London, 1999)

Victory's had originally been stepped in the hold. It is not clear how long *Victory* was in the yard and how soon her needs were attended. Her repairs and alterations may have just been completed when a new Order changed her status. It seems more probable though that the repairs necessary were still being considered late in 1807, for an Admiralty Order of 11 November ordered that *Victory* should be re-rated as a Second Rate of 98 guns and that her masts and spars should be reduced accordingly. Her lower-deck armament was reduced by two 32-pounders, and on the middle deck the 24-pounders were replaced by 18-pounder guns. At the same time her complement was reduced by ninety-nine men to seven hun-dred and thirty-eight in total. The reduced weight eased the burden on her now ageing structure and the reduced number of men on board improved her habitability.

After minor repairs made necessary by evidence of fungal decay, *Victory* was commissioned in March 1808 as the flagship of Rear Admiral de Saumarez, appointed C-in-C in the Baltic. By mid-November, however, *Victory* was back in Portsmouth. The work during the summer season in the Baltic had been successful, but with closed gunports for most of the time in the chilly damp of the northern climate, the ill-ventilated gundecks were unhealthy. The fleet had such a huge sick list that it had required two ships to send the worst affected back to

---

2. Bugler p29.

3. A situation strongly reminiscent of what had occurred 36 years earlier and no doubt the cause was the same.

This sketch of the quarterdeck of *Victory* was made by Turner while the ship lay off Sheerness at the beginning of 1806. He seems to have erred here, perhaps completing it from memory later, for the masts appear to have wooldings (rope strengthening a made mast) rather than the wrought-iron bands substituted for them in the 1803 repair. (Tate Gallery, London, 1999)

England. Minor repairs were again carried out and on 10 December *Victory* sailed as a private ship under Captain J C Searle, for the Peninsula to assist in the evacuation of the British Army from Corunna. This service successfully completed she returned to Portsmouth and was made ready for the new season in the Baltic. *Victory* spent the next two summers with Saumarez, but in each case the success was modest, for Saumarez was unable to tempt the Russian fleet into a major action.

Victory had required little attention between her Baltic campaigns, and on her return in December 1810 she needed only minor repairs together with partial conversion to troop-carrying. In January 1811 she sailed as a private ship in the squadron taking reinforcements to the army in the Peninsula. After this second winter interlude had been successfully concluded, *Victory* returned to Portsmouth and a brief re-conversion to a flagship again for Saumarez, now Vice Admiral, and left again for the summer campaign in the Baltic. The year 1811 proved much the same for *Victory* as had the preceding three: small-boat actions and a concentration on safeguarding the convoys of naval stores on their way to England. This time she did not reach Portsmouth until Christmas Day.

4. The cost of *Victory* when floated up had been £63,176; the Great Repair of 1814 cost £79,772. See also Ch. 2 footnote 9.

The winter refit was minor but at least not hurried, and in April she sailed yet again for the Baltic. On her return after a summer campaign as successful but as uneventful as the others, *Victory* arrived at Spithead on 7th November 1812. This time, however, she was paid off, and placed in Ordinary.

The survey carried out in 1813 recommended a small repair. In the November estimates it had prudently been upgraded to a middling repair. When, however, the repair began in April in No 3 Dock near *Victory*'s present berth, it became evident that even the revised estimate had been optimistic. The middling repair became a major reconstruction which was to last until January 1816[4].

The great repair of 1814-15 had a far greater effect on the change of *Victory*'s appearance than had the repairs of 1803 which had closed in her stern. When she emerged from the dockyard at Portsmouth in 1816 *Victory* had been brought up to date. Gone was the eighteenth century beakhead with its square bulkhead, which had itself improved upon the low beakheads fitted from about 1580 until late in the seventeenth century. Instead, an Admiralty Order of 31 May 1811 directed that

in future all line of battleships, including those of three decks, which may be laid down shall be built with round bows instead of beak heads as heretofore, and

An engraving of *Victory* in Portsmouth Harbour, drawn in 1828 by E W Cooke, which clearly shows the round bows of her post-Trafalgar refit.

Victory was rammed by HMS *Neptune* in 1903. This photograph was taken by Vice Admiral L H K Hamilton seconds before the impact. The alert young Hamilton was a 13-year-old Osborne cadet on board HMS *Racer* at the time. (HMS *Victory*)

that those now in hand and under repair which shall not be too far advanced to admit of the alteration without incurring an additional expense shall be finished in the same manner . . .

Accordingly, *Victory* was altered without further specific order.

The idea of the round bow had been conceived by Robert Seppings, Surveyor of the Navy 1813-1832 when, as Master Shipwright at Chatham, he had been responsible for reducing *Namur*, 90 guns, to a Third Rate 74-gun ship. The refitted *Namur* was a success and the decision to make the round bow a standard design was undoubtedly influenced by the severe damage suffered by a number of ships including *Victory*, at Trafalgar. The beakhead bulkhead between the upper and forecastle decks was a relatively light structure which laid the ship open to serious damage by raking fire from ahead. The

round bow however made the bulkhead virtually a continuation of the ship's side, with all its much greater strength.

The damage caused at Trafalgar also led to changes in the orlop of major warships. Bulkheads now had to be constructed so that there was ready access to the ship's side behind them. Presumably the dispensary was fitted at this repair – by the Admiralty Order of 22 July 1809 – in lieu of the surgeon's store-room which was removed. At the same refit the mizzen mast was altered so that it was stepped on the lower deck.

It is possible that 1814 also saw the introduction of iron knees in *Victory*. Arthur Bugler rather thought so, but adduces no argument as to why iron had not been introduced in the post-Trafalgar repair of 1806[5]. He quotes the Navy Board standing order of 6 May 1805 as evidence that iron knees were being made in the dockyards at that time. Presumably the idea was still considered too new and radical for it to be applied to a First Rate in 1806.

Whilst *Victory* was in the hands of the dockyard, the practice of painting the double streak along the line of

5. Bugler p32.

the gunports was formalised. A Navy Board standing order of 4 December 1815 required that ships of the line in commission should be painted with double streaks in a straight line. A ship of the line in Ordinary was to be painted with a single streak, which would form the upper streak should she be commissioned. At the same time it was ordered that the streaks should be white as opposed to the Nelsonian yellow. There is no real evidence as to why the changes of colour were ordered, but it seems probable that it was to avoid the variety of shades of yellow created by the idiosyncrasies and depth of pocket of different captains. These ranged from delicate shades of primrose to the rather dirty-looking buff yellow of the dockyard. Lord Nelson and Captain Hardy were content to use the latter, for neither was ever rich enough to indulge in such fancies. This is the colour that is used on *Victory* today.

Victory was undocked on 13 January 1816 and placed in Ordinary. The following year she was again re-rated when it was decided that all three-deckers should be First Rates. She had the usual periodic attention during this period until 1823, when she was again docked and refitted. When she emerged on 21 January 1825 *Victory* became the flagship of the Port Admiral and bore 21 guns. Six years later her role was changed, and she became the residence of the Captain of the Ordinary, the officer responsible for all vessels in that condition at Portsmouth. A year later, *Victory* was again put into commission as the Port Admiral's flagship. At the end of August 1836 she was replaced by *Britannia* and returned to the Ordinary. However, twelve months later *Victory* was commissioned again, this time as flagship of the Admiral Superintendent of the Dockyard. This service continued until 1847 when she became the stationary flagship of the Commander-in-Chief. These years in a long settled period of peace, were not surprisingly also a time of severe economy for both the Army and the Navy, which equally understandably meant that the ships on harbour service, especially those that were stationary, received only the most minimal maintenance. By 1857 *Victory* required serious attention and she was docked for repairs and recoppering. It was perhaps at this time, her

first sizeable repair since it had been decided that she should be permanently moored in harbour, that the lead of the ship's hawse holes was changed.

Victory resumed her station as flagship in April 1858, but was paid off in 1869. She then suffered the indignity of serving as tender – spare accommodation and storage of odds and ends – to her successor the *Duke of Wellington*, nearly a hundred years her junior in age. She was docked in 1887 when it was evident that a severe leak could no longer be either ignored or dealt with by pumping. It was in the 1880s that *Victory*'s wooden lower masts were replaced by the hollow wrought-iron masts of the *Shah*, and the docking in 1887 is the likeliest occasion for the change. The wrought-iron masts were not only lighter – an obvious advantage in a hull over a hundred years old – but would long outlast any timber equivalent, with far less maintenance.

Otherwise, although details are no longer available, it is evident that the time and money spent on *Victory* during these years was kept to a minimum – except when action was forced upon the dockyard by some unlooked-

The damage inflicted upon *Victory*. The hole is approximately 6ft by 2ft. (HMS *Victory*)

for incident. This was the case towards the end of 1903. On 23 October that year the ship suffered serious damage below the waterline when rammed by the *Neptune* which, while under tow, had broken adrift from her tugs in bad weather. The *Neptune* struck *Victory* on the port side causing such damage as to put her in danger of foundering. *Victory* was quickly docked and the work, which took some months, undoubtedly involved more than just the repairs necessitated by the *Neptune*. A considerable fuss was made of *Victory* for the Trafalgar centenary in 1905, but perhaps because of the work carried out after the collision little was done other than the barest minimum to make her reasonably tight and a rather cosmetic 'smartening up'. By 1920 her condition had deteriorated to such an extent that she was in danger of foundering at her moorings off the old Gosport Hard.

Ten years earlier the Society for Nautical Research had been founded 'to encourage reseach into matters relating to seafaring and shipbuilding . . . and into other subjects of nautical interest'. The future of *Victory* had been raised in the early years of the society, but the opportunity to achieve any concrete results had been stifled by the outbreak of war in 1914. By 1920, however, members of the SNR had begun to voice their fears again, fears that became the official view of the Society in 1921 when its President, Admiral the Marquis of Milford Haven, tabled a report showing the parlous state of the ship. His suggestion that urgent action was required by the Society was unanimously accepted by its Council.

The preservation of *Victory* was the subject of the President's address at the Annual General Meeting of the Society for Nautical Research in June of that year. Letters to the *Times* followed but undoubtedly the most important act was that the President ensured that the Society's report and views were laid directly before the Board of Admiralty. As a result *Victory* was moved into Portsmouth's No 1 Basin on 16 December 1921, the first step towards her restoration and permanent preservation. With her ballast removed, she was prepared for docking. This always delicate operation was further complicated by the distortion of the keel which had hogged to such an extent that the scarphs on the keelson had opened by

more than an inch. Forward of the foremast the bow had dropped by 18in, and aft of the mizzenmast the stern had dropped 8in.

Victory was docked on blocks roughly 2ft high, but although this was safe enough for normal purposes it had always been evident that a more secure support would be required if she were to stay permanently dry-docked. On 20 March 1922 the Admiralty Board ordered that *Victory* should be preserved and that the No 2 Dock was to be her home. Accordingly a steel cradle was designed as a permanent support. Bugler describes its construction:

The cradle consisted initially of ten transverse sections on each side of the ship. The *Victory* now has eleven each side. The additional one situated at the aft end on each side was added in 1956 during the major repairs to the stern post. Each cradle section was erected upon the upper surface of a 20lb foundation plate which was laid and cemented over the steps of the dock bottom. Each section consisted of 20lb plates erected in a vertical transverse plane worked intercostally between triangular-shaped 15lb bracket plates, usually four, at right angles to them. The intercostal 20lb plates were secured at the bottom to the foundation plate by 6in x 3in x ½in double angles with 6in flanges vertical. The triangular-shaped bracket frames were secured to the foundation plates by 3½in x 3½in x ⅜in angles. Two 4in x 4in x ¾in angles, worked vertically in opposite corners, were used to connect the intercostal 20lb plates to the 15lb bracket plates. The top of the cradle was formed of two 6in x 6in x ¾in angles riveted to the top edge of the intercostal plates and with a 15lb sole plate secured to their horizontal surfaces. This gave an upper surface 12in in width; each section of each cradle was about normal to the curve of the bottom and about 6in clear of the bottom. The space between the top of the cradle and the outer planking of the *Victory* was filled with carefully fitted teak driven as tightly as was practicable[6].

The height of the docking blocks had been governed by the depth of water that could be obtained in the dock at high-water spring tides. However, this led to the ship sitting very low in the dock and the result was widely criticised, for as a spectacle *Victory* had lost much of her grandeur. The Society for Nautical Research again led the way in pressing for the ship to be raised to present a more acceptable and impressive spectacle. This was certainly a laudable aim, but it immediately presented the dockyard officials with severe problems, the chief of which was the hugely increased amount of windage that would be caused if the ship were raised. The force of the wind on the rigging and upperworks of a ship afloat is largely counteracted by the pressure of the sea on the hull below the waterline. In other words, the sea supports the hull structure. With the ship in dry dock this support is absent, and an enormous strain is consequently placed upon the hull. This strain would be considerably greater if the ship were to be raised the additional few feet necessary to present her at her best. The raising of the ship was itself a difficult but not impossible operation. The major problem it presented was whether the severely weakened hull would stand the strain.

To the delight of the SNR and others critical of *Victory*'s position in the dock, it was eventually agreed that the ship should be raised – a decision that appears to have been influenced in no small way by the opinion of His Majesty King George V on his visit in July 1922. Two schemes were put forward to raise *Victory*. The first, proposed by Sir Philip Watts, a former Director of Naval Construction, planned to achieve the lift in one operation using the latest technology of rivetted steel ballast tanks. It was expensive, not least because the use of fifteen such tanks would require alteration of the dock to allow their insertion. In the event the alternative method, that proposed by the dockyard officers, was used. This more traditional practice required the lift of 3ft 3in to be accomplished in three stages with the divers chocking up, the dock pumped out and the blocks checked and consolidated at each stage. There was rather more risk involved in docking so old and weak a wooden hull three times, but the method was well-tried and could be carried out by experienced officers within the existing dockyard resources. With the ship in her

new position, the method of supporting her described above was extended and adjusted to her new height[7].

There was, however, a price to be paid for the improved spectacle. Even though *Victory* already had the lighter iron lower masts from the *Shah*, it was felt that the hull could not possibly withstand the strain of southwesterly gales if they were to remain stepped in the time-honoured manner. The solution was ingenious and Bugler's description of the fittings that relieve the hull of the weight cannot be bettered:

Four 5in clearance holes were bored through the bottom structure near the keel at the correct positions. The 5in holes were cut at the corners of squares two opposite sides of which were parallel to the middle line. Four solid circular 5in diameter mild steel bars were driven in each set of holes, and the heels of the circular pillars were stepped upon flat 1½in thick mild steel plates fitted on the top surface of the concrete wall which supported the keel. A 3in x 3in x ½in angle collar connected each pillar to the base plate. The pillars were cut to the correct length and another flat 1½in mild steel plate was secured to their tops by similar angle collars. A solid, dummy teak mast fabricated with baulks securely bolted together was then closely fitted between this upper plate, on the top of the 5in pillars, and the underside of the mast step in the ship. The arrangement was completed in way of the steps of each of the three lower masts, and ensured that the weight of the masts, spars and rigging would be taken and supported by the concrete wall under the keel. Hollow pillars would have been lighter to handle and almost as strong, but solid ones were chosen because of possible corrosion over a period. The 5in holes were cut with a heavy duty pneumatic drilling machine using a long bar with a cutter. The boring of these holes was no mean feat. The cutting tools constantly

---

6. *Ibid* p38. One square foot of half-inch plate weighs approximately 20lbs and is termed 20lb plate.

7. *Victory* was not raised to her new level until March-April 1925, after the completion of the beak bulkhead. The method of her raising is described here to avoid breaking into the account of the restoration work.

A rather fuzzy snapshot of Victory, but interesting in that it was taken at by Mr L H Boyce at noon on 21 October 1905, the Trafalgar Centenary. Lord Nelson's 'England expects . . . ' signal is hoisted. Alongside *Victory* is a representative of the new menace, HM Submarine B1. The Royal Navy's first submarine had been launched just four years earlier. (HMS *Victory*)

fouled many of the old fastenings during the boring but fortunately most of the fastenings in way of the holes were of copper. The lengths of the pillars finally fitted were, approximately, foremast 11ft 6in, mainmast 8ft 4in and mizzen 10ft 10in[8].

The problem of increased windage on the masts, spars and rigging was solved by the provision of additional stays for each of the masts fixed to anchoring points on the dockside. This compromise with the integrity of the original had to be made if the ship was to be seen to its greatest advantage. Indeed, it would almost certainly have been necessary even had *Victory* remained in her lower position in the dock. The aim of the Admiralty Board, as prompted by the Society for Nautical Reseach, was to restore and maintain the ship as nearly as possible to her Trafalgar state; but if the compromise had not been accepted, there would probably by now have been no *Victory* at all – or certainly not one rigged with more than the rather ugly lower masts.

8. Bugler p44.

Chapter Four

RESTORATION AND REPAIR
1922 – 1964

THE MARQUIS OF MILFORD HAVEN, who as President of the Society for Nautical Research had been a key figure in persuading the Board of Admiralty to take some positive action to preserve *Victory*, died towards the end of 1921. He was succeeded as President of the Society by Admiral of the Fleet Sir Doveton Sturdee, who had distinguished himself at the Battle of the Falklands in 1914. At the Society's Annual General Meeting in June 1922 Sturdee announced that the Admiralty had agreed that the executive officers of the society should be the experts to advise on the restoration of *Victory* to her Trafalgar condition, although for reasons already discussed in the last chapter it was tacitly accepted that the term 'restoration to her Trafalgar condition' could not be absolute.

The Board of Admiralty also saw a difference between what might conveniently be termed repairs and restoration. As *Victory* was to remain on the *Navy List* the Board was prepared to accept the cost of such repairs as were needed to maintain her as a ship capable of serving such purpose as the Navy might require. However, as the Service would not require her to put to sea she would not, for its purposes, require sails, admiral's or captain's quarters, steering wheel or binnacles. These and similar fittings might reasonably be considered restoration for which the use of public funds in the Navy Vote would be improper. The Admiralty however was willing that such work should be done in the dockyard and were willing that the Society for Nautical Reseach should organise an appeal fund to pay for it. The Society accepted these proposals, and it was resolved that work should begin once the amount in the Save the *Victory* Fund had reached £50,000.

The Society for Nautical Reseach had accepted responsibility for two crucial functions: the organisation of the appeal with the attendant administration of the funds collected and the considerable amount of research that was necessary if the repairs and restoration were to be effective and accurate. Two sub-committees were formed: one, the *Victory* Appeal Committee, was chaired by Sir Doveton Sturdee, the other, the *Victory* Technical Committee, was under the chairmanship of Sir Philip Watts, the Director of Naval Construction from 1901 to 1912.

The Mariner's Mirror, the journal of the Society, records that the lion's share of the task of fund-raising was accepted by Sir Doveton Sturdee who worked tirelessly for the appeal. Times were difficult, however, and progress was slow, for the post-war boom had come to an end in 1922. By the time of his death in 1925, undoubtedly hastened by his great efforts on behalf of *Victory*, the initial three years of the appeal, which should have been the most productive had achieved only £30,000, some £20,000 short of the key figure of £50,000 at which it was considered appropriate to begin the restoration. However, the fact that work could begin was made possible by one man's extraordinary generosity. Early in 1923 an anonymous donation of £50,000 solved the Appeal Committee's immediate problem and it only came to light some years later that the benefactor had been Sir James Caird, a Dundee ship owner [1].

---

1. Perhaps to be multiplied by 20 for an appropriate guide to today's values.

From the figure of £80,000 in 1925, the fund reached £105,000 in 1932. The efficiency of the appeal's administration may be measured by its percentage costs: 3.5 per cent a year to 1924, which included the starting costs, and a mere 0.25 per cent a year thereafter.

The Technical Committee's task was also onerous although no doubt less wearing. It contained such luminaries – and pioneers – in the field of maritime research as R C Anderson, W L Wyllie, L G Carr Laughton, Admiral Ballard and Professor Geoffrey Callender among others whose contributions are most frequent in the journal of the Society before the Second World War. Typical of the

Work during repairs to the stern post in 1956. The temporary external shores can be seen on the right of the picture, while to each side of the shipwright are the internal shores. The massive timber behind him is the sternpost knee. (MoD (N))

depth of the research is the report by Carr Laughton, published in the 1923 volume of *The Mariner's Mirror*, of his findings relevant to *Victory*'s restoration, from documents in the Public Record Office.

Presumably two surveys were undertaken, probably during the winter of 1922–1923. The first, carried out by the dockyard, was concerned with the physical state of the ship and showed the extent of the decay throughout the vessel just below and above the water-line. The other survey must have been made – although it is not recorded – by members of the Technical Committee to see what needed to be done in the way of restoration to her Trafalgar condition, as opposed to repair.

Restoration 1922–1928

Although, as has been shown, it was impracticable to return *Victory* to her absolute state of 1805, one of the first tasks in her restoration was to reverse the most obvious alteration made since Trafalgar; the round bow was removed and replaced with the square beakhead bulkhead that formed part of her original design.

The beakhead was built of eleven baulks of teak bolted together and to the stem, the innermost one running down to become part of the stem itself. The face of the stem is protected by an elm sole piece covering it from the keel to the top of the beakhead. A thick board covers the end grain of the teak baulks and provides a firm fixing for the trestle frames which support the grating platform. A large oak knee is fitted between the stemhead and the beakhead. The trestles also support the three rails on each side running from the beakhead to the stem. Below these rails is a longer moulded rail on each side that begins as a scroll at the top of the beakhead and, following its line, terminates at deck level below the foremost middle-deck gunport. Below this again a similar moulding runs parallel for the same length. Between these mouldings is a sheathing of fir 5in thick running from the bow planking forward for 8ft 9in, providing additional strength for the gammoning slots.

The stem is reinforced by the stemson which is scarphed into the keelson at station 10. This section above the forward end of the keelson was removed when the round bow was dismantled. Perhaps original, it was in good condition and was replaced when the beakhead was fitted but was fastened with steel bolts and nuts instead of the earlier copper clench bolts [2].

Although it lacked the strength of the round bow, the beakhead bulkhead had also been designed to provide some measure of protection to those on the upper deck from raking fire from ahead, as well as preventing the flooding of the forecastle deck in heavy weather. In view of this it was probably constructed of solid timber 1ft thick originally but that built in the 1920s has a 7in cavity.

Little or nothing was done in the hold, presumably on the grounds that with limited funds available and little likelihood of the public being admitted to the hold owing to the difficulty of access, the money would be better spent elsewhere. In fact the hold was not restored until the repairs were begun again in 1955.

Wings were built on the orlop, so creating again the carpenters' walk. It is not known when the originals were removed. The carpenter's and boatswain's cabins were installed with their attendant stores and the gunner's store was fitted out. The hanging magazine, sail rooms and cable tiers were also re-built. Similarly, the bread room and the cabins and stores for the purser and the steward were built and fitted out, as were the captain's store and the lieutenant's store. The surgeon's cabin and dispensary were also reinstated and fitted out at the expense of Sir Henry Wellcome, founder of the Wellcome Historical Medical Museum and of the giant pharmaceutical company that bore his name [3].

On the lower deck the nineteenth-century iron tiller,

Bomb damage repairs below the grand magazine looking forward. The scarph has been cut in the keel ready to receive the new section and below it the false keel can be seen. To the right may be seen one of the steel supports for the foremast step. (MoD (N))

---

2. Domed nuts were used so that when the tail of the bolt was cut off flush the effect simulated the clenches used in the eighteenth century.

3. A number of these reinstatements of the 1922 restoration have been altered in the light of the more recent research by the Curator of *Victory*, Mr Peter Goodwin.

4. The softwood panelling was painted white in the 1922 restoration. The more recent restoration now has the panelling stained to give the appearance of mahogany. The material is certainly correct, for the Navy Board was not likely to supply expensive mahogany. The authenticity of the staining is more problematical, although it would have added an appropriate air of dignity at little extra cost.

installed presumably in the 1814 repair, was replaced by a wooden one similar to the original. Chain pumps in the eighteenth century style were fitted, together with the appropriate cranked iron handles, and the manger was re-built. The rollers for the messenger and the compressors for the cable were either renewed or repaired.

On the middle deck the wardroom and the senior lieutenants' cabins were restored and fitted out. Forward, the fire-hearth and Brodie stove were installed, the gift of Sir Philip Watts, and the galley was re-built.

On the upper deck at the stern, the Great Cabin and admiral's quarters – the day and dining cabins and the sleeping cabin – were restored and refurbished [4]. The quarter galleries were also refurbished.

Under the poop, Captain Hardy's day cabin, dining cabin and sleeping cabin were similarly restored as were the quarter galleries and the small cabins to port and starboard for the master and secretary respectively. At the break of the poop, a binnacle was installed, and the wheel was replaced and connected to the new rudder with hemp rope. Forward of this on the quarterdeck the skylight was removed and the space planked over. It had been installed at the request of an admiral in the later part of the eighteenth century to allow more light below, but subsequently it had been removed on Lord Nelson's orders because it inhibited the working of the quarterdeck guns. The skylight was restored after Trafalgar, perhaps at the 1814 great repair but more probably when *Victory* was refitted in 1830 as the residence of the Captain of the Ordinary.

The gangways were restored in the waist on either side of the skid beams on which the boats and spare spars were stowed. The skid beams had been planked over during *Victory's* long sojourn at moorings in Portsmouth Harbour. The davits on each quarter and at the stern were also replaced. Mr Lionel Foster, also a member of the Technical Committee, presented the belfry, which was installed on the forecastle as were the funnel for the new Brodie stove and new bitts.

On the poop, period flag lockers were built and the skylight over Hardy's dining cabin was restored[5]. From the taffrail to the beakhead bulkhead, hammock cranes and netting were fitted to the bulwarks, and at the poop rail was hung a row of twenty-one leather fire buckets.

All the gun ports except the first two to port and starboard on the middle deck were made to hinge upwards instead of the later half-lids fitted casement fashion. Outboard the chainwales were put back to their earlier positions above the upper-deck gunports and the anchors were refashioned in wood reinforced with aluminium. This was to reduce the weight on the sides of

5. The skylight was removed during the ship's long sojourn in Portsmouth Harbour, probably after becoming tender to the *Duke of Wellington* in 1869 and presumably because it was a source of leaks. The present skylight can still be troublesome in this regard.

6. Bugler p103.

the ship. For the same reason, the iron anchors, which in a First Rate weighed just over four tons, were set apart for display on the dockside. Finally, outboard, the carvings at the bow and stern were restored.

Repairs 1922–1928

Stern

The great repair carried out in 1803–1804 brought the design of *Victory's* stern up to date by closing in the open galleries, but this would have had no effect on its main structural members below the middle gundeck. The most important of these are the sternpost, sternson and the huge transom beams. This structure is not only in its original form, but is believed to contain some of the original timbers, notably the upper transom beams of which the largest, the wing transom, is just under 36ft long, 28in wide and 14in deep.

There is no record of any serious repair to this lower part of the stern in the 1920s, nor to the structure in the region of the hold and orlop. When Bugler asserts that 'the stern generally, including the gingerbreads and carvings, was restored' in the 'twenties[6], he is referring to that part of it above the middle deck. That this needed restoration is not surprising given the relatively light nature of the timbers that formed it above the middle deck and the hundreds of joints and small ledges that encouraged rot because they prevented rainwater from being easily shed. The only specific repairs he records, however, refer to the four poop transom knees which strengthen the taffrail and are secured at their feet through the planking to the poop-deck transom and the three beams immediately forward of it. Grown compass timber of the size needed for such knees (9ft on the lower arm and 15in at the throat) was not available in the 'twenties, so the four knees were fabricated in mild steel, secured with mild steel bolts as has been the practice since, and sheathed with teak.

A great deal of work had to be done on the hull at the level roughly of the lower and middle gundecks, just above and along the crucial area 'twixt wind and water', as the old description has it. Timber that is alternately

At the after end of the lower gundeck, on the starboard side, planking has been removed, exposing the decayed beam ends below the waterway. (MoD (N))

underside of the carling between the pillars at stations 16 and 24. The pitch pine pillars in the cable tier just forward of the main hatch had been replaced earlier, probably in the nineteenth century. The aftermost pillars on each side of the hanging magazine (three to port, four to starboard) were renewed in teak.

Lower to middle deck

Throughout the length of the ship, the timbers, *ie* the frames, are numbered from bow to stern and their positions are known as stations. These timbers were all of oak and those at stations 48, 49, 55-58, 61-70 and 72-80, roughly 40ft forward of the main mast, were repaired or renewed also in oak. It is not clear from the records which side of the ship these were on but in view of the survey report it seems probable that both port and starboard frames were repaired. Approximately 150ft each of beam shelf, spirketting and the three strakes of planking in between were renewed both port and starboard.

The planking of the lower gundeck may well be largely original and there is little doubt that it pre-dates Trafalgar. A small area had to be renewed in the 1920s restoration from strakes 18 to 20 on the starboard side from stations 55 to 70. It extends roughly from about 12ft from the starboard side to just beyond the port side of the main hatch and from the fore side of the capstan aft to the forward edge of the hatch. At the foremost point on the lower deck the manger was completely renewed using 4in fir planking.

Middle to upper deck

Frames between the middle and upper decks were repaired or renewed from stations 20 to 124 on both sides. Most renewals were in oak but a shortage of oak timber combined presumably with a reluctance to delay repairs led to frame numbers 45-46, 51, 53, 55, 60, 68 and 81 being made up with fir at the upper-deck level.

At the same time twenty-one beam knees were either renewed or repaired on the port side as were twenty on the starboard side.

During the hundred years in which *Victory* lay at her moorings her sides had been repaired so many times in

wet and then dry expands and contracts as the conditions vary. This opens joints and cracks allowing moisture to penetrate and cause rot. It has been seen that during a century as a static ship in Portsmouth harbour *Victory* had received only minimal attention and by the time of her final docking in 1922 the frames and planking over much of the hull in the region of the tumble-home were so rotten as to be near collapse. A great deal of timber had to be renewed.

Orlop to lower deck

The shaped pillars in the cable tier on the orlop and the four pillars on each side of the hanging magazine were renewed in teak. The pillars at station 19 were renewed in oak. The steel plate 12½in x ⅝in was fitted to the

small 'first aid' patches that the old fair lines of planking seams were no longer evident. To achieve the desired, original effect with a minimum of labour and expense it was decided to sheath with 2in teak the planking above the main wale. At the same time the wales, removed in the 1857 repair, were replaced. Including the sheathing, a hundred and one strakes were renewed, both port and starboard, from the foremast to 15ft abaft the mizzen and from about 2ft 6in above the lower deck upward, an area roughly 170ft long by 24ft on each side of the ship. Between the middle and upper decks repairs and (largely) renewals were made to beam shelf, and other inner planking between stations 27 and 135 on the port side, and stations 18 to 118 to starboard.

Upper deck

From stations 42–105, *ie* from a point level with the belfry to just aft of the main ladder from the upper deck, the frames were renewed, principally in oak but with some fir used, on both sides of the ship. The beam shelf on each side was renewed in oak from stations 46 to 77 and the inner planking was renewed from station 38 to station 104 port and starboard. Both teak and pitch pine were used for the latter.

Although none of the upper-deck beams were renewed in the 1920s restoration, one at station 28 had to be repaired. This was done in the time-honoured manner. Beams need to be of considerable size; even those of the upper deck are quoted in Steel's *Naval Architecture* of 1794 as requiring to be 13½in x 12in and 30ft long[7]. Beams of that length and section had almost always to be scarphed, but during repair, in order to make the best use of timber saved after the rot-infected end had been cut away, it was not always practicable to use a conventional scarph. Instead, the timbers to be scarphed were linked by the insertion of an anchor piece, so called not so much

A photograph, taken in 1960, showing how a draw knife is used to fashion a new spar. (MoD (N))

because of its function as because of its shape, which resembled the wooden stock of an anchor. A number of the upper-deck beams had so been repaired in pitch pine, presumably in the nineteenth century. In the 1920s repair, the pitch pine anchor piece in the beam at station 28 was renewed in oak. Several beams are of pitch-pine throughout and not original. Almost certainly nineteenth century replacements, they may have been put in at the great repair of 1814. The long scarphs are conventional, suggesting that the beams were renewed completely.

Eleven hanging knees to the upper-deck beams were repaired, largely in the lower ends of the arms at the ship's side. Twenty-six pillars were renewed in teak, all of them at the edges of either the gratings or the companion ladder.

7. Table of the dimensions and scantlings for ships of each class, folio xxxii.

8. This unlikely station number occurs because the centre of the beam is just aft of the centre of timber No 85.

9. This is apparently the case although we cannot be certain. The records were destroyed by enemy action in 1941.

Above: HMS *Victory* under way, *ca*1780, painted by Monamy Swaine. This painting shows her when first commissioned and the open stern galleries are clearly visible. Ships' names first appeared on the sterns of Royal Navy warships in 1778. (Caird Collection in the NMM)

Below: A watercolour by W Clarkson Stanfield depicting *Victory* being towed into Gibraltar by *Neptune* on 28 October. (NMM)

Above: Lord Nelson's sleeping cabin, forward of the Great Cabin on the starboard side. The cot hangings are replicas of those said to have been embroidered by Lady Hamilton. Like the men, officers lived and slept between the guns. The sheet lead squares were fitted to all guns to protect the firing mechanism when not in use. (MoD (N))

Above: Vice Admiral Horatio Nelson, 1st Viscount Nelson (1758-1805), painted by Lemuel Abbott. (Greenwich Hospital Collection in the NMM)

Below: The lower gundeck completed, 1994. (MoD (N))

Above: Lord Nelson's day cabin, the after part of the Great Cabin. (MoD (N))

Below: A view of the sick bay with some of the surgeon's instruments laid out. The modern fire hose is an inevitable addition. (MoD (N))

Above: The Surgeon's table in a corner of the sick bay. There is no hard evidence of exactly how the table looked but this mock-up is a realistic interpretation. (MoD (N))

Left: The current figurehead is a replica of the design carried by the ship at Trafalgar. It was completed in 1989. (MoD(N))

Below: A display in the hold showing how barrels were stowed. Most of the ship's food was supplied and stored in casks. (Peter Goodwin)

The upper-deck planking was completely renewed in 3in teak, fastened with brass screws with the heads inset, and covered with teak plugs of 1in diameter. The water-ways were secured with galvanised steel fastenings similarly recessed and dowelled.

Quarterdeck and above

At the quarterdeck level, the spirketting and other inner planking were renewed in teak. As with those for the upper deck, eleven quarterdeck hanging knees were repaired in the lower arms. The upper frame timbers at the forecastle deck were renewed, as were the head timbers that project above the deck level at stations 85 and 88 port and starboard. Of the fifteen oak beams to the forecastle deck, only one was renewed in the 1920s. The aftermost beam was replaced in Douglas fir, those forward of it being deemed in an acceptable state. The hanging and lodging knees of the renewed beam were reinstated but the former on the starboard side needed repair in the side arm. Above the forecastle the rails and bulwark planking were renewed in teak. Eight of the ten boom-deck beams were renewed in Douglas fir, the two remaining being of oak, at stations 85.5[8] and 88. Repairs to both port and starboard knees for these beams were carried out, principally to the side arms.

A number of the knees to the poop deck had been repaired prior to the 1922 work. The repairs were mainly to the side arms and were considered to be in a good enough condition to be left. The 1920s repairs were again to the ship's side arms of knees both port and starboard of the forward half of the poop. A number of the carlings on the forecastle, boom and quarterdecks were renewed in teak and fir. The planking was renewed on the quarterdeck, the forecastle and the poop decks. Brass screws were used for the fastenings, recessed and plugged with teak dowels.

After the completion of the restoration programme in 1928 little work was done on *Victory* during the 1930s other than maintenance[9]. The ship was regularly painted and kept clean, but the methods used may have led to problems that had to be solved later. The decks were scrubbed in time-honoured fashion, probably daily.

Unfortunately, instead of using sea-water as had been the practice at sea, fresh water was used. Any water leads to rot in timber as it finds its way into the thousands of joints in the ship's structure, and those timbers that are completely or partially enclosed suffer most. The salt in sea-water is only mildly inhibiting, but the use of fresh water positively encourages rot and the regular washing-down of the decks carried on for years is thought to have been one of the reasons why so much of the repairs of the 1920s had to be reworked later. If the principal cause of the damage was caused by damp-induced rot, it was run close by decay caused by the death-watch beetle which had no doubt been present in the ship long before her docking in 1922 (see Damage by Death Watch Beetle p100).

At all events, there was no significant repair work done until it was necessitated by enemy action in the Second World War, when on the night of 10-11 March 1941, during an air raid on the dockyard, *Victory* suffered damage from what a service report of the action would call a near miss. The high explosive bomb hit the masonry steps in

Breast hooks, looking towards the port bow, *ca*1963. (MoD (N))

the dock wall, destroying the first four transverse sections of the cradle on the port side and causing considerable damage to sections 2-5 on the starboard side. Half the breast shores on the port side were dislodged and about 18ft of the longitudinal concrete plinth, built to support the keel, was damaged and displaced. Thirteen pairs of keel blocks were damaged or destroyed.

As for the ship herself, a hole 8ft long and about 15ft in height was torn in the hull planking and its supporting timbers. A 5ft hole was made in the orlop between stations 29 and 33, and damage caused on the centre-line. Between stations 33 and 36 the underside of the orlop was scarred. The lower deck also suffered damage on the centre-line over an area roughly 6ft x 7ft between stations 29 and 33.

Temporary shores and keel blocks were rigged and 'first-aid' repairs were made to the hull to keep out the worst of the weather. Douglas fir and deals were used to effect temporary repairs to the orlop and lower deck respectively. Permanent repairs were not attempted because of the pressure of urgent war work in the dockyard in 1941. In the event, these had to wait until the major repairs to the hold fourteen years later.

It took some time for the dockyard to return to a proper peacetime programme after the war and it was not until the 1950s that a lengthy survey was carried out on *Victory*. Its detailed nature is evident in that it involved analysis of the borings from 6,252 test holes. The results showed that the ship's structure from the level of the orlop down to the keel, virtually untouched in the 1920s, was in a very poor state, and particularly so at the stern.

Repairs 1955–1964

This great repair, as it would have been called in the eighteenth and early nineteenth centuries, was begun in 1955. There was however an important difference from the 1920s repair, when fifty additional shipwrights were taken on for much of the restoration period and it is a difference that is bound to affect *Victory* for as long as she exists. *Victory*'s interests have to be subordinate to the requirements of the current Navy, of which she is no longer an active part. Inevitably this involves financial considerations, but perhaps its greatest effect is in the restriction it places on the manpower available. This means that progress will inevitably be slower than wished.

Nor is manpower the only factor. If the timbers which form the structural underpinning of the ship have to be cut out and renewed, great care is required to see that not only does she not collapse in the process but that she does not lose her form or shape. In the 1950s, technology, as it applied to the shipwright's trade, had not advanced greatly except in the use of power tools. The supports necessary to maintain the ship's form while work was in progress were bulky, heavy and laborious to set in place, especially on board where difficulty of access and lack of headroom made the use of machinery impossible. The bulky nature of the supports also aggravated the already cramped and restricted room in which the shipwrights had to work. In addition, the very heavy timbers used in the repair itself had to be manhandled into position. Frame timbers for example could be eight or nine feet long and 14 or 15in square, and might have to be offered up two or three times before the correct fit was achieved.

Repair and renewal of any structural timber that was enclosed on three or more sides was made in teak. Oak was used if the member was not to be enclosed and a reasonable air space lay around it. As established in the 1920s repair, fastenings were made using galvanised mild steel bolts with nuts so that any future removal of the timber need not involve wasteful and damaging splitting out. Nuts that would show were recessed and covered with a plug of the appropriate timber, as were the heads of the heavy brass screws used to secure deck planking.

Stern

The stern of a wooden vessel is literally held together and supported by lateral beams called transoms, which tie the aftermost frames on each side to each other and to the sternpost. The lowest four transoms, from No 1 on

10. Bugler p126.

the after end of the keelson to No 4 at the level of the orlop deck, were renewed in teak, together with the anchor pieces that connect each wing across the foreside of the sternpost. Eight feet of the sternpost in way of these transoms was also renewed in teak.

Below these transoms 13ft 6in of the inner sternpost was renewed. Much of the adjoining deadwood was renewed or repaired, the few upper lengths being renewed in teak.

All the riders in the hold had to be renewed or in a very few cases repaired. Riders are like huge additional frames superimposed on the inner planking, crossing the keelson and rising to a point 4ft 6in above the orlop. Their section, 18in x 15in, adds considerable transverse strength to the ship. Alongside each rider, both port and starboard, is a knee of similar proportions bolted to it.

Some rider knees also cross the keelson; others begin some 21in from it. The top of each rider knee ends at the underside of the orlop-deck beams. The riders and knees were renewed in oak which, Bugler states, required forty-eight large oak trees of top quality timber that the dockyard was most fortunate to be able to obtain in the mid-1950s[10].

Hold to orlop

As a result of the bomb damage, one length of teak 12ft 10in long was scarphed into the keel, most of which

The ship with only the lower masts and the bowsprit left during the refit of the rigging in 1956. The fore and main yards have been lowered out of the way of the scaffolding. On the mizzen mast the cross-jack yard is still in place. (MoD (N))

seems to be the original in English elm. Elm was a favourite timber for keels because it remains stable when immersed and has a firm curly grain that holds fastenings well. In addition a similar length of false keel was fitted to protect the keel itself from damage through the vessel grounding, a common enough occurrence before steam power brought a more certain control over the effect of

Swaying up the fore topsail yard, c1964. (MoD (N))

the wind and tide and of navigation. It was important to protect the keel because of the enormous cost in time and effort involved in repairing or replacing it. Traditionally the false keel consisted of two parts: the upper part next to the keel itself was hardwood, in *Victory*, 6in beech. This was the tough protective layer, but to give greater depth to the protection a second sacrificial layer was added, not uncommonly in a softwood such as fir. In *Victory* however, this outer false keel or sole piece is of 4in elm. The sole pieces were fastened to the keel and to each other, using heavy-gauge copper dogs driven in vertically across the seams.

The keelson was renewed throughout much of its length, oak being used as it is exposed on three sides. One 26ft length of keelson, in good condition and believed to be original, was retained between stations 90 and 108. The repairs to the keelson listed above include the 14ft section that had to be replaced because of the bomb damage.

The extent of the decay in the hold may be realised in that from bow to stern there are one hundred and forty-five timbers or frames on each side below the waterline. Of these, one hundred and one to port and a hundred and four to starboard had to be renewed or repaired, roughly covering an area which stretched from a line below the third gunport on the lower deck to a line below the sternmost ports on the same deck. This included the seven timbers needed to replace those damaged by the bomb blast.

Orlop to lower deck

Few repairs were made to the frames between these two decks, and those that were repaired were all on the starboard side at stations 16-26, 40-43 and 49.

The orlop beams themselves appear to have remained virtually untouched in the great repair, other than relatively minor work done to the beams damaged by the bomb blast at stations 29 and 33. A hanging knee was replaced in oak and four corroded wrought-iron hanging knees were replaced in steel.

Of the pillars that help to support the orlop, all were renewed except that immediately forward of the after hatch and its neighbour, on the centre-line and immediately abaft the hanging magazine. These two are very old and could conceivably date from the great repair of 1814 or possibly 1803. The number of pillars and their position at the time of *Victory*'s floating out in 1765 is unknown, and Bugler records that a large number of shores, mostly fir, had clearly been inserted in the 1920s and perhaps before[11]. These also were replaced.

A great deal of outer planking was replaced in teak, some 3,500ft to port and 3,300ft to starboard. It ran between the stations 19 and 133, as did the major outer planking repair of the 1920s but, as indicated by the widespread renewal of frames at the level of the hold, extended upwards from the garboard strake to a maximum of twenty-four strakes, port and starboard, at station 133.

Also in the region from the hold to the orlop the inner planking and beam shelf were renewed in teak from station 23 to the stern, that is both to port and starboard aft of the foremast, a total of 8,676 running feet as Bugler records[12].

Middle deck

In 1955 and 1956 eight beam knees were replaced, three lodging and five hanging knees, all on the starboard side. Unfortunately timber for grown knees was not available and they had to be cut from baulk[13]. At the same time, eight beam ends had to be renewed at the starboard side, three of which were at stations where the knees had to be renewed. The beam ends were repaired by scarphing in new lengths of oak ranging from 9ft-10ft long except in the case of that at station 22, where there is a shaped half beam. There the scarphed piece was 4ft 9in long. During the same eight month period (August to March) deck planking was renewed to starboard between stations 16 and 32.

Boom deck

Six of the ten Douglas fir beams to this deck, which had been renewed in the 1920s, received attention during the eight months from June 1957 to January 1958. Beams 47, 51, 71 and 77 had to be completely renewed; beams 56 and 66 also needed repair at the ends on the port side, the new sections scarphed in being 8ft 5½in and 7ft 3in respectively.

Bulkheads

In the hold, three-quarters of the after bulkhead of the grand magazine had to be renewed. About seven feet further aft is the first of two bulkheads which run parallel at stations 40 and 42 some 10ft each side of the centreline. The whole of the former bulkhead and nearly all of the latter were renewed.

The area round the mainmast step, roughly in the middle of the hold, is the lowest point in the ship, and it is to this point that any water taken in by leaks would normally drain and from which it can be pumped. The water is contained by the well bulkhead, which forms a 12ft square around the mainmast reaching to the underside of the orlop. This entire enclosure was renewed, but one or two strakes of the 3in oak planking were left out in order to allow a flow of air within and counteract any tendency to dampness leading to decay.

On the after side of the well bulkhead but nine inches shorter is the shot locker. Its transverse bulkhead and ends also reach to the underside of the orlop, providing a space 11ft 3in x 2ft 5in All three of its bulkheads were renewed in oak.

The transverse bulkheads at stations 104 and 111 were renewed except for 10 per cent of the former, and all the bulkheads, both transverse and longitudinal, that form the flour room, after magazine wing space and access passages between stations 111 and 125, were renewed.

---

11. Bugler pp128-29.

12. Bugler p119.

13. Traditionally any timber in which a curve was required was cut so that the grain followed the curve, giving greater strength. A knee cut from baulk would almost certainly have the curve cut across the grain. Compass timber, as grown curves were called, was always in short supply especially in the larger sizes. This shortage led to the introduction of the wrought-iron bracket early in the nineteenth century, known by the name of its designer Mr T Roberts, master shipwright at Pembroke Dockyard. In recent years the developments in laminating techniques and the accompanying resins has obviated the need for grown curves.

Chapter Five

COMPLETING THE GREAT REPAIR
1964–2000

THE REPAIRS UNDERTAKEN to the keel and lower hull from 1950 to 1964 provided a firm base for the ongoing restoration and gave reasonable assurance that the original shape would not be lost. A great deal of attention was given to this in respect of subsequent removals and replacements of structure and breakage readings were taken at regular intervals as a check on maintainance of form. The sequence in which the restoration work was carried out is illustrated in the diagrams on pages 110–111 in the Progress Report and the work involved is described in the following paragraphs.

Restoration of the lower hull from the turn of bilge to the lower gun deck gunports 1964–1973

The repairs begun in the 1950s proceeded to schedule and in 1964 the repairs to the lower hold and the World War II bomb-damaged area forward were reported as complete. A survey was carried out and this indicated that the upper works which had been partially restored in the 1920s were in fair condition, but the area between them and the recently completed lower hold structure was badly decayed, particularly on the starboard side.

A programme was devised to restore that portion of the ship from the termination of the lower hold repairs up to some 4ft 6in below the lower gun ports. The section was to extend for the whole length of the orlop on port and starboard sides and to include the cockpit. The work proceeded in a similar manner to that used previously.

Squads of four men were allocated an area of the hull to repair, each area being estimated as one year's work for the squad. The areas opened up at any one time were staggered port and starboard, forward and aft, in order to conserve the strength of the hull and maintain form.

As each area was opened up for repair it was confined to a size compatible with ease of working and the maintainance of form of the hull. It usually extended four timbers in width, of which for ease of working only three were replaced, the fourth being replaced along with two or more when the next three timbers were removed. The top ends of the timbers were secured to the scarphs of the structure above, temporary filling pieces being inserted as required to allow the planking to be fitted. These were carefully marked with plastic tallies so that they could be removed later when the time came to continue the restoration upward at that point.

The restoration of the ship from the turn of the bilge to the under side of the lower gundeck gunports over its whole length was divided into twenty-three such sections with a further three sections each on the port and starboard sides at the bow making twenty-nine sections altogether.

The following account gives some idea of the amount of work involved in the removal and replacement of just one section and as will be seen each section overlaps the next in order to give the good shift of butts necessary to avoid weakness and distortion.

Prior to the removal of any structure, temporary supports were fitted to adjacent timbers usually in the form of 12in x 12in fir baulks. Once this temporary shoring was in place, any remaining copper sheathing was removed from the outer bottom and two new butts were marked on the old hull planking between adjacent frames. Each butt was spaced four frames apart. Holes were drilled and using pneumatic powered saws, cuts were made down these lines. The section of old planking between these two parallel cuts was then split away from the timbers using chisels, bars, wedges, and shipwright's mauls. The thickness of this outer planking varied between 3in to 9in and was held in place by treenails, dumps, and clenched bolts, with the seams between planks caulked with oakum. Iron and copper fastenings had to be sawn through and punched out clear using iron wedges. In some places the planking just crumbled away where it was so rotten.

The four oak timbers were then split out working from the scarphs of the restored futtock section below and upwards to the next scarph above. As each section was exposed, measurements were taken, and where there was no distortion, batten moulds were made and bevels obtained so that replacement futtocks would correspond in shape to those removed. In the workshop new teak sections were made to the moulds and then trimmed to fit at the ship. The space occupied by the fourth timber was used to gain working access and to enable moulds to be made of the face of the next timber to be removed and also to facilitate cutting the fastenings securing it to the inner bottom planking. As the new timbers were erected they were held in place with temporary bolts through the inner planking and by ribbands and temporary shores erected from the dockside.

When a number of timbers had been erected in this way their faces were faired and the outer bottom planking lined in, moulds were made and replanking was begun. On completion of an area of planking this too was faired in and the seams caulked with oakum, payed up with pitch and finally roped using white sisal.

Internally, the beam end chocks, wrought-iron securing brackets, hanging and lodging knees, and all the remaining fastenings had then to be removed together with several strakes of internal planking. Butts were cut to allow removal of sections of waterway, spirketting,

beam shelf and planking exposing the inner faces of the renewed futtocks. The inner planking was then replaced and secured through the new structure. Once this was done the replacement of the knees and beam-end chocks was undertaken. The beam-end chocks were recessed to take the wrought-iron securing brackets.

In total this one section involved removal and replacement of some 1400ft of timber all individually shaped to the original form of the hull. It comprised hull planking, futtocks, knees and spirketting, ranging from 27 futtock pieces 14in x 132in by 13ft long to 500ft of outer bottom planking 10in wide by 7in thick. Additionally, because they were in the way of the repairs described, the carpenters' walk, cabin and storeroom bulkheads had to be removed and later replaced.

Renewal of the bow timbers in 1968. On the right can be seen the copper sheathing still in place. (MoD (N))

Each section of three or four timbers brought its own problems but had a similar work content to that described in the foregoing. This programme of repairs continued from 1964 to 1973 when it was stopped to enable the restoration team to concentrate their efforts on the restoration of the stern. One area of particular concern was the cockpit, both in terms of the history and the construction. This area had been altered several times since the building of *Victory* but no drawings are known to exist which depict the cockpit structure at the time of the Battle of Trafalgar. The only clue to its layout lies in the sketches for the contemporary painting of 'The Death of Nelson' by Devis. The 1926 attempt to re-create the cockpit was removed and the structure was reinstated to match the starboard side of the ship.

The workforce was mainly engaged on restoration

Repairs to the bow timbers in 1968. (MoD (N))

work but from time to time it was necessary for them to undertake routine tasks such as periodic load tests and surveys. The latter occasionally uncovered potentially serious structural weakness or longer term hazards requiring immediate attention. Typical of these was the need to fabricate and fit new steel mast steps for the fore and mizzen masts and the urgent need to caulk and pay up large areas of deck planking to prevent the ingress of rainwater.

The grand magazine and fore peak, bow to station 26 1968–1973

Whilst still part of the section from the turn of bilge to the lower gundeck, this area extends down to the keel and forward from the bomb damage repairs right to the stem. In order to maintain form, each side was tackled separately: starboard side first, and then the port side. Only the repairs to the starboard side are described here as the work done on each side was similar. Work to repair the bomb damage at the after end of the grand magazine had already been completed.

The work commenced at the keel and rose up to number 18 strake of planking. It involved the renewal of portions of the keelson, foremast step (below the steel plate) and floors, working from station 26 forward and upward towards the stem. At the bow additional work was required because of the twist needed in the outer bottom planking which made it impossible to force it home to the timbers either by wedges or shores as had been done elsewhere for positions with less curvature. The traditional but notoriously difficult technique of bending planks by steaming had proved no more reliable than in the past and as a consequence much expensive timber was wasted. The problem was overcome by laminating the planks.

From station 24, the tapering of the bow requires that the timbers are fitted as cant frames and in order to strengthen their connection to the keel, floors are fitted between those at stations 15, 17, 19, 24 and 26, port and starboard across the keel.

The wooden ventilation trunking between the for-

The yards are lowered alongside using modern equipment undreamed of when *Victory*'s restoration began, but it makes for economy of manpower, speed of operation and a greatly reduced risk of accidents. Here the main yard is being lowered during work in 1972. (MoD (N))

ward and after bulkheads of the light compartment was removed together with 70sq ft of light compartment decking. Butts were marked and cut across the planking of the forward bulkhead of the grand magazine and 90sq ft was removed, consisting of 3in thick rabbeted oak boards overlaid with a double skin of ½in and ⅝in fir boards. Butts were marked and cut across the foremast step and the starboard side was removed. One hundred feet of inner planking was removed and later renewed in way of the foremast step. Four hundred square feet of copper sheathing was removed from the outer bottom between the stem and station 15[1]. One hundred and thirty running feet of outer bottom planking was also removed and later replaced in teak. Two butts were cut across the forepeak bulkhead at station 19 on the starboard side of the keelson and 70sq ft of bulkhead similar to that of the grand magazine were removed. Half moulds of the starboard-side floors at stations 15, 17, and 19 were made to assist replacement and a pitch batten was taken of the keelson, indicating the relative positions of the knees from the centre line of the foremast.

The wrought-iron straps were removed from the floors at stations 17 and 19 and laid apart for later replacement. The three floors at stations 15, 17, and 19 were removed. One pillar between the keelson and the orlop at station 14 was removed. Five inner bottom planks between the stem and station 26 were removed.

Sixty square feet of grand magazine bulkhead at station 24 and 45sq ft of the forepeak bulkhead at station 19 were removed. One hundred and twenty running feet of inner bottom planking were removed and renewed. Twenty futtock sections of the starboard side timbers between stations 6 and 26 were removed and renewed, the average size being some 14ft 6in long and sided 14in, moulded depth at the keel 3ft 4in, 15in at the top end.

One hundred and twenty running feet of outer bottom planking 4.5in x 10in was removed and renewed between stations 6 and 11. Five new teak outer bottom planks, stations 6 to 10 were lined in, moulded, fitted and secured after being steamed and set in the jig to the gentle curvature of ship's bottom. On completion 160sq ft of new planking was faired. Work continued in a simi-

lar manner with 600sq ft of outer bottom planking removed to allow the renewal of the cant timbers between frames 1 and 24. These were faired in and new teak planking fitted up to No 30 strake. Twenty-three temporary teak filling pieces, average size 14in x 14in by some 3ft 8in long, were moulded, fitted, secured and tallied. These were to fit the scarph joints at the upper ends of the timbers between stations 1 and 7 and between stations 11 and 26 enabling the outer planking to be closed up. Six new teak outer bottom planks were prepared and fitted to strakes 32 to 37. These planks are tapered across their width to conform to the outer bottom curvature and vary in thickness; 32 strake is 4½in whilst 37 strake is 8in thick. Three new teak temporary filling planks at strakes 38 to 40 were prepared and fitted in like manner. Plastic tallies for these pieces were used to mark the limit of the repairs and at either end of 35 strake. One hundred and forty square feet of starboard longitudinal bulkhead of the grand magazine similar to the forward bulkhead was removed from between stations 24 to 36. Work now continued repairing the inner bottom planking and structure. Thirteen new strakes of teak planking, totalling 200 running feet were fitted between stations 11 and 35.

In 1970, repairs were commenced to the port side of the ship, which also facilitated the renewal of the fore deadwood, keelson and breasthooks. Only the latter renewals will be given here, as the port side repairs were similar to those already described for the starboard side.

Butts were marked and cut across three breasthooks with an average cross-section 29in x 14in on the port side of the keelson. Three sections of breasthook each 16in in length were removed to clear the keelson which was then removed between the stem and station 27, 18in x 22in by 23ft long. A butt was marked across the upper baulk of the fore deadwood at station 16, and the section of oak deadwood between station 16 and station 24, 18in x 18in x 13ft long was removed. A new section of fore deadwood was moulded, prepared, fitted and secured.

---

1. A conscious decision was taken by the VATC not to replace the copper sheathing because it would encourage rot, as water trapped behind it could not evaporate.

Butts were marked across the first and second breast-hooks and sections of average size 14in x 19in x 3ft were removed from port and starboard of the middle line. One section of deadwood between stations 7 and 15 was removed, 17in x 18½in x 14ft. A new section of fore deadwood was moulded in teak, fitted, and secured. It was sided 18in at its after end, tapered to 16in at the forward end, moulded 28in at the throat, tapered to 18in at the after end and 10in at the forward end, and was 14ft long. The after section of the new teak keelson between the stem and station 20 was moulded, prepared, fitted, and secured, sided 18in to 16in, moulded 22in wide,

length 15ft. Two teak wedges, 13in to 16½in x 18in x 5ft 8in and 14½in to 16in x 18in x 5ft 8in were prepared and fitted between the new keelson and the foremast sole plate. Four new oak pillars, each 11in x 11in x 10ft, were prepared and fitted between the new keelson and the orlop beams 2 and 5. A standing section of the breast-hook in the forepeak, 14in x 18in x 5ft 6in, was removed.

In 1972 work on the fore end was halted and the structure sealed, in order that the workforce could be concen-

Repairs to the poop in 1975 with new deck beams being fitted. (MoD (N))

trated on the restoration of the after end. Work forward was not recommenced until 1980.

Stern structure 1973–1980

The restoration of the stern aft of the main hold at the level of the orlop extended from station 100 to the transom and upwards to the poop deck. The following paragraphs describe the work undertaken on the hull structure from station 100 to the transom, in the wardroom area and gallery structure, the admiral's cabin area, and the captain's cabin area.

The precautions necessary to protect the stern cabins from the weather during the repairs are evident from this photograph. (MoD (N))

Inner structure and outer bottom from station 100 to the transom

The lower part of the sternpost and the adjacent associated structure had been renewed in the 1950s. Before removing further timber it was necessary to erect internal and external temporary supports. To gain access to the timbers meant the removal of deck stringers, spirketting, three sections of waterway and ten deck planks at lower gundeck level port and starboard, which were later to be replaced with new material. New futtock sections of the ship's side timbers were fitted between stations 131 and 142, the average length of each being about 5ft. Then new outer bottom planking, built up from 1in thick laminates, was prepared and fitted between 19 and 36 strakes. The port and starboard quarter knees, the two

The repairs to the stern are completed. (MoD (N))

outer sternson knees and the beam-end chocks from under beams 130 to 137 were also removed. This was to allow for the fitting of new teak endpieces to the number nine oak transom beam[2]. A new section of beam shelf and new inner bottom planking was then installed, prior to the fitting of new sternson knees and beam-end chocks. New end sections were also fitted to the port and starboard beams at stations 128 and 133 underneath the orlop, and new beams were fitted to replace the beams at stations 137 and 142.

2. It seems probable that the main part of each of the transoms, ie other than the ends, from number five and the whole of number eleven, the wing transom, pre-date Trafalgar and are original. *Victory* was never raked with shot from the stern as she had raked the luckless *Bucentaure* at Trafalgar.

and a new end scarphed on. This action was then repeated on number 6 transom, both the port and starboard ends being renewed. The after sections of the port and starboard outer sternson knees were removed, as were six strakes on inner planking under each section. New sections were made and fitted to the ends of numbers 7 and 8 transoms. Three new strakes of lower wale and nine of main wale were fitted between stations 112 and 142[3]. Two new fabricated teak quarter-knees were fitted between the transom beam and the underside of the middle deck, and more sections of beam shelf and waterway from station 100 to the stern were renewed. Fabricated teak lodging knees were prepared and fitted at each end of the three stations 138 to 140 on the port side, together with fifteen new deck carlings. New spirketting and inner planking was then fitted from station 133 to the stern, and then new hanging knees and quarter chocks were fitted. Finally, new oak deck planking was laid and caulked.

The wrought-iron brackets were removed from the stern knees and the transom beams, to be replaced later after completion of repairs to the new structure. A new deck transom was fabricated and fitted, together with new end sections to the tie beam above. The lower ends of number 4 port and number 3 starboard stern knees were cut away and renewed. The wrought-iron brackets were replaced, and new inner planking was fitted from station 131 to the stern at lower gundeck level. New beam ends were made and fitted to beams under the lower deck at stations 130, 135 and 138. New carlings were then fitted port and starboard between the beams at stations 130-133, 133-138, and from 138 to the knee at the stern. Twenty-one ledges were fitted between the beam shelf and the new carlings, thus completing the work at the stern from the lower hold up to the middle gundeck.

The graceful curve of the inner planking is seen in this view of the fore end of the hold. (MoD (N))

New pillars fashioned from teak were fitted between the keelson and underside of the beams at stations 133 and 142. Two laminated standard knees were fitted at the afterside of station 128, and the whole area of the orlop from station 128 to the stern was decked in, using Douglas fir planking. A total of 120ft of laminated outer bottom planking was fitted to strakes 37 to 42 starboard, and 180ft on the port side to strakes 36 to 41.

Work continued on the inner structure with the removal of the port centre and the port inner sternson knees and eleven strakes of planking, which then allowed access to the number 4 transom at the orlop level. The outboard end of this beam was then removed

---

3. Originally the wale strakes were made up of single planks. Steel, *Naval Architecture*, Table of Dimensions and Scantlings, folio VII, gives the dimensions laid down for the main wales of a First Rate as four strakes measuring five feet two inches from top to bottom (ie each 15½in broad) and ten inches thick. With the introduction of laminated planking it has sometimes been convenient to fit a wale strake in two separate thicknesses.

Wardroom area and gallery structure

The work described here is bounded by the middle and upper gundecks, together with the stern timbers.

All minor bulkheads, wardroom linings and transom carvings were first removed, together with the panelling from the transom and the quarter galleries and the tongued-and-grooved boarding that formed the galleries' deck. All windows were removed from the stern as were the pine baluster carvings from the galleries. The quarter galleries themselves were then carefully dismantled, after first removing the copper weather sheathing and the moulded teak chocks. This was followed by the removal of the decks at middle and upper levels, by the removal of the deckhead, side planking, and oak chocks at the middle deck, and finally removing the seven fore-aft mouldings and the corner-posts from each gallery.

The replacement of the quarter galleries could not be undertaken until the completion of the repairs to the main structure; the description of this is included with the captain's cabin and poop deck area later in this section.

On the starboard side of the middle gundeck the following items were removed from between station 100 and the stern, to be later renewed after the repairs to the hidden structure underneath: the moulded waterway, inner planking, upper and lower spirketting, beam-end chocks, hanging and lodging knees, beam shelf sections, and the filling pieces fitted between the shelf and the knees. The port side was treated similarly except that the ends of beams at stations 113 and 117 required

Area 11 on the upper gundeck completed, looking to starboard at the foot of the ladder leading to the quarterdeck. (MoD (N))

The after part of the wardroom. The panelling covers the rudder head. (MoD (N))

renewal. New ledges were fitted between the carlings and the lodging knees or beam shelf as appropriate. The wrought-iron brackets were recessed into and secured to the beam-end chocks, to the beams and to the ship's side.

The renewal of this structure gave a firm foundation for the continuing removal of the ship's side planking and futtock timbers. Planking strakes 43 to 60 were progressively removed, together with gunport sills and lintels and the gallery doors. New futtocks were prepared and fitted, suitably recessed in way of the gunports to take the new sills and lintels. At their lower ends the timbers at stations 144 to 151 were butted onto the top face of the stern quarter knees, whilst that at station 148 was fitted between the top face of the quarter knee and the underside of the gallery doorway on the middle deck. In conjunction with this work, new quarter knees were prepared and fitted.

New ship's side planking was laminated, fitted and faired, the seams being primed with flat white paint and then stopped with linseed oil putty. New wale strakes were prepared and fitted from stations 100 to 140, the seams being then painted, caulked with oakum and stopped with putty. The stern mouldings fitted between the outer sternpost and the port and starboard quarter knees and along the plank ends at the tuck were removed. New mouldings were made and fitted. Because of the amount of curvature and twist, these replacements were fitted in two sections.

Whilst the external work was being carried out, the deckhead of the wardroom was blasted to remove the many layers of paint and to enable the condition of the structure to be assessed. This had to be done with the minimum risk of damage to the wood surface. After detailed investigation and tests it was decided that the blasting contractor should use a form of non-ferrous grit as the abrasive medium, a technique that had been used elsewhere in the ship. The blasting revealed that the beams were in good condition and that a beam-end chock originally fitted at station 142 had been omitted during an earlier repair. It was therefore replaced at this time. Twenty-nine deck planks, of which fourteen were oak and the remainder of Baltic redwood, were removed, as was the margin plank. New Douglas fir decking and margin planks were fitted in its place. The new decking was secured to the deck beams with recessed brass countersunk screws, which were covered by diamond-shaped fir dowels to give a finished appearance similar to the original deck. Finally the new deck was caulked with oakum and payed-up with marine glue.

The oak bulkhead boundary, to which a demountable bulkhead might be bolted, and which was fitted to the middle deck at station 121, had the port and starboard fifteen feet removed and replaced with teak. The curved double doors from the starboard side were refurbished and new *jalousies* fitted before they were replaced. Three new portable sections of curved bulkhead, each containing a *jalousie* panel in the upper half, were made and fitted outboard of the doors.

At the stern, nine new strakes of teak planking were fitted between the mouldings at the top of the tuck and the stern moulding at the level of the wardroom windowsill. On completion, the planking was caulked with oakum and payed with linseed oil putty. The moulding on both sides of the tie beam was cut and, together with the five planks above it, was removed and renewed. The five teak sliding windows were refurbished, glazed and refitted at the stern of the wardroom, and a window seat fitted under them. New upper and lower mouldings were prepared and fitted to the deck beam above the windows. The deck was covered in marine-grade plywood with canvas stretched over it, painted in black and white squares to give a diagonal chequered pattern.

The bulkhead at the forward end of the wardroom was completed by the fitting of eight curved and ten straight sections, with double doors to port and starboard worked into the curved sections. Six turned teak stanchions were manufactured and fitted under the beams, three on each side between the middle and upper decks. The new

bulkhead and fittings were stained and coated with matt finish polyurethane varnish to complete the wardroom area.

Admiral's cabin area, station 107 to the stern

This area is bounded by the middle and upper decks, and includes the admiral's day cabin (the Great Cabin), dining and sleeping cabins.

The demountable portable athwartships bulkheads at stations 125 and 141 were removed and laid aside for survey, renovation and future replacement, and the bulkhead boundary framing at the port and starboard ship's side was split away. This, together with the removal of the cabin linings, gave access to the inner planking and knees. All the hanging knees were removed between stations 115 to 155, and new knees were prepared. It was found that although no knees were present at station 144, evidence showed that they had been fitted at some previous time, and they were therefore replaced with the other knees as the restoration progressed.

The wrought-iron quarter knees connecting the deck beam to the spirketting were removed, together with three strakes of inner planking. The upper and lower spirketting was also removed between station 110 and the stern. The curved and moulded waterway, the shaped margin plank, and the beam shelf were also removed from between these stations. This allowed the removal of the wasted oak lodging knees, and their replacement by fabricated knees made from teak.

New teak sections of waterway, spirketting and beam shelf were fitted. Two new lengths of deck margin, each 52ft long, were prepared and fitted, made up of four sections butt-jointed together. The inner planking was renewed and gaps left for the gunports and gallery doorways. The wrought-iron quarter knees were replaced and resecured. The quarterdeck planking was released, the deck beams underneath at stations 109, 112 and 114, together with their supporting ornamental pillars, were removed, and new laminated teak beams manufactured and fitted. The old and new beams were fitted in two sections and joined together by an eight-foot snaped scarph. The ornamental pillars were replaced and the deck planking re-secured. The newly-made hanging knees were fitted, but not at beam 109, which was fastened by means of two iron knees. Similar beam renewals were required at stations 117, 119 and 121.

A temporary screen was built across the ship so that the forward bulkhead of the admiral's cabin could be removed. New teak pillars and deck and deckhead cants of red deal were made and fitted for the bulkhead between the day and dining areas. The refurbished bulkhead panels and the ornamental pillars were then replaced. New deckhead cants were fitted, and the refurbished panels and doors replaced in the bulkhead between the dining area and the forward end of the sleeping-cabin area. Where the beams met the deckhead, yellow pine mouldings were fitted in all cases. Marine-grade plywood was then fitted over the whole of the deck area of the admiral's quarters, and sail canvas stretched and secured over it, which was finally lined out and painted with black and white squares to give a chequered pattern.

Lord Nelson's dining cabin, looking aft into the day cabin. The dining cabin is used by the Second Sea Lord for entertaining. (MoD (N))

In conjunction with this internal work, repairs continued to the ship's side planking and framing. Six strakes of wale and the underlying side planking, strakes 60 to 65, were progressively removed from station 109 to the stern for access to the framing underneath. New futtock sections were prepared and fitted, those at stations 125, 126, 133 and 134 being butted at their lower ends onto the lintel chocks of the middle-deck gunports. New gallery door chocks were prepared and fitted between stations 147 to 149 at upper deck level. The ship's side planking was laminated and renewed in teak and the seams caulked with oakum and stopped with linseed oil putty. Eight new strakes of wale were fitted, both the wale and side planking being terminated at station 143 to allow for the later fitting of the quarter galleries.

Captain's cabin area and gallery structure

This area includes the captain's day, sleeping and dining areas, the secretary's and the sailing master's cabins, and the quarter galleries.

In order to protect the admiral's quarters and the wardroom below, it was first necessary to seal the deck against the ingress of water. The stern seat, the ship's side linings, and the portable bulkheads were removed and the whole deck area was covered with plywood sheets, which in turn were covered with a layer of glass-reinforced plastic as a weather seal.

Before any internal work was undertaken, the poop deck above was repaired, together with the stern timbers. Four teak knees, two port and two starboard, were removed, together with the boxed-in galvanised steel T-section brackets underneath and also the iron horses fitted across each pair of knees, while the iron knee fitted between the stern timbers and the ship's side inner planking starboard was removed and laid aside for later replacement. On the removal of the ensign staff and the poop skylight, it was apparent from the remains of iron, copper and white metal fastenings in the beams that the decking had been renewed at least three times. The mizzen topsail bitts were also removed for refurbishing and later replacement, and two strakes of inboard stern planking and the associated teak waterway were

removed from the poop deck. All the teak deck planking and the waterways were then removed, giving access to the beams below. The weakened deck transom beam was removed and a new laminated beam manufactured and fitted in its place. Sixteen new deck beams were laminated and fitted to replace those removed. The port and starboard ladders and platforms leading from the quarterdeck to the poop were removed, refurbished and replaced. The hammock cranes and the taffrail, with its moulding and supports, were removed, together with the fir beam at the forward end of the poop deck. A new laminated teak beam was manufactured and fitted. Two new carlings were fitted between the beams, one each on the port and starboard side of the mizzen mast.

Access to the ship's side planking necessitated the removal of the mizzen mast chain platforms and their later renewal. The four boat davits and the ship's side brackets had also to be removed, with the deadeyes and anchorage links.

Ornamental mouldings were carefully removed from between station 120 and the stern, and laid aside for later replacement. Thirteen strakes of planking, including the wale, were removed from between station 118 and the stern. The quarterpieces and the stern boat booms were removed; new quarter pieces were made and fitted. The new futtock timbers as cants at station 152 and 153 were butted on to the quarter piece.

New ship's side planking was prepared, fitted, and caulked from strake 65 to the sheer strake. New lintels and sills were fitted at the gunports and gallery doorways. Seventeen new planks of upper wale were fitted from station 115 to the stern. Two new mizzen-chain platforms, each 20ft long, were fabricated and fitted to the ship's sides. The anchorage links for the deadeyes and the platform support brackets were renovated, galvanised and fitted to the platforms. Two new laminated teak stern boat booms were manufactured and fitted, as were new lodging and hanging knees. The refurbished wrought-iron brackets were replaced and resecured and the balustrade rails superimposed on the stern planking between the admiral's and captain's cabins were removed for renovation and later replacement. The copper sheathing between the mouldings was removed, and the area under cleaned off by sanding machine. It was then found necessary to remove and renew the end sections of three of the planks, after which the new and the old planking seams were caulked with oakum and payed-up with putty. New waterways were manufactured and fitted to the port and starboard sides of the poop deck. Sheets of ½in marine-grade plywood were laid over the the new deck beams, each sheet being scribed to simulate the deck seams and coated with preservative before being bedded and secured to the beams. New white seraya deck planking was then laid over the whole area and the seams caulked with oakum and payed with pitch. Seven new planks were fitted to the inside skin of the transom.

Work proceeded on the inner structure with the removal and renewal of the spirketting, inner planking, hanging and lodging knees. The upper and lower iron brackets connecting the beam shelf to the deck transom beam were removed to enable the stern portion of the beam shelf to be removed. Most of this structure was of pitch pine, replacing the original oak; all the renewals were made using teak. However, the inner planking between the taffrail and poop-deck waterway was split away and renewed, the new planking being caulked and payed-up with linseed-oil putty. New rails were fitted to the port and starboard sides of the poop deck. Four new fabricated knees were fitted between the inner stern planking and the poop deck, with the knees recessed to take the steel reinforcing brackets. The iron horse for the driver boom was fitted across the space between the inner two knees.

All the temporary weathersealing was removed from the deck of the captain's quarters. The poop-deck skylight was re-assembled and replaced, and eight sliding panels fitted under it. A new moulding was fitted to the foremost beam of this deck, and the hammock cranes were replaced. The capping of the taffrail and the first outboard strake of planking below it were found to be in good condition, but the centre section of the next seven planks below it had to be replaced. The renewal of their outboard ends was deferred until the gallery roof chocks

had been fitted. The seven stern windows were refitted and replaced, with new sashes and weight boxes. The shutters to each sash were renovated and new teak sills and lead flashings fitted, together with eight new teak mullions.

A new seat was made and fitted across the whole width of the stern below the window-sill level. The six vertical stern timbers were boxed in with seats similar to those fitted in the admiral's quarters and the wardroom.

The restoration of this part of the stern brought to light an ingenious means of combining habitability and convenience with the ship's fighting efficiency. It was important, if inconvenient, that the great cabin and the captain's cabin should have ports for the use of stern chasers when required. Standard gunports would have either destroyed the symmetry of the stern or reduced the window space, and perhaps both. However, the stern-chase gunport lids above the middle deck level were made as half ports hinged at their lower edges. When the panelling was removed from the stern timbers for action stations, the windows in way of the gunports could be removed to form the top opening section of the gunport. The lower section was hinged at the bottom and held in place by a draw-bolt on each side near the top edge. The stern moulding in way of these gunports was cut and fitted as short lengths across the gunport lids.

In the master's and secretary's cabins, new deck and deckhead cants were made from fir. Two new bulkhead panels were made and fitted to each cabin, the inboard panel glazed, the outboard panel fitted to the rake of the ship's side. Ornamental pillars were made and fitted between the deck and deckhead cants. Similar cants with pillars were manufactured and fitted for the fore and aft bulkheads. Each bulkhead comprised three panels and a glazed door. All the panels were hinged to the top cants, and bolts were fitted to their lower ends to retain them when closed. The ship's sides were panelled-in between the hanging knees, and the drop frieze was fitted. Five new panels and a double door were made and fitted at the forward bulkhead of the captain's quarters, the doors and three of the panels half-glazed. New cants were fitted to the deck and the deckhead.

Three ornamental pillars were fitted between the cants, and the space between them was panelled. The five bays formed by the hanging knees at the ship's side were panelled, and a drop frieze was fitted. Cants were fitted with two pillars and three panels, which, together with a double door, formed the fore-and-aft bulkhead between the dining and sleeping cabins, while the panels were fitted with hinges and bolts similar to those of the master's cabin. The remaining bulkheads were constructed in a similar manner and the ship's side was panelled in.

For the replacement of the quarter galleries, new support chocks had to be made and fitted. To the forward end of each of these a tapered corner post was fastened with the taper on the fore edge of the post rabbeted to take the gallery side planking, and similar posts of triangular section were fitted to the after end of the chocks against the transom. Four teak stiffeners were tenoned into each chock to support the planking, and teak mouldings were fitted at the window-sill of the lower galleries. The mouldings were shaped to the ship's side at the forward end and mitred into the moulding of the stern with a rabbet cut on the bottom edge. They were fastened to the four stiffeners with mortice and tenon joints.

Three strakes of gallery side-planking were then fitted between the support chocks and the mouldings. This planking was made up of laminates in order to achieve the required bend and twist in the fore-and-aft direction. Two mouldings were fitted to the lower edges of the chocks in way of the plank-end rabbets. Fillet pieces and bearers were fitted to the lower edges of the middle gallery, and triangular section corner pieces were then fitted between mouldings of the lower and middle galleries and two stiffeners fitted between the mouldings. A strake of laminated planking was fitted under the mouldings of the middle gallery, and an iron knee inserted between the mouldings and the stern timber.

At the quarterdeck level a fillet piece was fitted to the ship's side, then a bearer fitted between the corner post and the stern. Three bearers were fitted between the fillet piece and the stiffeners, and the deck planking was laid.

Similarly, mouldings were made for the galleries at the

New framing and planking. The pipes visible are the leads for the laniards to the gun port lid on the deck below. For all that such heavy timbers make up the ship's side, the elegant curves of the tumblehome are plain to see . . . (MoD (N))

. . . and they are just as elegant lower down. There is new framing beneath the waterline and new wales are visible at the top of the photograph. (MoD (N))

window-sill level of the captain's cabin, and bearers, side planking and deck planking fitted. The top of the gallery crowns were formed from teak planks laid over bearers running between a moulding on the ship's side and the crown of the galleries. Three strakes of laminated side planking were fitted between the moulding under the crown and the moulding at window lintel level. Fascia

Working on the beakhead in June 1987. (MoD (N))

boards were then fitted. Four teak mullions were fitted for the wardroom quarter gallery windows, and the three windows installed.

Three sets of mouldings were fitted between the forward end of the galleries and the mast-chain platforms. In the galleries port and starboard, twenty balusters and four mullions were fitted between the mouldings at the top of the wardroom gallery windows and the sills of the windows above. Similarly a further twenty balusters and four mullions were fitted between the top of the great cabin's gallery windows and the sills of those above.

Across the stern between the mouldings at the top of the wardroom windows and the window-sills of the great cabin, sixty-nine balusters were fitted, with a similar number below the window-sills of the captain's cabin. Window frames were fitted at all levels and the windows glazed. Except for the carvings, cleaning, and polishing, this completed work on the stern.

During the restoration work on the stern, the programme of surveys and tests prescribed in the maintenance schedule was continued. These indicated the need to effect urgent repairs in other areas for the safety of the ship or the public. These included repairs to Nos 5 and 6 cradle supports in the dock bottom, removal and replacement of the quarterdeck beam at station 81, and the bitts to the main mast. The skid beam at station 71 was renewed using teak laminations and two supporting pillars fitted. The skid beam forward of the main mast was replaced by a new laminated beam, with new fore and aft carlings. The half-beams fitted on each side of the mast and their intercostal carlings were renewed; new half-beams were also fitted port and starboard between the after main beam and the middle line of the mast half-beams. Similar half-beams were fitted between the middle line half-beams and the forward main beam. The second skid beam aft of the mainmast was also renewed. The timbers supporting the heel of the bowsprit were found to be so weakened that the figurehead was in danger of being crushed, and although restoration of this area was soon to begin, a temporary steel bipole support was made and placed under the bowsprit to prevent it resting on the figurehead.

Bow Structure, 1980-1989

Stem to station 31

The early 1980s saw the start of a very difficult period. This included the reduction of the dockyard labour force, and the change in 1984 from a Royal Dockyard to a Fleet Maintenance Base, while in the middle of this the Falkland Islands crisis occured. Inevitably these factors affected progress of work on *Victory*. Fortunately this was ameliorated to some extent in the mid-80s by a temporary increase in the number of workers allocated to *Victory* and by the introduction of improved techniques. Both factors enabled the restoration to be brought back on schedule. As the work on the stern diminished, the workforce was diverted to other tasks, including work around the mainmast and the starboard entry port and a detailed survey of the bow structure. This latter revealed that the fore end was more decayed than at first thought and complete renewal was deemed necessary.

Restoration work on the forward end, stem to station 31, commenced with work on the inner planking on the port side by the main magazine. The planking, which was mainly laminated, was secured to the existing ship's side timbers, some 25 per cent of which had been renewed in the early 1970s. At that time several sections of oak laminated breasthooks had been prepared and stored. These were fitted as the restoration proceeded. The fore-and-aft light room bulkhead was removed on the port side of the grand magazine, together with the fore-end gratings and the deck planking on the orlop. New ceiling planking was fitted port and starboard from station 31 to the stem up to the orlop. Because of the shape of the hull, it was necessary to fit this planking in laminates and to work some of the planks as stealers. All the planks that fitted to the bow were cut on a snape to fit against the faces of the apron, stemson, or keelson. Sections of the stemson and the apron were removed from behind the stem to just below the orlop, and new sections were fabricated and fitted. A new futtock was made and fitted close against the after face of the apron, and although originally one of the hawse timber futtocks, for reference purposes it was counted as No 1 station.

View of the starboard side of the lower gundeck between beams 4 and 6. (MoD (N))

Parts of No 1 (lower) and No 2 breasthooks had already been fitted using the sections previously fabricated and stored. The new arms and centre sections were fitted and secured. No 4 breasthook and the ceiling underneath it were removed and new planking laminated and fitted.

In the meantime the foremast and the bowsprit had been unrigged and laid apart for refurbishment and later replacement; the bowsprit was to be fitted with a new steel cap. The beakhead bulkhead was burned off to remove all paint, so that its condition could be surveyed and the positions of the fastenings determined. The structure of the beak itself was found to be satisfactory but the head timbers, quarterpieces and the hawse pieces were badly decayed and needed replacing. Datum marks and levels were fixed so that the beak could be removed for access from behind. All of the beak and its supporting rails, knees, and figurehead, and the marines walk gratings, were removed for renovation and later replacement. In order to prevent any drop of the bow structure whilst renewal of the stem was taking place, a steel cradle was manufactured and placed to support the forefoot. A section of the stem and apron were then removed, new sections made and fitted. Number 3 breasthook was made and fitted in three sections. Upon completion, the original iron buttstrap was fitted across the after face, the total length of which was 19ft 8ins.

Temporary closing planks in the bottom and temporary filling sections in the timbers were also removed and new timbers fitted to complete the futtocks up to the lower deck level, from the stem to station 23. The inner planking was removed from the stem to station 14 between the orlop and lower decks. Number 5 breasthook was removed, and a new teak breasthook manufactured and fitted, with the original iron buttstrap being replaced on completion. The lodging knees were removed from No 1 beam at the orlop and lower-deck

The manufacture and trial assembly of deck beams and their associated carlings (longitudinals) and ledges in the workshop makes the final fitting on board much easier. Here two shipwrights and an apprentice are seen with the assembly between beams 3 and 4 of the upper gundeck. (MoD (N))

levels, and new knees were fabricated. The steel hawsepipes were removed as their alignment was found to be different from that of the hawse holes in 1805, probably because this made them more convenient for permanent mooring whilst *Victory* remained afloat in Portsmouth harbour. The lower sections of Nos 2 and 3 hawse timbers were fitted.

A section of the lower-deck planking was removed, as were the bulkheads forming the manger. The gunners' store and carpenters' walk bulkheads were also dismantled and removed, together with the deck planking back to station 26 at the level of the orlop. This gave access to the orlop and enabled the removal and renewal of No 1 deck beam and its lodging knees.

New ceiling planking was laminated and fitted as strakes 25 to 36 port and starboard, thus completing the inner planking up to the lower-deck level. Removal of the old bottom planking revealed that there was a slight difference in the make-up of the bow timbers, there being ten on the port side but twelve to starboard. The extra timbers were given letters to identify them, and the original numbers picked up again at timber No 7, port and starboard. This completed the hull inner planking and futtocks from stem to station 23 and from the limit of the repairs to the lower deck level undertaken prior to 1970.

Work continued internally with the removal and renewal of the structure between the lower and middle decks from the stem to station 29. This included the waterway, spirketting and inner planking. During the removals of the old spirketting and sections of waterway in the manger area, two lead scupper-heads and attached lengths of lead piping were discovered; these were the original drains to the manger, one port and one starboard.

Removal of the planking on the orlop revealed severe decay and beetle infestation to No 2 beam. All the carlings between Nos 2 and 3 beams on the orlop were numbered and photographs were taken for identification to ease replacement. Moulds were then made of No 2 beam before its removal. The beam, together with its two standard and two lodging knees, was then removed. A new laminated beam and fabricated knees

Renovation of the forward end of the middle gundeck which were completed in 1987. (MoD (N))

were then made and fitted. The carlings between the beams were replaced.

Sixteen strakes of laminated bottom planking, strakes 13 to 29, were fitted port and starboard over the new futtock sections, to below the orlop. The remaining sections of the old stem, apron and stemson were removed, and the new teak sections prepared and fitted. The deck hook at the lower deck level was removed, together with its iron strap, and a new replacement was fabricated. The old inner lining was removed and new laminated planking was fitted, followed by the new deck hook and its iron band.

Six new fore and aft carlings were fitted at orlop deck level between No 1 beam and the stem. New gratings were made and fitted to the carlings to form the deck. All

The new figurehead carved in the workshop and unveiled on 19 May 1990 to mark the completion of the fore end repairs. It is a replica of the figurehead borne at Trafalgar.

The restoration continued in this manner, with the removal and replacement of a futtock length at a time, up to the upper deck level. Inboard the work was arranged to be slightly in advance of this, with the replacement of the waterways, spirketting and beam shelves to give support and maintenance of form before renewing other structure.

Number 3 deck beam under the middle deck was found to be badly fractured and so a new beam was made and fitted, using iroko, following the satisfactory trial of an iroko beam to the quarterdeck. New laminated oak hanging knees were fitted, one each to port and starboard. A new outboard end was fitted to the starboard curved half-beam. New sections of beam shelf were laminated and fitted in way of No 3 beam. Similarly, the No 2 beam and its knee were removed and renewed; the hanging knees were also removed from No 1 beam in order to fit the new inner planking. A new section of beam shelf was fitted and the beams replaced.

Moulds were made of the old breasthook on the middle deck which was then split out together with the inner planking and spirketting underneath. A new breasthook was fabricated from iroko and fitted to the new planking. At the upper deck level the old beakhead deck was removed together with the beak bulkhead.

The waterway port and starboard was removed and renewed from the stem back to station 20. A new deck hook was made and fitted under the middle deck after laminating and fitting a new beam shelf. Number 2 beam on the underside of the upper deck was removed together with its shaped half-beams and beam-end chocks. The inner planking in way of the beam-ends was renewed and a new beam and two new half-beams fitted, all fabricated from iroko. New beam-end chocks and a new beam shelf were also fitted.

Similarly, No 1 beam was renewed together with its hanging, lodging knees and carlings between No 1 and No 2 beams. The bowsprit was refitted and three half-beams making up the bowsprit partners on the port side of the bowsprit opening were renewed in iroko. A new section of Douglas-fir deck planking was laid from the stem back to the bowsprit step and was caulked with

the carlings and ledges between Nos 1 and 2 beams were renewed and fitted in position. All the ship's side planking and futtock timbers from the stem to station 22 were removed and renewed up to the third tier, at middle gundeck level. The stem was now completed with the fitting of a new section, the stem pieces, and knighthead timbers.

oakum and payed with marine pitch. The old deck hook was removed from the underside of the upper deck and moulds were made from which a new iroko deck hook was manufactured. New futtock timbers were made and fitted to the underside of the beak-deck capping and an emergency exit was cut on the port side forward[4]. New futtock lengths were fitted to the cant timbers to bring them up to the level of the bulwarks or to end as timber-heads. New teak side planking from 37 to 57 strakes was fitted over the futtocks port and starboard from the stem to station 23. The realigned hawse holes were cut and faired through strakes 48 to 50. The old No 1 beam at the middle-deck level was removed, and a new iroko beam fitted with two new laminated oak knees.

Except for the fitting of the top strakes of planking and the replacement of the beak structure, this completed the restoration of the external hull from the stem to station 23, up to upper-deck level.

The 1980 survey had indicated that an area in the vicinity of the starboard exit (the gangway position) was in an advanced state of decay, and so repairs were put in hand. At the lower deck level, the five hanging knees were removed from the beams at stations 77 to 91 together with three strakes of clamp from stations 75 to 85. The inner planking was removed from between the gunports between stations 89 to 94, and laminated planking and clamps fitted. At the middle-deck level a temporary exit was cut in the starboard side, incorporating the third gunport aft of the permanent exit. Two strakes of planking and spirketting were removed and later renewed in stations 71 to 94. The waterway and inner planking were removed from stations 72 and 92 and later renewed together with the beam shelf. The hanging knees, beam-end chocks and associated wrought-iron brackets were removed over the same distance. The lodging knees at stations 71 to 74 and stations 83 to 86 were removed, together with five carlings.

A new section of beam shelf and two new lodging

knees were fitted with filler chocks between the beamshelf and deckhead. New hanging knees and beam-end chocks were fitted and new inner linings, deck margin planks and carlings were fitted from station 65 aft.

Other work which was carried out as a result of the 1980 survey included the renewal of a quarterdeck beam

The bows were finally completed with the unveiling of the new figurehead, 19 May 1990. (MoD (N))

---

4. Over the years, the requirement to meet ever more stringent safety regulations has led to the creation of emergency exits, wooden handrails on the ladders, a fire main and other precautions, none of which existed before 1922.

Rot in the futtocks on the starboard side of the lower gundeck in 1993. (MoD (N))

ing items were also removed, either for refurbishment and later replacement or as patterns for renewals: the top of the false cat tail from the middle line to the ship's side; the shot garlands for the carronades; carlings from the steel cathead support knees; the fore and aft steadying knees on the after side of the cathead; mouldings; fife rail; planksheer, from the beak bulkhead back to the third timberhead; and two hammock cranes. Numbers 10, 11, and 12 cant timbers were then renewed up to the bulwark level and a new section of sheer strake No 76 fitted together with the first strake below. The support knees were removed and the planking and timbers under renewed. This planking was laminated and fitted as strakes 69 to 74, from stations 8 to 16.

In order that the bowsprit might more easily be refitted, the centre section of the beak bulkhead had been removed. With the bowsprit back in position the repaired beak structure could be replaced and work begun on the beak bulkhead.

The waterway and spirketting was removed and renewed from stations 17 to 29 at the upper-deck level, port and starboard. This was followed by the removal of the inner planking and hanging knees. The three strakes of inner lining were replaced using iroko in three equal laminates.

The knee of the head structure, including the gammoning knee, its extension, capping and hairpin brackets, were replaced and resecured. The key chocks, teak cappings, facing pieces, cheek rails and gammoning doublers were refurbished and refitted; minor modifications were required because of the realignment of the hawse holes. The ship's side planking in way of the wales was caulked and payed with hard stopping and new wales were fitted port and starboard.

Numbers 3 and 4 beams and the upper-deck carlings between them were removed; new iroko beams and carlings were fitted in their place. The waterway and spirketting to port and starboard were removed and renewed between stations 26 and 32 and new sections of iroko planking and beam shelf were fitted from stations 21 to 32. The lodging knee fitted on the port side between beams Nos 3 and 4 was renewed using iroko; recesses

just abaft the mainmast. The new beam was fashioned from iroko, the first large iroko section to be fitted in the ship and an experiment that proved highly successful. At the same time four carlings and the mouldings between the top of the beam and the underside of the quarterdeck planking were also renewed. Extensive repairs to the steel cradles supporting the ship were also undertaken at this time.

Upper deck, forecastle deck, deck fittings and associated structure

The port and starboard catheads, which were removed for access to the ship's side planking and futtock timbers, were surveyed and fitted with new sheaves. The follow-

were cut and new ledges fitted on the port and starboard sides at beam No 3 and a new iroko lodging knee and three ledges were made and fitted to the starboard side between beams Nos 3 and 4 supporting the upper deck. The old ship's side planking and top timbers 32 to 44 port and starboard were removed and renewed, working down to the gunport lintels on the middle deck with new sills and lintels being fitted as the work progressed. The timbers were renewed using teak, while the planking was of iroko fitted in four laminates for strakes 58 to 75.

The bowsprit was adjusted to give a clearance of 10½ins between the top of the crown on the figurehead and the underside of the sprit. New chocks were fitted between the stem head, stem pieces, and the underside of the bowsprit. The gammoning fish was repaired and fitted to the bowsprit, the seams being caulked with oakum and payed with mastic. A new retaining bridge was made and dovetailed into the knighthead timbers to secure the bowsprit in position. Moulds were made and bevels taken of the ship's side to enable tapered pads to be fitted to take the vertical cathead support brackets. The catheads were then positioned and secured to the brackets which were afterwards sheathed in teak. The bulkhead planks, planksheer and fife rail were prepared and fitted in way of the cathead. A new cat beam was manufactured and fitted. Although the original beam was solid timber, in order to reduce weight the replacement was constructed as a hollow box structure as it was no longer required to support the weight of the catheads and anchors.

Two new iroko beam-end chocks were made and fitted together with their Roberts brackets, one each to port and starboard under No 4 beam at the underside of the upper deck, whilst at the same time two cast hanging knees were fitted under No 5 beam. The foremast wedges were removed, surveyed, repaired, replaced and caulked at the middle-deck level. Two new pillars were fitted at the after end of the mast surround up to the underside of No 3 beam.

At middle-deck level, the waterway and spirketting were removed and renewed from stations 34 to 50 starboard. This completed the renewals from the stem to

station 50, and connected up with the earlier restoration of that side.

When the mast wedges were removed and the foremast surround at upper-deck level was surveyed, it was evident that it had been infested with beetle and was badly decayed. A new teak surround was fitted and the refurbished wedges were replaced and caulked.

The forward section of the upper gundeck from the stem to the beak bulkhead was renewed using Douglas fir. The seams were cauked with oakum and payed with pitch. The beak bulkhead, bulkhead stanchions and deck beams were removed, made anew and fitted. The waterway and spirketting at upper-deck level were removed and renewed from stations 40 to 44 on the port side. The inner planking at the upper-deck level port and starboard was renewed using iroko laminates. The beam shelf was similarly renewed between stations 35 and 49. The hanging knees and lodging knees which had been fitted in 1985 were removed to give access for this work, and were afterwards replaced. The upper, middle, and lower rails to the beak and their mouldings were refitted and replaced together with the head timbers. The marines' walk gratings and supporting structure were renewed and fitted. The futtock timbers from the planksheer down to the middle-deck levels between stations 24 to 44, port and starboard, were renewed. New laminate iroko side planking was fitted to the new timbers for strakes 57 to 75. The port and starboard fore chainwale platforms were removed, refurbished and replaced after the renewal of the wale and planking underneath. The remaining wale was fitted after the seams of the planking had been caulked with boat cotton and payed with Sikkens hard stopping. The waterway and spirketting were removed from the lower deck port side between stations 29 and 37, and renewed. Similarly, the old knees and beam shelf on that side were removed and renewed from stations 25 to 37. This completed the renewals from the stem to station 44 of the beam shelf, waterway, and spirketting at this level.

The port and starboard beam-end chocks were removed from under No 6 upper-deck beam. The beam shelf and inner planking were removed and renewed and

The periodic surveys and test of structure, guns and fittings as described in the Maintenance Schedule[5] led to miscellaneous repairs being carried out, and to the renewal of fourteen strakes of poop-deck planking and the recaulking of the whole deck to eliminate leaks. All the gunport lids were repaired and new hinge pins fitted. Number 16 beam on the underside of the upper gun-deck was renewed, with its hanging and lodging knees. A new lodging knee was fitted to beam No 15 and the carlings replaced between beams 16 and 17.

At the middle-deck level a new beam-end chock was fitted to No 20 beam and a new beam end to No 17 beam. New sills and lintels were fitted to the new gun-port openings cut in the restored bow areas.

Restoration of the port and starboard sides above the orlop, 1989-1999

With the completion of the earlier restoration work in the lower regions of the hull and at the extreme after and forward ends, there remained a lot of repair work necessary in the port and starboard sides and some tidying-up of internal deck areas. The restoration of these areas was carried out concurrently with the ship's side repairs, as were the internal beam and deck replacements. The starboard side was progressed first, as it could have prejudiced the maintenance of form if too much of the ship had been opened up by working on both sides at the same time. Also a conscious policy of providing the general public with a national monument that was of good appearance from at least one viewpoint was adopted at this time. Thus from the late summer of 1992 one side of the ship remained of whole appearance for them to photograph: the port side until the completion of the starboard repairs in October 1995, and thereafter the starboard side whilst the port side work was continued.

The starboard ship's side was divided into three main work areas and the task was progressively undertaken between timbers 40 to 68, 69 to 87, and 88 to 104 from the level of the previous repairs in the vicinity of the lower gunports up to the top of the bulwark. This portion of the hull included most of the gunports on all three

The replica Brodie stove presented by a former Director of Naval Construction, Sir Philip Watts, for the 1920s restoration. The copper condenser provided distilled water for use by the surgeon.
(MoD (N))

the new beam-end chocks fitted. The cast knee under No 7 beam to starboard was renewed. Numbers 5, 6, 7, 8, and 9 beams and the two half-beams at station No 6 on the underside of the forecastle deck were removed and renewed, together with their associated carlings, lodging and hanging knees, and topsail bitt supports. This concluded work on the bow structure up to February 1989. The foremast was then fully re-rigged and the refurbished figurehead replaced. The First Sea Lord, Admiral Sir William Staveley formally unveiled it on 19 May 1990 in a ceremony to mark the completion of the fore end restoration work.

5. A maintenance schedule prepared by the Manager of the Constructive Department and endorsed by the VATC was issued in 1966. The current schedule, also endorsed by the VATC and issued by the Project Manager *Victory* in 1993 brings the earlier document up to date with regard to the latest practices and techniques as well as separately identifying maintenance tasks.

decks and the starboard entrance port, and also required the removal and replacement of the chainwale platforms of the main and mizzen masts. In preparation for the work, additional dockside stays were added to the mainmast, while the shrouds were released and made up temporarily to the bulwark in order to retain the ship's appearance. This was also done later with mizzen mast shrouds.

Late in 1991 a minor setback occured when the Douglas-fir planking in the beak deck was found to be rotten. This had been laid only two years previously, and was a sharp reminder of the speed with which rot can set in. The fungus present was identified by the Technical Support Directorate at Woolwich as *penicillium spinulosum*, a type commonly found in soil but not normally associated with wood rot, although capable of degrading wood in certain conditions. Fortunately the area of the beak deck is not large and it was relaid in teak with associated waterway, carlings and ledges in iroko. Two additional scuppers were carefully sited in the deck, making four in all, to improve the drainage of this cramped area which is sheltered to some extent from the wind and thereby more subject to persistent damp. Although not 'as at Trafalgar', this measure was felt necessary to reduce the risk of the rot recurring.

The technique used for replacing the defective ship structure was very similar to that developed for other hull renewals, except that because of the tumblehome it was found best to remove and replace the inner hull planking using temporary fastenings and to renew beam ends and associated knees and so forth first. Then areas of outer hull planking and wales were removed to give working access to the decayed futtocks. Replacement sections of teak futtocks were then moulded and fitted to the renewed inner planking, using this to maintain shape while working over an area which embraced some four or five timbers at any one time. When sufficient timbers were completed in this way, the external planking and wales were carefully lined in over the section, usually some 12ft to 15ft in length, and the external planking was moulded and fitted.

This planking consisted of two iroko inner laminates and one outer laminate of teak, arranged so as to form planks approximately 6in thick in total and to provide for an authentic shift of butts. As work moved aft, each beam was inspected, with its associated knees, carlings and ledges. Most of the beams were sound throughout or only needed their ends renewed. New beams were fitted at Nos 6, 7, and 8 on the lower gundeck, 11 and 12 to the middle gundeck and 28 to 33 to the quarterdeck. Most carlings and ledges were sound and were replaced during the repair work. In December 1993, the removal of No 12 beam to the middle gundeck revealed a paper on its upper side. It read 'This deck was laid October 27 1886 by Naval Shipwright Pensioners James Lockyear, Leading Man, Mr N Philips Chief Carpenter RN in charge'. The gunports were then lined in, cut, and faired. Finally the gunport lids were refitted and the gunport sills sealed with glass-reinforced plastic, arranged with an outward slope to shed rainwater. On completion the planking was caulked with oakum and paid up with soft

The removal of No 12 beam on the middle gundeck revealed a note placed under the planking by shipwrights when the deck was renewed in 1886. (MoD (N))

The renewed starboard entry canopy. (Simon Murray)

stopping before painting. All the through fastenings used were of specially made galvanised steel nuts and bolts. To give the authentic 'clenched end' appearance of the original copper fastenings, the nuts were manufactured in the form of a dome and the projecting threaded ends of all the long bolts were cut off flush.

The restoration of the ship's side in the vicinity of stations 79 and 80 at middle-deck level enabled the starboard exit to be re-established in its original place in April 1994, and the subsequent repair work to the structure aft of this permitted the temporary opening made in 1980 to be filled. The carved entrance canopy was renewed and gilded. The chainwale platforms were replaced, and this enabled the shrouds to be correctly re-secured. With the final painting of the side from stem to stern the starboard side repairs were completed during September 1995.

Similar repair work on the port side was commenced soon after, but not before photographs of the ship were taken, as this was the first time since the commencement of the restoration in the 1950s that *Victory* was not encumbered by scaffolding.

In March 1992, it was realised that the forecastle deck appeared to be inadequately supported aft of the foremast partners, and that this had almost certainly been the case in the ship's early years. On beam No 8 there are two hinge plates similar to those fitted on the middle gun-deck adjacent to the jeer capstan head. The plates hold the heads of stanchions, but enable them to be swung up out of the way when necessary. While there is no direct evidence that such stanchions were in place in 1805, it is extremely likely, as the ship would then have been forty years old and the majority of the wrought-iron work that might be said to be part of the ship's structure, such as the Roberts brackets, had been introduced during the great repair of 1803. It was decided therefore to have a pair of stanchions made and fitted.

There remained areas of the hull at orlop level and in the hold which had not been restored during the earlier repairs, and these were tackled as labour resources became available. The work in the forward part of the hold and orlop had been suspended in 1972 because of the need to deal with the stern repairs and this was picked up again. Beams 1-5 to the orlop proved to be sound, although the anchor stock piece in No 5 was badly cracked and had to be renewed. From the state of the surrounding timbers it seemed probable that the fracture had been caused by the bomb which exploded on the dockside in 1941. The knees and chocks which had to be removed in order to replace the decayed inner planking were found to be generally sound, and were replaced later during the restoration. At lower-gundeck level a lintel and sill were worked in between stations 23 and 26 and an opening left in the hull to provide an emergency exit for personnel. A steel brow was attached in 1993 leading to the dockside, thereby providing a means of escape from the ship at this level as advised by the local fire officer. The opening was 'disguised' by a door which when closed carefully matched the lines of the plank edges and external contours of the hull.

Internal work continued commensurate with the ship's side repairs and beam ends, chocks, knees, and so forth were renewed as found necessary and finally bolted through the restored hull structure. On the lower deck, knees, beam shelf, waterway and inner planking were renewed between stations 29 and 37 and also from station 71 to 94. A new end was fitted to No 17 beam on the middle deck and new chocks to No 20. The knees, beam shelf, waterway, spirketting and inner planking were also removed. The wrought-iron Roberts brackets that had been removed were refurbished and refitted. The sides were caulked with oakum, payed up with soft stopping, and finally painted. The six hammock cranes removed for refurbishment were now replaced and rigged with netting.

Two major goals had now been achieved: first, the restoration of the lower gundeck was largely completed in 1994 so that it was totally clear of any significant restoration work and thus could be seen by the public throughout its entire length for the first time in many years; secondly, by October 1995 the restoration of the starboard side was completed. This meant that since the work began in 1955 every floor, futtock and top timber had been inspected and renewed where deemed necessary and the whole starboard side replanked. The final task was the refitting of the main chainwale platform on that side, 34ft 11in long, 4ft 1in wide and in thickness tapering from 6½in from the ship's side to 5¼in outboard.

The beam-end chocks of the orlop beams 2 to 8 were removed, together with associated Roberts brackets. They were found to be in good condition suitable for re-use, with the exception of that from beam No 2 on the port side, which needed replacing. With the refurbished Roberts brackets, all the remainder were later refitted. Similarly the oak standard knees for those beams were also removed and inspected; all proved sound except that at No 2 beam, port side, for which a replacement was manufactured in teak.

The chocks and knees were removed to give access to the inner planking and beam shelf, which was split out. On the port side, the beam shelf was replaced between timbers 11 to 23, 26 to 36, and 73 to 91, together with the three strakes of planking below. To starboard, the beam shelf and four strakes of planking below it were renewed from timbers 12 to 24, 21 to 45, and 77 to 96.

On the orlop, planking was completed from the stem back to No 9 beam, all seams – 1,272ft in total – being caulked with three strands of oakum and payed with marine glue. Following new research, the section between beams 2 and 6 was raised to create a platform. On this platform a transverse bulkhead was erected, from which the cabins for the boatswain and the carpenter were later extended with adjacent storerooms. A hatch was fitted immediately forward of No 9 beam together, with scuttles for the three storerooms, the magazine, the magazine light room and the cartridge store. In the wings

The galley. Placed directly aft of the Brodie stove on the middle gundeck, the dimensions of the galley (6ft 2in to the front of the stove and 8ft 6in athwartships) it seems more than probable that the preparation of the food spread to adjacent mess tables whenever the ship's situation allowed. The paddle shaped board against the meagre range of cupboards is a replica of that used with the oven. (MoD (N))

three gratings of Douglas fir were fitted port and starboard, one each between beams 3, 4, 5, and 6.

It was now possible to attack a large area on the port side without serious danger of losing the form. Planking and timbers were split out from about the waterline up to the capping on the top timber between stations 44 and 73, using the standard method of removing four timbers at a time and working in three. As before, all the futtocks were replaced in teak, with an adequate shift in butts to avoid weak spots. This section alone involved the preparation and installation of some 90 pieces of timber 14in x 11in, roughly half of which were between 7ft and 9ft long and weighed in excess of 300lbs. Preparation in the workshop was easy, but offering up such timbers once or twice to get the size and shape exactly right when working in the necessarily confined space available was both difficult and frustrating.

As the futtocks between stations 44 and 73 were renewed, so too were all the gunport sills and lintels: Nos 6, 7 and 8 on the lower gundeck, 6, 7, 8 and 9 on the middle gundeck and 5, 6 and 7 on the upper gundeck. This area was then planked in 5½in teak, using three laminates. When the inner planking was renewed, ¾in spaces were left between planks not abutting on spirketting or beam shelf, in order to encourage the movement of air between the inner and outer planking. Between stations 75 and 93 the final section of waterway on the lower gundeck was renewed in one piece of teak 22ft 5¾in long, with overall measurements in depth 9¾in and width 1ft 1⅞in. The two strakes of spirketting above were renewed in teak 6in thick, made up from two laminates glued and screwed together using Cascophen Resorcinol resin R S 126 and catalyst hardener.

Between beams 12 and 16, eight iroko ledges were fitted between the ship's side and the first carling. New beam ends had to be fitted to Nos 13, 14, and 17 to the lower gundeck, and the No 16 beam arm end was also renewed. A lodging knee and hanging knee were fitted to No 13 beam; a cast knee to No 14; two lodging knees and a hanging knee to No 15; one lodging, one cast and one hanging knee to No 17, and a cast knee to No 18 beam. All these knees were fabricated in teak.

The last remaining area of the ship's side was opened up by the removal of the outer planking between timbers 78 and 90 and strakes 40 and 58. All the futtocks, together with the lintel and sill to gunport 10 on the lower gundeck, were renewed in teak. The work in this area also necessitated the removal of the steps and other structure pertaining to the entry port. The canopy and carvings were also removed, the canopy to be renewed and the carvings to be refurbished.

The removal of this length of the ship's side structure revealed serious deterioration in the deck planking at its outer edge. There has always been a reluctance to interfere in any way with the planking on the lower gundeck, because it is reliably believed to be pre-Trafalgar and therefore quite possibly the original deck laid in 1764. However, it was found necessary to replace an approximately 60ft run consisting of the margin plank and the two adjacent strakes between stations 51 and 52. The replacement planking was of 3in oak.

At the time of writing the Great Repair is not complete, and there are factors that may jeopardise the timetable as planned. For example, work on *Victory* must quite properly be subordinate to the requirements of the modern Royal Navy; shipwrights and riggers have other employment elsewhere in the yard. More problematical is the supply of timber. Teak, the favoured timber, is currently priced at about £4,500 per cubic metre. All timber used by the Ministry of Defence must come from genuinely sustainable sources, and it is not clear that plantation-grown hardwoods have the same durability as those from natural forests. Political decisions about certain sources may also create problems. Fortunately, the dockyard authorities and the VATC included a safety margin in the planning, and we can be certain that the work will be completed for the bicentenary of *Victory*'s greatest day.

The restoration of *Victory* began in 1923 as a result of the efforts of the Society for Nautical Research. By virtue of its trusteeships of the Save the *Victory* Fund, the Society has an ongoing commitment to meet the cost of such items as rigging. At the end of this account of the ship's restoration and the latest Great Repair, it is appropriate to refer again to the Society's generosity, and especially to the men whose skill and craftsmanship is evident throughout the ship.

In 1980 it was decided to award a medallion to retiring shipwrights who had given long service to the ship. A three-inch bronze medallion was designed and struck by Austin Farrar, FRINA, a stalwart of the Society and long-serving member of its Council. The first awards were made in 1980 and presented to shipwrights Bill Paice,

Bob Williams and Bob Smith by Admiral Sir Richard Clayton, Commander-in-Chief Naval Home Command. The medallion is still awarded as and when appropriate and it is presented on board on the occasion of the Society's yearly visit to the ship in midsummer.

The quarterdeck waist and forecastle viewed from near the place where Lord Nelson fell. (Simon Murray)

Chapter Six

THE WAY AHEAD

THE PLAN NOW is to complete the restoration and repair of *Victory* by the bicentenary of the Battle of Trafalgar in 2005. Although restoration is all but complete, active measures are required to ensure that the best possible benefit is gained from the work done in the past.

The most important factor in this will be the need to maintain the structure in as tight a manner as possible to prevent rainwater coming in. This can only be achieved by a continuous progamme of caulking all seams that are either in direct contact with the weather or subject to the necessary cleaning activities of the ship's staff. The internal structure too, must be kept dry and well ventilated. Despite these precautions, in so complex a wooden structure the possibility of rot appearing is always present, particularly in enclosed timber. To keep the need to replace defective timber to a minimum in the future it is essential that thorough surveys are conducted at regular intervals. Generally, the intervals between surveys/repairs are ten years for the outer bottom structure and five years for the decks, beams and knees.

To determine the presence of decay the surveys will continue to be undertaken using the following methods:

a. visually;

b. with bore tests using a ⅝in spoon auger, where hammer or pricker test indicate a possible problem. The borings are collected and retained in bags for further investigation.

c. using a special instrument, a small diameter 'detecting' drill, to produce a virtually undetectable test hole giving an instantaneous read out from which the internal density of the timber can be ascertained.

From the results, the condition of each timber will be assessed and classified. Concurrently, sample galvanised bolts will be removed for examination and replaced by new. In order to minimise cost, save time and reduce disruptions onboard, as much use as possible will be made of trestle ladders and mobile hydraulic platforms instead of conventional tube scaffolding.

Confirmation load-testing of deck structures and access brows will also continue at regular intervals. Similarly, regular measurement of the breakage of the ship (vertical hull deflection along its length), and the maintenance of its shape (transverse beam spread, vertical height between decks and vertical height of outer bottom above dock base—all taken at positions along the ship's length) will be made as in the past.

All masts, yards and spars and associated equipment will continue to be surveyed every two years, generally aloft, by mastheadmen using a safety chair. Those yards and spars which can conveniently be brought down will be lowered for survey. Similarly, any items found aloft to be suspect or defective will be brought down for a more detailed survey, repair or renewal. The lower masts and the largest yards and spars, and the mast caps that are fabricated from mild steel or iron and are fitted with inspection/access plates, will be surveyed internally and have ultrasonic thickness measurements taken. The fore, main and mizzen lower masts step on the lower, orlop and middle gundecks respectively, and their extensions through to the top of the concrete plinth in the dock will also be surveyed every two years and repairs carried out as necessary.

Surveys of the rigging and blocks will be carried out concurrently with the masts, yards and spars, and rectification work undertaken. Black polypropylene cordage used for the rigging is specially manufactured for the purpose, to resemble the original blacked-down hemp rigging, and is set up at intervals until the stretch has been fully taken up.

Four replica boats are stowed onboard *Victory*: a 34ft launch, 32ft barge, 28ft pinnace and an 18ft cutter. These boats are surveyed biennially and any first-aid repairs are carried out with the boats in their stowage positions. Every six years the boats are removed for any significant repairs.

Consideration is being given to slinging a specially constructed 25ft cutter (listed in the Establishment of

The 'magic' Sibert drill, used to identify the state of timber several inches in from the surface. (MoD (N))

Boats *c*1805) from the starboard quarter davits on *Victory*. In this event, load testing of the davits will be required every four years following survey and any necessary repairs.

A miscellany of hull items will be surveyed at regular intervals and repaired as in the past, including the chainwale platforms, davits, catheads, anchors, guns and carriages, gunport lids, carved entry ports, figureheads, furniture and panelling in the senior officers quarters, steering gear, capstans and galley range.

The supporting arrangement for *Victory* in No 2 Dry Dock comprises the keel blocks and concrete plinth, the outer bottom cradles and the breast shores. The survey periods and requirements for these are as follows:

Keel blocks; every five years there will be a visual examination and hammer and spike tests. One or two sample blocks are rammed out at each survey and the condition of the ship's keel in their way is examined and recorded.

Dock cradles; every five years there will be an ultrasonic examination of steel plates, hammer tests of rivets if failure is suspected and a check on the condition of teak capping pieces fitted between the top of the cradles and the hull.

Breast Shores; will be removed, surveyed, re-preserved and set up in a different place using new packing and wedges, every two years. A quick routine check of shores and wedges is carried out monthly and recorded.

As the overall safety of the ship is dependent upon these checks, any important defects are rectified promptly and will continue to be. Two other safety-related systems are also given close attention. First, the electrical distribution system is regularly surveyed and tested; following the thorough examination of the installation in 1992, the whole system has been renewed in accordance with the latest IEE Regulations. Second, the ship is equipped with a fire-alarm system and fire main, which are regularly surveyed, maintained and tested.

Keeping *Victory* and its equipment well preserved and of good appearance is a continuous task. It is the responsibility of a small and skilled painting force permanently employed on and around the ship. They work to a well-established and proven painting schedule, which sets out the preparation and treatment processes with accompanying paint specifications for all exterior and interior work. No significant developments in the future are anticipated, although there may be colour or tint changes where substantiated by further reseach.

Research into the internal design of *Victory* and other comparable ships of the period is actively being pursued. Much had already been achieved by the valuable and painstaking work undertaken by the ship's Curator, appointed in 1991. Projects initiated by his research and already completed include the refurbished galley with its numerous additions, the sick bay, complete with de-mountable canvas bulkheads and authentic period glass jars, and the spectacular stowage layout in the forward part of the hold. Hammock battens have been fitted and hammocks slung; the complement of guns is now correct and examples are shown lashed up for sea and also ready for action. Currently in hand is the creation of the cabins and stores on the forward platform of the orlop. Associated with these in the hold below will be the Grand Magazine which, when completed, will be the only one of its kind in the world.

By the time all the planned work is complete, the total restoration period will have amounted to eighty years since the ship was originally placed in No 2 dock in 1922. No other major maritime exhibit in the world is known to have been given such treatment for the benefit of posterity, for the thousands who come to see *Victory* and tread her decks. There is an aura about the ship that stems not merely from her great age of nearly 250 years, but principally from awareness of the stirring events she witnessed during her first fifty years, the time of her active career, and from the courage of all who served in her during those years of hardships and danger. That aura is only heightened by the fact that *Victory* is still a ship in commission, the flagship of the Second Sea Lord and Commander-in-Chief, Naval Home Command.

Admiral of the Fleet Lord Fraser of the North Cape, C-in-C Portsmouth 1947-48. (IWM)

Admiral of the Fleet Lord Lewin, photographed aboard his flagship when C-in-C Naval Home Command, 1975-77. (IWM)

Admiral Sir John (Sandy) Woodward in the Great Cabin when C-in-C Naval Home Command, 1987-89. (MoD (N))

The Victory Advisory Technical Committee with the Second Sea Lord/CinC Naval Home Command on 11 May 1998. L to R back row: Lieutenant V Arden RN (Flag Lieutenant), Dr A F Bravery (Director, Centre for Timber Technology and Construction), Mr G Rodgers (Ships Support Agency), Captain R G Melly RN (Superintendent Ships), Dr D Pattison RCNC (Director of Naval Architecture), Mr B Lavery (NMM), Mr J Munday (SNR), Front row: Mr J Coad (SNR), Commodore Iain Henderson RN (Naval Base Commander), Dr A P McGowan. (Chairman), Admiral Sir John Brigstocke KCB (2SL/CinCNavHome), Mr P Goodwin (Secretary), Lieutenant Commander F Nowosielski RN Commanding Officer, HMS Victory. (MoD (N))

Victory's craftsmen at the break of the poop in 1996, led by PTO Mr Ray Caruana. (MoD (N))

Aspects of Restoration

1. BOATS

Victory would normally have carried six boats in all, four of them stowed on the skid beams in the waist. These were the 34ft launch, the 32ft barge, the 28ft pinnace and one of the cutters. Aft, on davits at the quarters or lashed above the mizzen chainwales on each side, were the two remaining cutters. All the cutters were clinker-built, that is with each strake overlapping and fastened to the strake below it. The launch, barge and pinnace were carvel-built, the planks edge to edge, fastened to internal frames.

The cutters were most commonly used for moving light stores and people, their lighter construction making them easier to handle. The largest boat, the launch, was used for the really heavy work. Fitted with a windlass, it could transport a gun, an anchor or heavy stores and water. The barge and occasionally the pinnace were decorated, the latter being used by subordinate officers. On a flagship the use of the barge was the prerogative of the admiral. The extent of the decoration depended upon the personal wealth of the captain or admiral, and in 1805 *Victory*'s boats would have had only such decoration as might have been coaxed out of the dockyard, for neither Captain Hardy nor Lord Nelson was a rich man. With the exception of the pinnace, all the boats had sails as well as oars.

It seems to have been common practice to have at least one boat rigged to the tackles – later at the davits – at night so that it might be hoisted out without delay in an emergency[1]. In an emergency of course, all boats might be used for any duty. In sloops and even the smaller frigates for example, all the boats might be used to tow the ship out of calm windless waters if necessary, physical labour for hours at a time that it is now difficult to imagine[2].

There seems to be no hard evidence as to which boats *Victory* actually carried at Trafalgar. It has always been assumed, for no other reason than that it would have been the norm, that she carried the carvel-built boats as listed above, but there is conflicting evidence about the cutters. Without giving his source, Bugler asserts that two 30ft cutters were fitted, 'one on each quarter'. He merely quotes the Navy Board Standing Order of 18 November 1798, which permitted the use of eight-oared cutters instead of barges[3].

Steel, *Naval Architecture*, contains a draught of an eight-oared cutter of 30ft at plate xxx. In the text, folio LV11 shows the 30ft cutter as the largest of the type. However, the Survey of the Boatswain's Stores for *Victory*, dated 27 March 1805, lists the boats as: launch, barge and pinnace, a Deal cutter of 33ft and two yawls of 26 and 18ft respectively[4]. The reference to yawls is not significant: cutters were commonly so rigged. The term 'Deal cutter' also means little, for most of the Navy's cutters came from yards there, where clinker-building was the norm. Royal Dockyards invariably produced carvel-built boats. The length of the cutter is unusual, but W E May's excellent monograph *The Boats of Men-of-War* shows that there was a considerable variation in cutter sizes, perhaps because they did not come from Royal Dockyards, which is borne out by Steel's table quoted above, which makes no mention of 18ft cutters, listing them as 30ft, 25ft, 21ft and 16ft.

Unfortunately, despite its having been written in 1805, the Boatswain's Survey cannot be considered conclusive evidence. It was made while *Victory* was reprovisioning in the Gulf of Palmas in southwestern Sardinia. Between then and September, when she left for the Mediterranean again, there was the long chase to the West Indies followed by a brief refit at Portsmouth. It is quite possible that the boats on *Victory* at Trafalgar particularly the lightly-built cutters were not the same as those of the survey.

Further confusion was added when in 1993, the

---

1. Lavery p154

2. Rodger p41

3. Bugler p26

4. RNM 14/84 (195-200)

Society for Nautical Research filled the complement of boats for *Victory* – one of them to be a working boat – and chose 25ft cutters. These boats were built to commemorate the service to the Society of the late Lieutenant Commander Peter Whitlock, who had expressed the hope that one day the complement of boats might be completed by the addition of 25ft cutters. Peter Whitlock's knowledge of the *Victory* and the Navy of the late eighteenth and early nineteenth centuries was unsurpassed, but it is not clear on what his opinion was based. It may be that he felt that anything larger would have been too unwieldy to launch or recover using the davits that had only entered widespread use in 1804. This could certainly have been true of the 33ft cutter.

Before the introduction of the quarter davits, which in any case could only handle the lightly-built clinker boats, all boats had to be hoisted out using tackles and the yard arm of the main or mizzen mast as appropriate.

At all events, *Victory*'s two additional boats are 25ft cutters, and it should be noted that the working cutter, manned by volunteers, has been a great success in representing the ship and the Society both at home and abroad.

The 25ft cutter – the Peter Whitlock Memorial Boat – under sail, before her colour scheme was updated, based on recent research. Now, her wash strakes are buff, the rubbing strake varnished, the plank sheer and strake below black, the hull white, and her interior buff. (The Society for Nautical Research)

2. MASTS AND SPARS

Long before the middle of the eighteenth century, near-ly all the timber used for the manufacture of masts and spars was imported, mainly from New England and the Baltic because it was difficult to obtain the required size of trees in the United Kingdom. The fore and main lower masts and the bowsprits and mizzen lower masts for ships of the line were 'made' masts. That is to say, they were built up, the diameter being achieved by fastening together six lengths of shaped mast-timber. The diameters ranged from 39in for a First Rate mainmast to 22in for the mizzen mast of a Third Rate of 74 guns, these dimensions being taken at the partners.[5] Even the topmasts were approximately 20in in diameter, and if a mast was to be made from a single tree it had to be at least 2in greater in the rough.

At sea masts could be damaged by heavy weather, especially the upper masts and spars, and of course they were the principal casualties when the ships were involved in action. Many of the British ships at the battle of Trafalgar lost one or more masts, and eight of the twenty prizes taken were wholly dismasted. The extensive damage to *Victory*'s masts and spars is detailed in an earlier chapter of this book.

Wooden spars and masts also deteriorate quite quickly due to the effects of the weather. Consequently when a vessel was not required for sea service she was placed 'in Ordinary'. She was stripped to her lower masts, and all the other masts and spars were set aside in dry airy conditions and marked with the ships name. Similarly the sails and rigging were repaired and properly stored ready for use again when the ship was recommissioned.

Victory had wooden lower masts until 1887, when, because they had become rotten, they were replaced with hollow iron masts removed from the armoured frigate *Shah*. *Victory*'s lower masts, therefore, now date from 1870. The fore- and mainmasts can be surveyed internally by means of access holes near their heels and are considered to be in good condition. The workmanship involved in their manufacture is first class, shown by the accuracy of the close-fitting joints. The design is also good, ensuring that the T-shaped sections for longitudinal stiffening are each run in one length from the top to the bottom of the masts. The present good condition confirms the fact that the material of the lower masts is wrought-iron. They were given a 'Trafalgar' appearance during the 1922-28 restoration when the mainmast was extended.

It is believed that at the time of the battle all *Victory*'s masts were stepped on the keelson. An order of 26 January 1807 stated that when ships came in hand for repairs, they were to have the mizzen mast stepped on the lower deck, a measure intended to utilise shorter masts and so save money and timber. In 1880 *Victory*'s mizzen mast was stepped on the middle deck, a measure of economy commensurate with her virtually static role at that time in Portsmouth Harbour. Although all three masts are now stepped on the keelson (supported through to the dock floor), they are not in their original positions as-built, because changes were made in 1787.

Until the late 1960s the majority of *Victory*'s spars were of wood, necessitating a survey every two years. This task was usually carried out by two mastheadsmen, shipwrights by trade who had been given training in the use of a boatswain's chair for working aloft, and who were thus able to undertake the survey work with the mast and spars in position. Each mast and spar was methodically examined, spiked with an awl to detect soft spots, and sounded by hammer. If a more detailed survey was required then the spar was unrigged and lowered to the dockside. Deterioration usually appeared on the top and weatherside first, as the wood shakes (splits) with age and the effects of weather, thereby permitting water to lodge and create rot.

For many years Douglas fir was used for the replacements. Unfortunately, the timber available was not of the quality of that previously used, very few logs were avail-

---

5. Steel, *Rigging and Seamanship* Vol I p49.

able over 50ft in length, and the cost was vastly increased. Whilst Douglas fir is an excellent timber in many respects, the logs are large, the knots are big, and it is not always possible to arrange the heart of the log at the centre of the spar for its entire length, a requirement that is essential for a long-lasting spar that will not twist or bow. Some idea of the rapid deterioration of wooden spars can be gained from the fact that although the fore topgallant mast and yard had been replaced with new in 1964, only six years later in 1970 they were condemned as unsafe.

The difficulties of replacing wooden spars were exacerbated by the provisions of the Health and Safety at Work Act (1968), which required that for every man working aloft in a boatswain's chair two trained men had to attend him from the deck. This doubled the labour costs of survey and inspection and, coupled with the frequent unsuitability of the spar timber on its arrival and the relatively short life even of suitable timber, led to most of *Victory*'s spars being replaced using mild steel. Renewals in steel became the general policy, and the remaining spars on the mainmast were so renewed in 1972 and on the mizzen the following year.

The striking (lowering down) of spars has been set at eight-year intervals for a thorough survey coupled with an annual *in-situ* survey, mainly as a safety check, using the boatswain's chair. Steel, of course, is susceptible to corrosion if exposed to the atmosphere, and the annual surveys are aimed particularly at highlighting areas where the paint coating may have broken down, such as where moisture may have been retained on the steel surface by the rope rigging or where the chafe has removed paint. Detailed surveys of suspect areas are carried out with the assistance of modern ultrasonics or even radiography. Repairs to steel spars generally involve un-rigging and lowering, whilst mast repairs require the erection of scaffolding with tenting to afford good access and provide weather protection.

Although the original tops had been built of oak, an Admiralty instruction of 30 November 1802 laid down that they were to be constructed of fir to save top weight. During the 1922-28 restoration, with masts firmly stayed from the dockside, weight was considered secondary to

durability and the tops were replaced in teak. However, in 1973 the mizzen top was replaced using steel.

Fibreglass Treatment of Yards

Mizzen topgallant yard, spritsail, topsail and spritsail yards were treated as follows:

1. Mizzen topgallant yard, and spritsail, topsail yard were cleaned off, planed back to bare wood and lightly sanded.
2. 2oz strand mat cut to shape in 3ft lengths.
3. Polyester resin and hardener was mixed to the following specification and applied to the spars; any shakes are filled with resin.

Polyester resin:	Crystic	189	-	2oz
	Pregel	79	-	4oz
	Catalyst paste	H	-	1½oz
	Accelerator	E	-	10cc

(quantity according to requirements.)

4. The mat was applied to the spar and lightly rolled until resin appeared evenly through the mat.
5. Items 2, 3 and 4 were repeated until the whole surface of the spar was covered.
6. The surface was lightly sanded.
7. Items 2 to 6 were repeated for the second thickness, with butts and laps staggered.
8. Epothen resin and hardener were mixed to the following specification and applied with mat as in items 2 to 6 until a further two thicknesses had been added; Epothen resin EL5-4 parts, EHM3-3 parts. A little black pigment was added, quantity according to requirements.
9. A final two coats of epothen resin and hardener with a little black pigment was added, applied and allowed to harden.

The epothen resin mixture was used in items 8 and 9 as having faster setting properties.

10. A new spritsail yard was made from Douglas fir, ⅜in smaller in diameter than the original, and coated with fibreglass in accordance to above specification.

These yards were treated in 1969 and are still in good condition; wooden untreated spars would have decayed in five to seven years.

Details of Masts, Spars and Yards

	Length		Diameter				Material	Renewed
	ft	ins	Head ins	Heel ins	Bunt ins	Ends ins		
flying jib boom	54	0	7	7⅝			mild steel	1970
jib boom	53	1	10½	15⅜			mild steel	1970
bowsprit	68	0	21⅝	32			steel	1936
spritsail topsail yard	43	0			8⅜	3¾	Douglas fir	1948 GRP coated
spritsail yard	65	1			13⅝	6	Douglas fir	1969 GRP coated
dolphin striker	18	0	5¼	8¼			Douglas fir	1982
boomkin port	24	6	6⅞	12			Douglas fir	1982
boomkin starboard	24	6	6⅞	12			Douglas fir	1970
fore topgallant mast	50	8	5⅝	14			mild steel	1970
fore topgallant yard	43	4			8¾	4	mild steel	1970
fore topmast	63	0	11⅛	27			steel	fitted during restoration
fore topsail yard	65	0			17⅜	6	mild steel	1970
studding sail boom port	32	6			6½	6½	Douglas fir	1985
studding sail boom stbd	32	6			6½	6½	Douglas fir	1980
foremast	107	0	33	36			iron	restored during restoration
fore lower yard	91	2			21	9	steel	fitted during restoration
studding sail boom port	45	0	5⅞	8½			Douglas fir	renewed 1985
studding sail boom stbd	45	0	5⅞	8½			Douglas fir	1964
fore hand mast	14	3	7	8			teak	-
main topgallant mast	60	6	6⅜	14¼			mild steel	1972
main topgallant yard	49	2			10	4¼	mild steel	1972
main topmast	70	0	11⅛	24			steel	fitted during restoration
main topsail yard	74	4			15½	6⅝	steel	1972
main studding sail boom (port)	36	7	7	7			mild steel	1972
main studding sail boom (stbd)	36	7	7	7			mild steel	1972
mainmast	119	0	30	36			iron	restored during restoration
main lower yard	102	2			24	10¼	steel	fitted during restoration
main lower studding sail boom (port)	51	3	7½	9¾			mild steel	1972
main lower studding sail boom (stbd)	51	3	7½	9¾			mild steel	1972
main studding sail boom (port)	60	0	8½	11⅞			Douglas fir	1980
main studding sail boom (stbd)	60	0	8½	11⅞			Douglas fir	1965
main hand mast	16	2	9½	9½			teak	
mizzen topgallant mast	39	8½	4½	9¼			mild steel	1973
mizzen topgallant yard	32	5¼			6⅜	3	mild steel	1973
mizzen topsail yard	49	2			11⅞	5	mild steel	1973
mizzen mast	102	0	21	24			iron	restored during restoration
mizzen cross jack yard	65	9			14¼	5¾	mild steel	1973
mizzen gaff	58	0	7⅝	13¾			mild steel	1973
driver boom	73	0	9½	13¾			mild steel	1972
mizzen hand mast	10	5	6	5¼			teak	-

Details of Cross-trees, Trestle-trees, Mast Caps, Fighting Platforms, Ensign and Jack Staff

	Length ft ins		Width ft ins		Depth ft ins		No	Material	Renewed
Cross-Trees									
fore topmast	10	3		7		6	3	teak	1964
foremast	21	10½		10½		9½	2	teak	1964
main topmast	11	3		6⅝		6½-3¾	3	mild steel	1972
mainmast (fwd)	22	10		10¾		10⅛	1	mild steel	1972
mainmast (aft)	23	6		10¾		10⅛	1	mild steel	1972
mizzen topmast (fwd)	8	6		5		5	1	mild steel	1973
mizzen topmast (aft)	8	6		5		5	1	mild steel	1973
mizzen topmast (centre)	2	3		5		5	1	mild steel	1973
mizzen mast	16	7		7½		7¼	2	mild steel	1973
Trestle-Trees									
fore topmast	6	1		7		4½	2	teak	1973
foremast	16	6		15¼		10½	2	mild steel	1956
main topmast	6	9		7½	5	3¾	2	mild steel	1972
mainmast	17	4		16		11	2	mild steel	-
mizzen topmast	5	1		6		4	2	mild steel	1973
mizzen mast	12	2		11		7½	2	mild steel	-
Mast Caps									
bowsprit	6	6	2	9	1	3		mild steel	1985
fore topmast	3	10½	1	9		9¾		mild steel	1970
foremast	7	1	3	6	1	8		mild steel	-
main topmast	4	1	2	0		11		mild steel	-
mainmast	7	3	3	7	1	7½		mild steel	-
mizzen topmast	2	11½	1	5		8		mild steel	1973
mizzen mast	5	1	2	6	1	1¾		mild steel	-
Fighting Top Platforms									
foremast	17	2	22	7		3		teak	repaired 1983
mainmast	18	2	24	3		3		teak	refurbished 1972
mizzen mast	13	1	17	3		¼		mild steel	1973

Diameter at Head and Heel

							No	Material	Renewed
ensign staff				4¼		7⅜	1	Douglas fir	1970
jack staff	16	6		3		4	1	Douglas fir	1970

3. SAILS

There are no sails that can be hoisted on *Victory*, nor have there been, one suspects for more than one hundred years. At Trafalgar, however, fresh from the dockyard a matter of weeks before, she probably had two suits (or sets) of sails as well as boat sails and other canvas for repairs, awnings and the thousand and one requirements on board, including the shutes used to convey fresh air to the lower decks and orlop, known, rather curiously, as windsails. When the ship was in a region of light winds the older of the sails were set to save the best canvas to carry her through stormy weather. It was also a prudent

practice, if there was sufficient time, to use older though serviceable sails in action. When captain of HMS *Excellent*, and about to engage the *San Isidro* in the battle of Cape St. Vincent, Collingwood was heard to call out to the boatswain, 'Bless me! Mr Peffers, how came we [to] forget to bend our old topsail. They will quite ruin that new one. It will never be worth a farthing again.'[6]

Victory's Trafalgar topsail as shown at the International Festival of the Sea at Portsmouth in August 1998. The No 2 canvas is in remarkably good condition but it is now backed with Kevlar netting for display purposes. The battle damage speaks for itself although the tear in the centre is now larger. The tallest building available in the old part of the dockyard is still not high enough to display the 54 feet in the depth of the sail. (Peter Goodwin)

6. GLN Collingwood fn p178.

The making of canvas for the Navy was strictly regulated and delivered in bolts 38yds long and 2ft (a cloth) wide. The different qualities of canvas were distinguished by weight: thus a bolt of No 1 canvas weighed 44lbs and No 8 canvas 21lbs. Each bolt had a blue thread running through it to mark it as Navy canvas, the fine for illegal possession of such canvas being a massive £200.

Sailmaking for the Navy was also strictly controlled in great detail. The regulations covered the quality and manufacture of the twine and the beeswax used to make it waterproof, the breadth of the seams, and the number of stitches per yard–between 108 and 116. There were also requirements in the method of making sails. For example, reef bands might not be put on until all the cloths were sewn into place.

The lowest sails, the courses, were made of No 1 canvas while the royals, those highest on the mast, were of No 8 canvas. The sail plan for major warships changed little during the course of the eighteenth century the addition of the royals being the last. *Victory* probably had royals when she joined the Mediterranean Fleet under Samuel Hood in 1793.[7]

---

7. *Victory* does not have her royal yards crossed. At sea they were sent up or struck as required.

There were probably thirty-seven sails in a suit for *Victory* at Trafalgar. The sails were: spritsail, spritsail topsail; jib, flying jib; fore course, fore topsail, fore topgallant sail, fore royal, and similarly on the mainmast, main course *etc*; on the mizzen mast the lowest sail was the spanker or driver, and above it the mizzen topsail, mizzen topgallant sail, mizzen royal; the staysails were fore staysail, fore topmast staysail, main staysail, main topmast staysail, middle staysail, main topgallant staysail, mizzen staysail, mizzen topmast staysail, and mizzen topgallant staysail; fore studding sails, fore topmast studding sails, fore topgallant studding sails, main studding sails, the main topmast studding sails, and main topgallant studding sails.

Perhaps the most important point to make with regard to *Victory*'s sails is that her fore topsail at Trafalgar still exists. Despite the many years since 1929 that it was folded in a glass case on the orlop, the canvas is in remarkably good condition. It was removed from the ship during the restoration of the orlop, and has been conserved and backed with a Kevlar netting. Suitably thus fortified, it was displayed from a replica yard in No 4 Boathouse during the International Festival of the Sea in August 1998.

4. Rigging from 1965

A ship's rigging is made up of two parts: standing rigging and running rigging. The former is that holding the masts in place and supporting them, such as the shrouds and the stays. The running rigging is that which is actively worked while the ship is at sea, to move the yards or to handle the sails. From the completion of the 1920s refit – and no doubt long before, when it was evident that *Victory* would never sail again – until the mid-1990s, only the standing rigging and the running rigging for the yards was in place. Recently however, to improve the appearance and make it more authentic, the running rigging has been virtually completed to include that necessary for the sails.

At the same time as the surveys of the masts and spars, every two years the rigging has been examined and any chafed or worn items renewed. The masts and yards were undressed and lowered in rotation one mast at a time for detailed surveys to be carried out, usually during the winter months. This entailed un-rigging the mast and setting it up again upon completion of the survey. For example, in 1965 the mizzen mast was surveyed and the mast was re-rigged using Italian hemp. New wire shorestays were also fitted at that time. On completion the rigging was tarred, the shrouds were given a final set up and the battening and rattling down followed immediately. This is the term used to describe the technique for putting in place the ratlines on the shrouds. Starting from the deck level, wooden battens are temporarily lashed to the shrouds one above the other to form a convenient ladder up the length of the shrouds to the trestle trees. Then, working down from the upper levels, the ropes which form the actual ratlines are progressively secured in place and the battens removed. This method is adopted not only to afford safe working access for the riggers but also to ensure that the space between each pair of shrouds is correctly maintained at all the various positions. The hammock nets and gunport pendants were also renewed at this time. The following autumn saw the need for 25 to 30 per cent more of the rigging to be renewed, with the blacking down following on during 1966.

During the winter of 1968-69 the rigging on the mizzen and the main was again renewed, followed in turn by the foremast during the next winter.

In 1973 an additional 3in standing stay was rigged from the lower foremast to the bowsprit as a temporary support to keep the bowsprit clear of the figurehead. Subsequently this was replaced with the bi-pole support described earlier.

Because of the worldwide shortage and relatively high cost of good quality hemp, trials were carried out using rigging made of polypropylene. In the meantime the mizzen was again re-rigged using Grade 1 Manilla instead of hemp.

In 1979, with the commencement of the restoration of the bow area, it was recognised that the complete unrigging of the foremast and bowsprit would become necessary. A survey of the existing rigging indicated that it was generally in a poor condition and required renewal. The full restoration of the bow was expected to take at least five years, during which time the mainmast rigging and

Rot in the deadeyes for the main topmast shrouds in 1991. (MoD (N))

The bowsprit, jibboom and the spritsail yard. (MoD (N))

possibly the mizzen also would become due for its major overhaul. A decision was therefore made to carry out the rigging programme using polypropylene rope. During the winter period, 1981-82, all the rigging was removed from the foremast and bowsprit. The spars were brought

The bowsprit's massive gear. (MoD (N))

down and laid apart, while most of the old rigging was labelled and laid apart to be measured for use as patterns for the new replacements. The cost of the rigging was met from the Save the *Victory* Fund, administered by the Society for Nautical Research.

Whilst work was proceeding on the bow structure during 1983, the mainmast was unrigged and surveyed and its associated rigging examined. This led to the re-rigging, using polypropylene, of first the mainmast in 1985, then the mizzen, and finally the foremast and bowsprit by the winter of 1989-90. This was the first time that ropes of man-made fibre of this size had been used for rigging work in Portsmouth Dockyard. Trials had been carried out, and although it was evident that stretch would occur it was considered that the change would be both satisfactory and worthwhile. The expected longer life of the synthetic material was, however, the biggest factor affecting the decision to change from natural hemp or manila, together with its more stable characteristics. The use of synthetic fibre would not only reduce the cost, it would also significantly reduce the workload on the riggers. The number of riggers employed in the dockyard had steadily declined since the First World War and by the 1960s there were too few to be able to provide even a monthly attendance on board *Victory*. This was necessary because natural fibres constantly stretch or shrink depending upon the weather and the loading imposed. When the ship was sea-going, the rigging had received continuous attention from experienced seamen under the watchful eye of the boatswain. Polypropylene does not have need of such frequent adjustment, although it does stretch under heavy loading. This problem was partially overcome by employing the traditional practice of stretching the new rope prior to making up the new lengths. The re-rigging of the mainmast using black polypropylene 'hemp look-alike' was completed in 1985, and this marked the beginning of a notable new phase in the restoration techniques adopted for *Victory*'s rigging. In the event the main lower shrouds were set up six times and the circumference of the rope reduced from 11in to approximately 9½in. Notwithstanding the earlier trials, it was necessary to monitor the new material under actual 'ship conditions' for the amount of stretch, the changes in diameter, resistance to wear and chafe and the effects of prolonged exposure to the sun's ultraviolet light rays.

The manufacture of the new rigging took the same time as the previous natural fibre materials, but the times taken to rig the ship were slightly less due to its lighter weight. The rigging installed in March 1985 has not required significant adjustment since the initial stretching. Although slightly more susceptible to damage by chafing, which can be prevented by traditional methods using canvas and spunyarn servings, the man-made fibre has shown no obvious signs of bleaching or powdering, which are the most likely effects of prolonged exposure to sunlight. The periodic surveys have shown that the

polypropylene is lasting better than originally expected and as a result the planned intervals for detailed surveys of the rigging have been extended to eight years to coincide with that of the steel masts and spars. However, an annual inspection will still be undertaken for safety reasons and to detect and rectify any occurrences of chafe.

Research has highlighted that running rigging was never 'blacked' with tar as this would have impeded its ease of turning through blocks, been difficult to make up on cleats, and been generally awkward to handle. All such cordage would have been natural hemp, manila or sisal and hence of a light colour. Accordingly, the running rigging has progressively been replaced using light coloured polypropylene cordage, as have the tackles which support all the gunport lids.

Lanyards for the fore topsail shrouds. (Credit?)

A new triple jeer block, used for hauling up the main yard. (The Maritime Workshop)

5. ANCHORS AND GROUND TACKLE

Victory carried seven anchors, four large and three small, the large anchors being the best bower, small bower and two sheet anchors. The bowers were secured one on each bow ready for use, while the sheet anchors, one with a cable permanently bent on ready for any emergency, were secured outside the foremast shrouds. These anchors each weighed between four and four-and-a-half tons. The exact weights are irrelevant because, being made by hand, it was impossible for the smith to be precise, but all were several hundredweight (cwt) heavier than the 81cwt minimum specified in the table in Steel's *Rigging and Seamanship*.

The three smaller anchors were the stream anchor, the large kedge and the small kedge, which were required to be at least 21cwt, 10cwt and 5cwt respectively. Again, in each case *Victory*'s anchors were very properly rather above the mimimum weight.

The best bower was the working anchor normally used. The principal anchors were all much the same in size and weight, but the best bower was so called because in practice it was always the heaviest, although the difference in weight might be relatively slight. In *Victory*'s case it was a mere 76 pounds. Normal weather patterns always required a particular bow anchor to be used first. In the northern hemisphere winds tend to veer in a gale: that is, they move in a clockwise direction. Consequently, when anchoring, the port anchor was always let go first. Should a gale arise and the wind shift from say the prevailing south-westerly to a north or north-westerly direction, the starboard anchor could also be let go without the risk of the cables fouling each other as the ship's head swung round. In the southern hemisphere this procedure was reversed.

The large anchors were used with a cable of 24in circumference and, as with the manufacture of sails, the making of all sizes of cordage for the Royal Navy was prescribed in detail, down to the material (hemp), the number of yarns and strands, and the weight per fathom.

Cables were made from three yarns laid up (twisted) to make each strand, three strands laid up to make each rope and three ropes laid up to make each cable. While yarns and strands were laid up with a right-handed lay or twist, in the final stage of making the cable the ropes were laid up left-handed. The advantages were that cable-laid rope was less inclined to kinks which would make it difficult to handle. John Harland (*op. cit.*) also avers that the consequently tightly-bound fibres make it less pervious to water when not in use. A First Rate was normally allowed nine 24in cables and one 14in.

A cable was laid up in lengths of approximately 120 fathoms—the limit of the ropewalk—and at Trafalgar *Victory* would have had three such lengths spliced together on each of her bowers and the sheet anchor. The power that restrains a ship at anchor comes from the weight of the cable laid out rather than from the anchor itself, which really only positions the end of the cable. A cable of 120 fathoms weighs just over seven tons.

The anchor was heaved up using both main capstans, the lower driving the messenger, a continuous 16in cable running from the lower deck capstan to the rollers situated abaft and between each pair of hawse holes and back again. The capstans were linked one above the other on the lower and middle gundecks. The cable was nipped, that is temporarily secured to the messenger with short lengths of rope by the nipper men—a heavy job not without its hazards. The nippers (ropes) were then handed to boys who walked aft along the deck, straining to keep the wet and heavy cable and messenger clear of the deck until they reached the main hatch. There the nippers were released to allow the cable to go down through the orlop into the hold, where seamen wrestled to stow it to the satisfaction of the boatswain or his mates, while at the same time endeavouring to avoid trapping fingers or hands or the ever-present threat of hernia, for working the ship too frequently required them to move heavy weights while at the stretch. Where the cable entered the hatch, iron-bar compressors were fitted as a brake on the cable in the event of a sudden surge.

Once the stock of the anchor had broken water it was hoisted so that the ring was close under the heavy beam of the cathead. The shank was then hauled to the horizontal and the inboard fluke secured. Further lashings were added in order to secure the anchor firmly for sea.

The stream anchor, bent to the 14in cable, was used to hold the ship temporarily while mooring, or similarly to anchor for a short time if the holding power of the sea-bed was good and the conditions calm. The advantage was that its smaller size made handling easier.

Kedge anchors were used to warp (heave) the ship in a calm. A kedge would be taken by the launch and let go, whereupon by use of the capstans the ship could be hauled forward close to that point; if necessary the process could be repeated. Just as some of the guns have been replaced by replicas—first in wood and now in GRP—in order to reduce the weight high in the ship, so the anchors currently displayed on board are wooden replicas.

In 1995 it became apparent that the anchor cable had deteriorated noticeably in appearance and that it ought to be replaced. Wide-ranging enquiries finally established that the only source at present for a cable of this size is in the Netherlands. A new cable was ordered, to be paid for also out of the Save the *Victory* Fund, courtesy of the SNR, and it was installed in May 1996.

The anchor cable removed is of interest, but it was certainly not in use at Trafalgar and probably dates from the late nineteenth century.

Anchors on the starboard bow of *Victory* (Peter Goodwin)

6. MATERIALS AND TECHNIQUES

In the early 1960s a steam kiln was installed and a heavy channel bar frame was erected nearby, so that the thick bottom planking for the bow and stern sections could be steamed and bent in the traditional manner. The steaming was carried out for a minimum period of 24 hours, after which the plank was removed and placed in the jig which had been adjusted to give the required shape. The plank was bent and held in position until cold by means of adjustable tie bars and wedges. Unfortunately, sometimes as many as two out of every three planks, particularly in the thicker sizes, tended to break. Because of the considerable improvement in the quality of modern adhesives, in the early 1970s this method was abandoned in favour of lamination. Several laminates are used to build up the required thickness, being secured with Cascophen resin and hardener. The laminates are held together with long brass woodscrews, whilst the adhesive sets. This practice was later extended to the construction of knees.

Teak was used increasingly after the Second World War for those structural members which were enclosed on three sides, such as the frame timbers (futtocks), outer planking, internal deck stringers and linings. Oak was only used for members which were exposed on three sides, such as riders, beams and keelson, so that seasoning of the timber might continue in place after fitting.

Oak in the bulk sizes required was becoming more difficult to obtain and was invariably not seasoned. Teak is a tropical hardwood more resistant than oak to wood-destroying fungi and wood-boring insects, but because of diminishing world supplies the Procurement Executive of the Ministry of Defence has long since been allowed to purchase only from sustainable sources. The price of teak has risen alarmingly over the past thirty years, and at the time of going to press is in the region of £4,500 per cubic metre. For these reasons alternatives have had to be considered. In consequence, since the late 1970s the *Victory* Advisory Technical Committee has had a timber sub-committee keeping alternative materials and restoration methods under review.

As a result of the sub-committee's initial report a beam was manufactured in iroko and fitted under the quarter-deck abaft the mainmast for trial purposes. This wood is of similar natural durability to teak but, there being no available experience of the fitting and subsequent behaviour of a large section of this timber as a structural member, the performance of this beam was carefully monitored after installation. The trial was considered successful and as iroko is less expensive than teak its use has been permitted in other areas of the ship's structure such as replacement beams in the bow (referred to in Chapter 5), laminated planking and knees.

7. Rase Marks

When wooden ships were built a means was devised by which the various parts of the structure could be identified during the building process and their positions determined. It had to be a long-lasting method of marking, as often the timbers would be transported over considerable distances on bad roads and in all kinds of weather. Consequently marks were carved into the face of the timber about ⅛in deep using a special tool called a rasing knife which consisted of a V-shaped blade attached to a hooked handle. These marks, called rase marks, were scrieved onto the timber or logs in their original state by the Admiralty timber buyers, and until the early 1980s were still used and recorded at the saw mills. Once the timber had been selected it would be marked with the same identifying marks as those on the wooden mould of the ship's structural member, and this marking would accompany it throughout the process of manufacture, including cutting, shaping and erection at the ship. Good timber removed from vessels being broken up or repaired was sometimes used for repairs to other ships, so not all rase marks found necessarily refer to the vessel on which they appear. Today logs are marked by plastic tallies, and with only a few sections of the ship being worked on at the same time it is easy to keep the marking simple using pencil or wax crayon. However, as an aid to any future repairs some new structural members have a restoration date cut into them. Most of the rase marks found on *Victory* are dated between 1814 and 1815 from the Great Repair carried out at that time.

Top: Number 10 cant timber at the orlop deck, rase-marked 442 and dated 1812. (MoD (N))

Right: Repairs to the bow structure in 1985 show a rase-marked timber (1814) just below the breast hook and to the right of the access opening. (MoD (N))

8. FASTENINGS

Many different fastenings are used to ensure the security of the structure of *Victory*. Most of the deck and outer and inner planking was attached to the beams and frame timbers by means of treenails. These were long wooden dowels made from good-quality, straight-grained, well-seasoned oak, and of round section. The treenail was dipped in tallow and driven into a drilled hole by using a pin maul. The surplus ends were cut off and caulked to bell the ends slightly and prevent withdrawal or loosening. Very few treenails are being used in the restoration work except to hold large laminates together, and these are usually made from teak.

Dumps are manufactured from ¾in diameter round bar in Muntz metal or a lead gunmetal. They were generally about 12in long with a chisel point at one end and fashioned into a dome head at the other. Dumps are still used, but are made from mild steel rod and are galvanised.

Clench bolts for use below the waterline were mainly of copper, and those for use above it were of wrought-iron. Clench bolts are no longer used. They have been replaced by galvanised mild steel long bolts and threaded nuts. Where appearance is important these are domed to give the impression of the original clenches.

Coaks are cylindrically shaped pieces of timber, usually oak or sometimes Lignum Vitae, 2in to 3in in diameter and roughly the same length as the diameter, fitted as location fasteners to prevent slip of the faying surfaces at scarph joints of beams and between beams and knees. Not all of these have been replaced during the restoration but some were fitted in the scarphs of No 2 beam under the upper deck when it was renewed in 1986.

A shipwright looks at a handful of rot. Any fastening would long since have become useless. (MoD (N))

9. Caulking and Drainage

Leakage of rain into the ship creates the risk of inducing rot into timber. Since early in 1970 trials of various caulking materials have been carried out. As each new material has been made available, trials of limited areas of caulking have been arranged but to date none has proved to be as effective for *Victory* as the traditional method of driving oakum into the seams and paying-up with pitch. This is partly because the oakum hardens or stiffens the seams between adjacent members, but also because while the large scantlings of the wood involved move with the variations in temperature and humidity the pitch used can move a similar amount, thereby remaining the most effective water seal. The caulking of the seams in this traditional manner will continue for as long as *Victory* exists, especially on the weather decks and external hull.

The use of glass-reinforced plastic (GRP) to line the-underside of a deck or as a cover for deck seams was also tried as a means of excluding rain water, but this achieved only limited success. Mild steel trays were fitted to the gunport sills to prevent water finding its way down between the timbers to the decks and hold below. This too was only partially effective, and in 1983 it was decided to fit GRP trays to the gunports. These were laid up in place over a teak fill-in piece arranged so as to give positive slope out of the ship and so shed any water. The trays are bedded to the sill and sealed to both the teak chock and the ship's side. This method has proved effective.

To prevent water from lying on the decks, additional scuppers have been fitted to the upper and middle gundecks. A GRP cover was designed and fitted over the skid beams in 1984, and this was covered with a canvas to present a more authentic appearance. This arrangement was so successful that GRP gaiters were fitted around the masts where they pass through the open deck, and each was then also covered with canvas.

10. Surveys

The survey of the hull structure and its fittings is, and will always remain, an ongoing and continuous task. Its objective is to identify any defective material so that plans can be made for the necessary rectification work. Even after the major restoration is completed, surveys will continue to be carried out at regular intervals. Generally the periods of time between surveys are ten years for the outer bottom structure and five years for the decks, beams and knees.

The detection of defects in heavy timbers that are apparently sound is an important factor in the maintenance of such a large and complex structure as *Victory*. Various methods are used besides visual examination. Drill tests are carried out using a spoon auger about $5/8$in diameter. This method involves drilling holes in selected positions along the length of a beam and carefully collecting the wood drillings for subsequent examination to determine if rot is present. Obviously this method creates large numbers of holes which have to be plugged, and in any case it only gives random samples of the wood's condition at the precise position of the hole. Rot could exist close to this position but not be detected. Considerable skill is therefore needed on the part of the surveyor in selecting the site for the hole so as to reveal the condition of the timber and also in making the correct interpretation of the wood drillings. The use of endoscopes has been tried, permitting examination right to the bottom of the holes where results of drill tests are uncertain. Radiographs have also been used to try to identify internally decayed timber. This latter technique, however, is now rarely used for safety reasons, largely connected with the unacceptable constraints which its use imposes on the movement of personnel. Ultrasonics have been used to measure the wood thickness in way of the public tour areas, where it was suspected that the visitors might be wearing down the deck planking. This showed that the amount of wear was in fact negligible and further monitoring in this way has not been considered necessary. The latest tool to assist with structural survey is the Sibert testing drill. Hand-held and battery-operated, this drives a fine needle-like drill only 2mm in diameter and some 350mm long into the wood at a constant drilling rate while the operator maintains a steady pressure. The speed of advance into timber is therefore a measure of its hardness, and is recorded on a paper trace. Because the hole produced is so small, many such probes can be made deep into the wood to determine the extent of any softening without risk of causing structural damage. This has become the main tool which *Victory*'s surveyors use to detect and define areas of rotten timber.

In addition to the hull structure itself a miscellany of items need to be surveyed at regular intervals and repaired as found necessary. These include the chainwale supports to the rigging, davits, catheads, anchors, guns and carriages, gunport lids, carved entry ports, figurehead, furniture and panelling in the officers quarters, steering gear, mast supports to the deck bottom, dock cradle, dock blocks and breast shores, capstans and galley range. The steel support cradle in the dock bottom, the dock blocks and the steel breast shores are of particular importance because of their role in supporting the ship. The blocks and cradle are surveyed every five years and the breast shores every two.

During the reconstruction of the hull great care has been taken to ensure that the original shape or form of the ship was not lost. The areas for restoration were carefully selected so as not to weaken the structure significantly whilst being worked on, the same positions on both port and starboard sides were not opened up at the same time, beams and beam-end supports were only renewed one at a time in any particular area, and large temporary shores were used to compensate for the removal of structure, these being left in place until the ship's structure had been restored. In a similar way the permanent shoring of the hull in the dry dock with numerous breast shores and steel plate bilge cradle supports also contribute to the maintenance of form. The geometrical shape of the ship is regularly checked by taking overall breakage readings, using a theodolite to establish a true data plane, from which measurements of internal deck heights at various tallied positions along the length of both the upper and middle gundecks can be taken. These breakage readings are taken approximately once each calendar month, and successive readings compared to detect any permanent movements or deflections. In addition, measurements are taken monthly at numerous positions internally, using sliding gunter battens to detect if any changes are occurring to the heights between decks and to the beam width of the hull. All of these readings are logged and retained for reference.

11. IMPROVED DOCKYARD EQUIPMENT

The period between 1980 and 1985 saw some significant changes in the use of equipment by the dockyard as a drive for greater efficiency was sought. The 14in x 14in Douglas fir breast shores had to be surveyed every month and hardened up when needed. Every two or three years they required renewal. The steel shores that replaced them only require survey every five years and they have a life expectancy of over fifteen years.

Grit blasting machines used in conjunction with hot air strippers greatly speeded the removal of old and often thick layers of paint.

Increasing use has been made of hydraulically-operated high-rise platforms, which obviate the need for the erection of so much conventional scaffolding, and also to some extent reduce the need to use a bosun's chair for certain tasks.

Several lengths of roller conveyor were obtained to assist manoeuvring large sections of timber into and out of the ship. Hydraulic lift platforms were purchased to assist with lifting beams up to the deck head when renewing them. Screw-threaded steel tubular shores (Acro-jacks) were purchased to be used for temporary shoring in way of the restoration work instead of the cumbersome wedged wooden shores used previously.

In 1995, a valuable addition to the equipment was made with the introduction of the Sibert drill used in testing for decay as described in the previous section.

In much of the shipwright's work, although the processes have not changed, the modern power tools—saws, drills and planes—have made them easier and certainly faster. However, skill in the use of traditional tools such as the adze is still required occasionally.

The traditional tools of the shipwright which, despite the advent of power tools, have all been used during the postwar restoration of *Victory*. (Simon Murray)

The bowsprit is removed in November 1982. (MoD (N))

12. PAINTING AND PRESERVATION

Various paints have been tried on *Victory* in the attempt to find a combination of lasting decoration and preservation. The problems caused by woodwork that is alternately wet and dry, combined with variations in temperature, are those that seamen have struggled with for centuries. The hull of *Victory* had reproduced all these difficulties since the 1920s restoration, but a satisfactory solution was not reached until developments in paint technology in the early 1980s.

Ten years earlier, the Dockyard Chemical Laboratory produced a formula for a low-sheen black paint that

A demonstration patch that shows the effect of shot blasting using a special grit that does not destroy the surface of the timber. (MoD (N))

would not chalk and which could be washed down successfully. Experiments were also carried out to remove old paint by burning off in small areas at a time, but following a fire in 1973 this method was abandoned and has not been used since. Shot blasting to remove chipped paint from the wardroom deckhead was however successfully demonstrated. The Durbane non-ferrous grit used produced an extremely clean finish down to bare wood, and rase marking was revealed on many of the pitch pine beams and oak intercostals.

Considerable painting effort had to be expended each year to keep the ship in good condition and to present a good appearance to the public. After a short trial the paint formula was once again changed in 1976. An area of the port side was washed down with fresh water and detergent and rubbed down with glasspaper. This was followed with two coats of low-sheen black supplied by the manufacturer. The weather during the paint application was dry and mild. After acceptance of the trial the starboard side, *ie* the weather side of the ship, was also coated in a similar manner. Bare areas were primed with two coats of pink primer, all abraded areas were filled with 'Dufay' fairing compound, and the ship's side was coated overall with the approved paint in coats of low-sheen black and buff.

The heavy work on this section of the upper gun deck has been completed and it is almost ready for painting. From top to bottom: beams, carlings, ledges and beamshelf; left to right: hanging knee, lodging knee, cast knee; the blue is the protective coating painted on all faying surfaces. On the deck a variety of shipwright's tools may be seen. (MoD (N))

By 1983, in spite of washing down with water and detergent and an annual repaint of bad areas, the ship's sides were looking very untidy, with large areas of paint peeling off. The problem seemed to be caused by the combination of prolonged exposure to the weather and the large thicknesses of teak involved, because the natural oil in the teak came to the surface, causing blisters which later allowed moisture to get behind the protective paint surface. Clearly, further trials were necessary.

The first of these involved the use of polyurethane primer, but this was not successful. Then several heavy-duty hot air strippers were tried as a means of removing the old paint instead of using paint strippers, in the hope that the heat would tend to remove the natural teak oil from the surface of the wood and thus allow the paint to key in better. A paint system based upon a finishing coat of the low-sheen paint of the appropriate colours was then applied. Records of the atmospheric conditions were kept during the trial. At the same time an alternative system using a Sikkens microporous paint was also tried to provide a comparison. Large sections of teak were coated and placed in an exposed position on the boathouse roof. By October 1984 the trial areas of the ship's side were showing signs of blistering, whilst the teak on the boathouse roof was still good after eighteen months exposure. It was therefore proposed that the ship's sides should be cleared back to base wood, to be prepared and painted using the Sikkens paint. Accordingly, all the paint on the port side was removed using hot air strippers, and the starboard side paint was removed by shot blasting. Although the non-ferrous grit shot blasting was quicker, the areas had to be rubbed down to remove the slight scouring effect. The adoption of Sikkens microporous paints has proved successful and they continue to be used in all areas of the ship in appropriate shades.

Protection of the timber by the use of paint is crucial, but constant vigilance is also required. Paintwork needs regular inspection to ensure that cracks or peeling, especially in hidden places, are dealt with and not allowed to undermine what on a more obvious surface may seem adequate protection. Scuppers and other drainage passages must be kept clear. The most important factor is to keep water off the ship and then to ensure that water that cannot be avoided–from rain–is made to drain off through appropriate and protected channels.

Stopping and filling must be checked regularly, and remedial work tackled with the minimum delay. Puddles, sometimes unavoidable on an open deck, should be mopped up as soon as possible. Puddles on a covered deck should also be mopped up and an attempt made immediately to discover the source of the leak. Wooden decks need to be kept clean, but a minimum amount of water should be used and any surplus taken up with squeegee or mop. The use of a hose invariably puts down far more water than is either necessary or can be easily contained with mops, and so encourages rot, especially in corners.

It is important that mast coats, conical canvas covers fitted over the wedges where a mast protrudes through a deck, are tight.

It is tempting to cover a small area of deck with sheets of plywood sheathing, especially if it has been difficult to make a particular area watertight by caulking. There is a considerable risk in this practice however, for unless the sealing of the joints is perfect, water can eventually find its way under the sheathing and rot the deck underneath without the problem becoming apparent until it is too late.

In effecting restoration or repair it is essential that in opening up any section of the hull the minimum is removed that will allow access and repair. This reduces the risk of loss of form and also allows the possibility of protecting the area from the weather, and if the opened area cannot be covered the amount of timber exposed to the elements is at least reduced. All faying surfaces should be coated and end grains in particular should be thoroughly treated.

If the exclusion of water is the first priority, the second is to obtain or at least allow the movement of air wherever possible. This is helped at least by keeping all drainage passages clear. On *Victory* more positive action has been taken by clearing a narrow gap in the inner planking between frames just below the deck above.

13. DAMAGE BY DEATH WATCH BEETLE

Death watch beetle, *xestobium refuvillosum*, is a notorious pest of oak structural woodwork in ancient buildings and churches throughout the United Kingdom. It was first discovered in HMS *Victory* in 1932. However the counting of the emerged beetles was not put onto a regular basis until 1937, under the direction of the Commanding Officer and the scientific guidance of the Forest Products Research Laboratory. This process continued until 1988 and was carried out every year except for the years 1941 and 1948 to 1960.

Three fumigations of the entire ship were carried out in 1954, 1955 and 1956 using methyl bromide. The results of these showed that not only had they been successful in destroying the adult beetles, but that they had also killed a large number of the grubs. Complete eradication of the beetle had not been achieved, but two considerations led to a decision to postpone any further treatments. The first was the desirability of assessing the extent of the survival of the grubs by recording the post-fumigation emergence of the adults, and the second was the decision taken by the Admiralty to carry out a complete hull survey and structural repair of the ship. This work would involve significant removal of affected timber, which served as a breeding ground for the beetles, and subsequent replacement by sound material. It was thought justifiable therefore to allow a period to elapse during which it could be determined whether the repair was preventing a resurgence of the attack by the beetle. Furthermore, the final effect of this long-term major repair would be that if further fumigation treatment was deemed necessary, the sounder condition of the hull should result in a much higher retention of the fumigation gas, which would have an even greater effect on those insects remaining.

An unexpected result of the fumigation was the continued high emergence of the predacious beetle, *corynetes coeruleus*, throughout the three fumigation years and also the following year. In 1956 and 1957 the emergence of the predator was higher than its host. It is not known

Annual Totals of Death Watch Beetle

Year	Beetles	
1954	953	Fumigation 1-3 March
1955	889	Fumigation 18-20 May
1956	230	Fumigation 24-27 May
1957	72	
1958	74	
1959	65	
1960	72	
1961	172	
1962	115	
1963	139	
1964	113	
1965	44	
1966	16	
1967	120	
1968	84	
1969	67	
1970	32	
1971	286	
1972	408	
1973	260	
1974	404	
1975	257	
1976	1283	
1977	1516	
1978	2710	Insecticide emulsion and smoke treatment annually
1979	2723	,,
1980	3103	,,
1981	2541	,,
1982	2919	,,
1983	3708	,,
1984	6635	,,
1985	3749	,,
1986	1997	,,
1987	392	No treatment due to restoration work
1988	1175	No treatment due to restoration work

whether *corynetes* is more tolerant of the methyl bromide than the death watch beetle but as would be expected, the decrease in the population of the latter eventually resulted in a corresponding decrease of *corynetes* because of the reduction in its food supply. The annual beetle emergence records for subsequent years do show the fumigations to have had an impact on the beetle population lasting twenty years. With some annual fluctuations numbers showed only a small increase to 404 in 1974, a small drop to 257 in 1975 followed by a dramatic increase in 1976 to 1283 beetles; this upward trend was maintained in following years. The reason for this increase can only be attributed to the environment onboard being suitable for their development. One possibility is that an increase in the moisture content of the timber occurred with consequential fungal decay and possibly a slight increase in temperature, which lead to better breeding conditions for the beetle. Whatever the cause, it prompted a need to consider further insecticidal measures. Since the ongoing programme of replacement of decayed timber would ultimately deny the beetles their food supply, it was decided that only localised application of insecticide was appropriate. The treatment programme was initiated in 1978 and consisted of an annual spray application of an emulsion containing 0.1% of the synthetic pyrethroid insecticide premethrin. This formulation was selected as not presenting a significant fire risk, and the use of one of a new generation of insecticides was preferred for its greater safety for humans. This treatment was applied by dockyard personnel to those areas found to be yielding significant numbers of beetles, mainly the forward parts of the lower, middle, and upper gundecks and the orlop. Application was by surface spraying of the deck timbers up to 6ft from the hull and by flooding the gaps between inner hull lining and timbers. A total of eighty gallons of the fluid was used each year. In addition an insecticidal smoke treatment was carried each year using twelve 40-gramme lindane smoke generators.

These treatments were carried out for the five years up to and including 1983. The beetle population over this period continued to rise, reaching a count of 3708 in

that year. It had been expected that any affects on the beetles during the first year of treatment (1978) would have been evidenced by a reduction in beetles emerging after five years, this being the average life span of the beetle larvae. Failure to contain or reduce the beetle population suggested that the majority of them were emerging from decayed oak timbers deep within the hull where the treatment fluid could not penetrate. A decision was therefore made to restrict the fluid application to the most severely infested areas in the bow and to

The death watch beetle, and his effect on wood.
(Centre for Timber Technology & Construction)

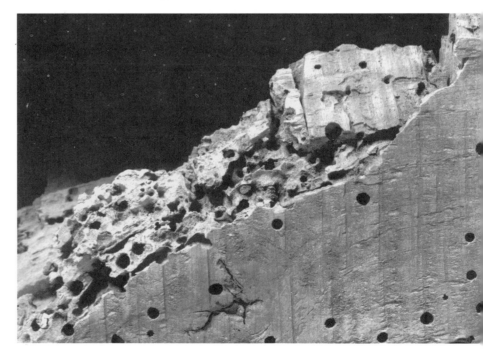

reassess the situation once the programme of replacement of the decayed timbers had been completed. The Building Research Establishment staff who carried out the inspections at this time concluded that the beetles collected from the hold were probably dropping down from the orlop deck above and that the beetle activity in the hold was minimal. The insecticidal smoke treatment on the hold was therefore stopped.

The numbers of beetles collected continued to rise to a peak of 6635 in 1984, after which numbers began to decrease so that by 1986 the number was 1997. Throughout the period 1978-86 the distribution of the beetles suggested that the infestation was somewhat localised, with the most severe areas being on the port side of the ship forward of the mainmast. In 1986 it became difficult to apply further treatment because of the major replacement work then proceeding on the hull. It was decided to abandon further treatment until the effects of the replacement of the rotted timbers upon the beetle population could be assessed.

Only 392 beetles were collected in 1987, but this must be regarded as misleading since major disruptions due to the restoration works prevented any consistent collection procedure. Despite the continuing work in the bow area, reliable collections were possible in 1988, when the number of beetles was 1175. This figure, the lowest for twelve years, was taken to indicate that replacement of the decaying timber by teak and iroko was having the predicted effect on the beetle population in producing a significant reduction. The beetle count is currently in abeyance pending completion of the major restoration.

14. PROGRESS REPORT (SEPTEMBER 1991 – FEBRUARY 1992)

1.   GENERAL

a)   Good progress has again been maintained during this period. This is in spite of the need to transfer labour for short periods to priority tasks elsewhere within the naval base. It is regretted that there has been very little labour available during this period for any work to be carried out on any maintenance tasks. It is planned that in the near future 2 in no shipwrights will be allocated the task of progressing the routine maintenance, which is considered essential to the upkeep of the ship.

b)   It has been agreed that there is far too much of the ship opened up and therefore no further unnecessary work is to be started until such time as the present areas in hand are near completion. It is with this in mind and the importance of trying to minimise the disruption of the ship, that a new schedule has been produced. This new schedule is intended to be a simple guide that separates the ship into different areas and provides key estimated dates for milestones to be achieved. The areas and their given ref no's can be found at ANNEX 1.

c)   The main areas of restoration on which effort has been concentrated during this period are:

1.   Area 1. Stb side (69-87 timbers)

2.   Area 3. Upper gundeck (fwd back to approx 6 beam)

3.   Area 4. Renewal of no 7 beam on lower gundeck (under side of middle gundeck) together with associated knees.

d)   The quartermasters lobby, along with all electrics, has been temporary resited just fwd of its permanent position, to enable access for the restoration of the ship's side.

e)   A small section of area 7 is presently in hand. This is on the middle gundeck and consists of the renewal of the waterway, spirketting, innerplanking, beamshelf and knees between No's 89-100 timbers. This area is being progressed in order that the quartermaster's lobby can be resited in conjunction with the reinstatement of the starboard brow. A temporary bulkhead has been erected to segregate this area from the visitors.

f)   The deck head beams on the underside of the quarter deck (Area 11) have now been deferred until a later date. It was decided that it was unnecessary to disrupt another area of the ship when there was a considerable amount of work still outstanding elsewhere. However, prior to this decision, the fabrication of certain items had already been achieved. Therefore these items have been laid apart ready for fitting at a later date. Details of these items can be found at section 4:h:2 of this report.

g)   The caulking and paying up of the hull below the wale strakes stb aft of temporary brow, complete with painting, has now been achieved.

h)   The renewal of futtocks, both port and starboard, has progressed, although work on the port side futtocks has now been temporarily deferred.

i)   Progress continues on the starboard restoration with the aim of installing the starboard gangway back to its original position. The renewal of futtocks in this area is now complete and good progress has been achieved on the renewal of the ship's side planking. (Area 1)

j)   The new canopy for the starboard exit has now been carved and is presently in the paint shop being painted. In order to achieve this it was necessary to bring in an outside contractor. The contractor concerned was Mr I Brennan, and a photograph of himself with his completed work was published in the *Times* on 31.1.92.

k)   The renewal or refurbishment, and fitting of the gunport lids on the lower gundeck (stb) is progressively in hand. This includes all associated fittings and ringbolts. The gunport lids on the port side are now complete and are awaiting the fitting of GRP sills.

l)   On investigation of the completion of the beak bulkhead, it was found that rot had set in to the beak deck planking. This had been replaced in 1989 using softwood. On analysis, it was reported that this was *Penicillium spinulosum* caused by the ingress of water. See ANNEX 11. Therefore work is now in hand to rectify this matter and is being progressed in conjunction with area 3. Full details will be contained in the next report.

m)   The drawings for the manufacture of the fwd port side brow, have been returned to the drawing office for validation and work will be put in hand on its manufacture, on the return of the drawings.

n)   Work commenced on the relaying of the cobble stones around the dockside (Port) by contractors. This task had only a minor disruptive effect on the restoration, due to close co-operation and mutual agreement with the contractors.

o)   The routine load testing of decks has been carried in accordance with drawing Po MCD 0339920. Full details are given at ANNEX 10.

p)   All checks on breakage and maintenance of form of the structure have been carried out. Full details are given in ANNEX 9.

q)   There has been no progress on repairs to dock cradles during this period, but this is not of immediate concern.

2.   RESOURCES

a)   The labour distribution throughout the period is shown at ANNEX 2 and indicates both shipwrights and craft painters allocated to HMS *Victory*. The joiners and other trades are not included as their contribution on board ship is minimal. Their work is invariably carried out in the joiner's shop or other workshops and is in response to ship staff job cards.

NOTE:– The distribution chart takes account of sickness and leave of one or more weeks duration only. Any sickness or leave of less than one week's duration is disregarded.

b)   The complement still stands at 15 in no. shipwrights, with a bearing at 12, and a complement and bearing of 2 in no. craft painters. It is to be noted that there were no painters available for any work on *Victory* during the months of December and January. There have been requirements to loan several shipwrights to other centres within the naval base to assist with priority tasks on deploying warships.

Within the 12 in no. bearing shipwrights, there is 1 in no mastheadman shipwright, who performs other work within the naval base in addition to work on *Victory*, and 1 in no shipwright liner who is heavily involved in the production of the VATC reports. Other duties that he carries out are, maintenance of form readings, surveys, drawings and supervisor substitution periods that are required when the PTO is absent.

3.   MATERIAL

a)   *Teak*
The current stock of teak held within the naval base for use on the restoration of HMS Victory now stands at:-
176 in no baulks of 16' x 16" x16" or longer

b)   *Iroko*
The current stock of iroko in the naval base for use on the restoration of HMS *Victory* now stands at:-

   8 in no baulks at 25' - 0" x 21" x 17"
   1 in no baulks at 25' - 0" x 20" x 17"
   3 in no baulks at 25' - 0" x 18" x 15"
   31 in no baulks at 16' - 0" x 16" x 16"
   3 in no baulks at 25' - 0" x 18" x 14"
   3 in no baulks at 25' - 0" x 17" x 18"
   1 in no baulks at 25' - 0" x 16" x 14"
   1 in no baulks at 29' - 0" x 13" x 10"
   5 in no baulks at 25' - 0" x 13" x 10"

making a total of 56 in no baulks, together with 2 in no. logs yet to be converted, sizes of these being:-

   27' - 0" long x 3' 3" dia
   34' - 0" long x 3' 0" dia

c)   There has been no stock ordered during this current 6 monthly period.

4. PROGRESS OF ACTIVITIES

a) *Restoration of the starboard side*

1. The extent of outer planking and futtocks progressed and renewed during this period is fully illustrated at ANNEX 4A whilst ANNEX 4 provides the legend.

2. The full details of sizes and renewals of futtocks on the starboard side are given at ANNEX 6.

3. Outer planking starboard

Outer planking renewals have progressed on the starboard side, between approx 69-87 timbers and from approx 44 to 60 strake. Each strake is made up of iroko laminates and full details can be found at ANNEX 7.

4. Wale strakes

There has been no progress to the starboard wale strakes during this period.

b) *Restoration of the Port side*

1. The extent of outer planking and futtocks progressed and renewed during this period is fully illustrated at ANNEX 4B whilst ANNEX 4 provides the legend.

2. The full details of sizes and renewals of futtocks on the port side are given at ANNEX 5.

3. Outer planking renewals have progressed on the port side and full details can be found at ANNEX 8.

4. Wale strakes

The renewal and fitting of port side wales have been progressed as follows:-

no 1 wale strake: consisting of 2 in no. laminates of teak, making up a total thickness of 4 - ⅝" on the top edge and 3¾" on the bottom edge.

From no 26 timber back to no 37 timber
16' - 1¼" long x 12⅛" wide fwd x 12¾" wide aft

From no 37 timber back to no 47 timber
16' - 3½" long x 12¾" wide fwd x 12½" wide aft

c) *Lintels and sills (starboard)*

The lintels and sills to the 7th and 9th gunports on the middle gundeck, have been fabricated in teak and fitted.

Each is housed into the timbers fwd and aft and shaped to the contours of the ship's side. Sizes are as follows:-

no 7 gunport
lintel: 3' - 3" long x 8¾" thick x 10¼" wide
sill: 3' - 3" long x 10¼" thick x 8¼" wide

no 9 gunport
lintel: 3' - 5⅜" long x 9¼" thick x 10½" wide
sill: 3' - 5½" long x 10⅛" thick x 13¼" wide

d) *Lintel and sills (port)*

All lintels and sills in the current restoration area on the port side are complete.

e) *Deadeye channel starboard*

There has been no further progress on the starboard deadeye channel during this period.

f) *Lower gundeck*

1. no 6 beam cast knee port: Has been fitted at ship by securing through the ship's side with 3 in no ¾" dia. bolts with nuts, and through no 6 beam together with lodging knee, by 2 in no ¾ dia. bolts. It has been radiused at the ends with a quirk worked around the edges. Sizes are as follows:-

length at beam   4' - 2"
length at shipside   5' - 6¾"
width at throat   1' - 9"
thickness   9½"

2. no 6 beam lodging knees port and starboard: Have been moulded and fabricated out of iroko and are awaiting fitting at ship. Sizes will be given on completion.

3. no 7 beam: Fabrication of no 7 beam, underside of middle gundeck is now in hand. Account was taken of sizes, offsets and camber and work has progressed along with the manufacture of associated hanging knees. Full details will be given in the next report.

4. Gunports starboard side fwd: The fairing in of no's 1 to 5 gunports, complete with fitting of lids is well in hand. Each gunport has been faired and a lining of teak fitted. No 1 gunport lid has been moulded and fabricat-

ed from teak off cuts from the ship's side planking. No's 2 - 4 gunport lids have been refurbished as required and will be re-used. No. 5 gunport lid has yet to be surveyed. It was necessary to manufacture a new pair of hinges for no 1 gunport, these are presently at the heavy plate shop being fabricated.

5.   Gunports port side fwd: No's 1 - 5 gunports on the port side are now complete. The rigging holes have been lined out with lead and all leather top hats have been fitted in readiness for final rigging. An order has been placed on the GRP Shop for the fitting of GRP sills to the gunports, but as yet the work has not commenced.

g)   *Middle gundeck*

1.   In order to renew the starboard side inner planking, between 89 - 100 timbers, it was necessary to temporarily resite the quartermaster's lobby. This involved a complete rewiring of all electrical and telephone cables.
On removal of the qm's lobby, it was found that the deck in the immediate area had undergone considerable wear due to being continuously walked on by the quartermaster. In its worst position, the deck had worn down from the original thickness of 3" to only ½".

Therefore, on final resiting it will be necessary to incorporate a small area of sacrificial decking to prevent re-occurrence.

2.   The starboard side inner planking, between 89 - 100 timbers, along with spirketting, waterway and beam shelf has been split out and all securings have been cut back flush with existing timbers.

3.   Renewal of waterway: Consisting of a total of 4 in no laminates of teak, each laminate being glued and screwed together to give an overall thickness of 8" from no 90 timber fwd back to no 96/97 timber aft

9' - 9⅞" long x 13" thick x 11½" wide

4.   Spirketting: Renewal of spirketting has progressed as follows:-

1st strake of spirketting: Consisting of a total of 3 in no laminates of teak, each laminate being glued and

screwed together to give an overall thickness of 6" from no 90 timber fwd back to no 96 timber aft

10' - 0½" long x 9¾" wide fwd x 9⅞" wide aft

2nd strake of spirketting: Consisting of a total of 3 in no laminates of teak, each laminate being glued and screwed together to give an overall thickness of 6" from no 90 timber fwd back to no 96 timber aft

10' - 8⅜" long x 12½" wide fwd x 12½" wide aft

5.   Inner planking
Renewal of inner planking has progressed as follows:-
1st strake above spirketting: Consisting of a total of 2 in no laminates of teak, each laminate being glued and screwed together to give an overall thickness of 4" from no 88 timber fwd back to no 97 timber aft

7' - 10¼" long x 12" wide fwd x 12¼" wide aft

2nd strake above spirketting: Consisting of a total of 2 in no laminates of teak, each laminate being glued and screwed together to give an overall thickness of 4" from no 88 timber fwd back to no 97 timber aft

7' - 10¼" long x 12" wide fwd x 12" wide aft.

6.   *Middle Gundeck Knees*
Account was taken and moulds manufactured to enable the fabrication of the following knees:-

i)   Lodging knee to after side of no 17 beam (stb) was manufactured from iroko and is awaiting final fitting at ship.

ii)   Lodging knee to fwd side of no 19 beam (stb) was manufactured from iroko and is awaiting final fitting at ship.

iii)   Beam end chock to no 18 beam (stb) was manufactured from iroko and is awaiting final fitting at ship.

iv)   Beam end chock to no 20 beam (stb) was manufactured from iroko and is awaiting final fitting at ship.

Full details of sizes will be given on completion of final fitting at ship.

h)   *Upper gundeck*

1.   Ship side planking (starboard)

i) Intercostal packing pieces were fitted between beams above the beamshelf and made up of 3 in no. laminates of iroko, 2" thick, and a final laminate of teak, 2" thick, making up an overall thickness of 8".

From no. 19 to no 20 beams (57 - 60 timbers)
5' - 7⅞" long x 9¾" wide fwd x 10" wide aft

From no. 20 to no 21 beams (62 - 66 timbers)
5' - 8⅝" long x 9¾" wide fwd x 9¾" wide aft

From no. 21 to no 22 beams (67 - 70 timbers)
5' - 8½" long x 9¾" wide fwd x 10" wide aft

ii) Beamshelf
Fitted under beam ends and made up of 3 in no iroko laminates, 2" thick and a final laminate of teak, 2" thick, making an overall thickness of 8".

From no. 58/59 timber fwd back to no 67 timber aft:-
11' - 4⅝" long x 8½" wide fwd x 8½" wide aft

From no. 67 timber fwd back to no 75A timber aft:-
13' - 4" long x 8½" wide fwd x 8½" wide aft

iii) Inner planking (quickworks)

4th strake above spirketting
Fitted over no's 6, 7, and 8 gunports, thickness made up of 1 in no. laminate of iroko and a top laminate of teak, making up an overall thickness of 4".

From no. 57 timber fwd back to no 67A timber aft:-
15' - 2¾" long x 9" wide fwd x 8¾" wide aft

From no. 67A timber fwd back to no 78 timber aft:-
13' - 10" long x 8¾" wide fwd x 10⅛" wide aft

3rd strake above spirketting
Fitted between no's 7 and 8 gunports, thickness made up of 1 in no. laminate of iroko and a top laminate of teak, making up an overall thickness of 3".

From no. 68 timber fwd back to no 74 timber aft:-
8' - 3¾" long x 10⁵⁄₁₆" wide fwd x 10¾" wide aft

2nd strake above spirketting
Fitted between no's 7 and 8 gunports, thickness made up of 1 in no. laminate of iroko and a top laminate of teak, making up an overall thickness of 3".

From no. 68 timber fwd back to no 74 timber aft:-

8' - 3¾" long x 10¼" wide fwd x 10¼" wide aft

2. Beams no's 27 - 33 (underside of quarter deck)
The manufacture of beams, no's 27 - 33, along with associated hanging knees has been progressed as follows:-
Account was taken of sizes, offsets and camber of no's 33, 31 and 30 beam. These beams were then fabricated from iroko in no 4 Boathouse, each consisting of 2 in no sections and bolted together. Also a total of 4 in no knees were manufactured out of iroko, these being:-

Hanging knees to no 30 beam (2 in no. pt & stb)
Hanging knees to no 29 beam (2 in no. pt and stb)

All of the above items have been laid apart with green left on them and full details and sizes will be given on completion of fitting at ship.

The fabrication of beam no's 27, 28 and 32 has now been deferred until a later date.

3. Fwd decking (upper gundeck Area 3)
In order to complete the forward end of the upper gundeck, so that it can be handed back to ship's staff, work on the renewal of the deck planking, complete with associated carlings and ledges has progressed as follows:

i) Deck planking between beak bulkhead back to approx no 6 beam (Allowing for shift of butts)

No. of lengths	Length	Width	Depth
1	9ft – 7in	10in	3in
8	9ft – 7in	8in	3in
2	10ft – 8in	8in	3in
10	5ft – 6½in	8in	3in
8	16ft – 7½in	8in	3in
8	17ft – 5½in	8in	3in
2	7ft – 6½in	8in	3in
1	14ft – 8in	13in	3in pt margin
1	11ft – 3in	14½in	3in pt margin
1	11ft – 6in	7¾in	3in pt margin
3	17ft – 7¾in	8in	3in
8	16ft – 9in	8in	3in
5	9ft – 11in	8in	3in

No. of lengths	Length	Width	Depth
1	7ft–9½in	8in	3in
1	14ft–8¾in	9½in	3in stb margin
1	10ft–10½in	11½in	3in stb margin
1	9ft–3½in	6¼in	3in stb margin

ii) New carlings fitted between 2nd and 3rd beams (see Annex 1C).

	Length	Width	Depth
Starboard side			
A (forward):-	2ft–4½in	8in	7in
A (aft):-	2ft–10in	8in	7in
B:-	4ft–6in	8in	7in
Port side			
C:-	4ft–10½in	8in	7in
D (forward):-	2ft–2in	8in	7in
D (aft):-	3ft–2½in	8in	7in

iii)   New ledges fitted between carlings (see Annex 1C).

Ledge No	Length	Width	Depth
Port side between carling A and shipside			
8	4ft–6in	4in	4in
9	4ft–6in	4in	4in
Port side between A and B carlings			
5	2ft–9in	4in	4in
6	3ft–11in	4in	4in
7	3ft–11in	4in	4in
Port side between B and foremast			
1	5ft–0¾in	4in	4in
2	5ft–0¾in	4in	4in
3	5ft–1½in	4in	4in
4	5ft–1¼in	4in	4in

Ledge No	Length	Width	Depth
Stb side between C and foremast			
1	4ft–9¾in	4in	4in
2	4ft–11¼in	4in	4in
3	5ft–1in	4in	4in
4	5ft–2½in	4in	4in
Stb side between C and D carlings			
5	3ft–8in	4in	4in
6	4ft–1¾in	4in	4in
7	4ft–2in	4in	4in
Stb side between carlings D and ship side			
8	4ft–4¼in	4in	4in
9	4ft–2½in	4in	4in

5.   GENERAL MAINTENANCE AND REPAIR

a)   The caulking and paying up of the hull below the wale strakes, starboard aft of the temporary brow has now been achieved.

6.   MAINTENANCE OF FORM

a)   Readings taken of outer bottom, beam spread and height between decks are tabulated and the results given in ANNEX 9.

b)   Breakage readings were taken on the 22nd October 1991, 19th December 1991 and 31st January 1992 and are given in ANNEX 3.

c)   The load testing of decks was carried out in accordance with drawing No. Po MCG 0339920 in November 1991, and the results are given in ANNEX 10.

7.   ASSIST CENTRES

a)   Joiners
Good service has been maintained by sawmills and joiners shop for the cutting of futtocks, decking and planking. Assist request for coaming has been transferred to C261 as C263 were unable to undertake, due to heavy work load.

b) Riggers

An informal meeting was held between F(C)11 and the master rigger to discuss the striking of the main mast. It was felt that a complete survey of the main mast was most important and work would start as soon as possible. As at 1st March 1992 work on the survey was still not started due to other commitments elsewhere within the naval base.

c) Painters

1. Priming and stopping up of the underside of the foc'sle deck is now complete. Attention to the beak bulkhead has been temporarily deferred due to priority tasks elsewhere within the naval base.

2. The weathered varnish to the binnacle has been stripped back to bare timber, prepared and given 3 coats of Sikkens Microporous Cettol 7. (teak)

3. The ship's wheel support and barge line has been sized and regilded.

4. The bulwarks and guns on the quarter deck have been reconciled as to colour and given 2 coats of Leigh Low Sheen Finish throughout. (buff and black)

5. The painting of the hull below the wale strakes, starboard aft of the temporary brow, is now complete. It has been given 1 coat of primer followed by 3 coats of Sikkens Microporous Paint. (outer bottom black)

8. SURVEY OF FIRE MAIN

The survey of the fire main was carried out by the fire prevention officer on the 22nd October 1991. A copy of his report can be found at ANNEX 12. Work is currently in hand to rectify this matter.

Annex 1

Key Milestones

Area No		Start	Finish	Area No		Start	Finish
1	Stb side, 69–87 timbers		Nov 92	8	Port side, 88–104 timbers	Jan 96	June 97
2	Stb side 40–68 timbers	July 92	May 94	9	Port side, 69–87 timbers	June 97	Dec 98
3	Upper Gundeck Forward		Apr 92	10	Port side, 50–68 timbers	Aug 98	Dec 99
4	Lower Gundeck (u/s of M.G.D. 7–12 beams)		June 93	11	Upper Gundeck (u/s of Quarterdeck, 28–33) beams	June 93	June 94
5	Lower Gundeck (u/s of M.G.D. 92–102 timbers)	Jan 93	May 94	12	Orlop Deck (u/s of Lower Gundeck, 1–4) beams	June 94	Nov 95
6	Port side Forward, 16–50 timbers	June 94	Dec 95	13	Hold (u/s of LGD 1–4) beams	Nov 95	June 98
7	Stb side, 88–104 timbers	May 94	Dec 95				

Annex 1a

Profile of the starboard side

H.M.S. VICTORY
PROFILE - STARBOARD
Forecast Dates:
AREA No. 1:   to Nov., 1992
AREA No. 2: July, 1992 to May, 1994
AREA No. 7: May, 1994 to Dec., 1995

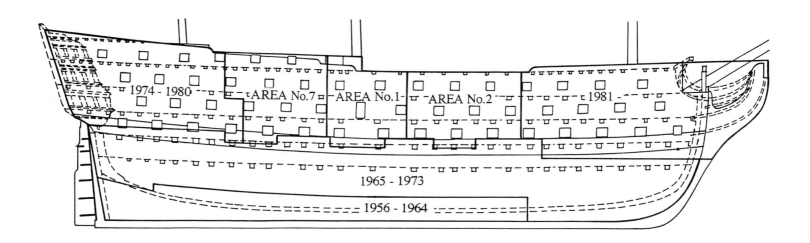

Annex 1b

Profile of the port side

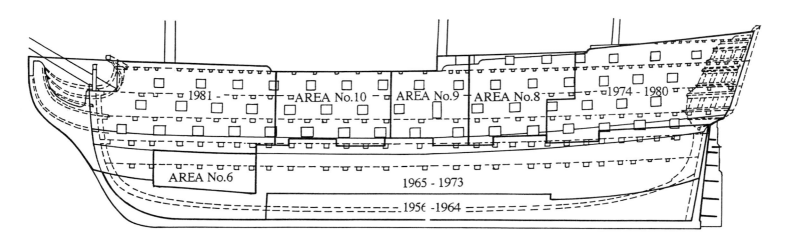

H.M.S. VICTORY
PROFILE – PORT
Forecast Dates:
AREA No. 6:   6 June, 1994 to Dec., 1995
AREA No. 8:   8 Jan, 1996 to June 1997
AREA No. 9:   June, 1997 to Dec., 1998
AREA No. 10   10 Aug., 1998 to Dec., 1999

Annex 1c

Upper gundeck forwsard, Area 3

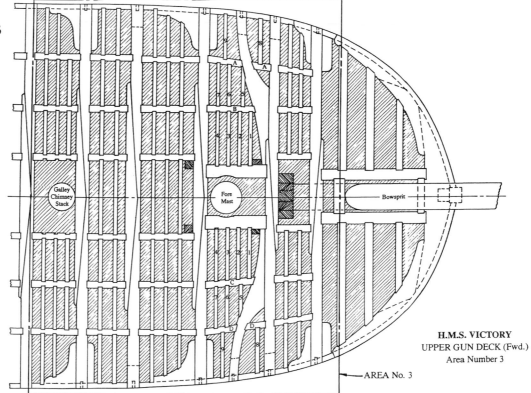

H.M.S. VICTORY
UPPER GUN DECK (Fwd.)
Area Number 3

Annex 1d

Middle gundeck
forward

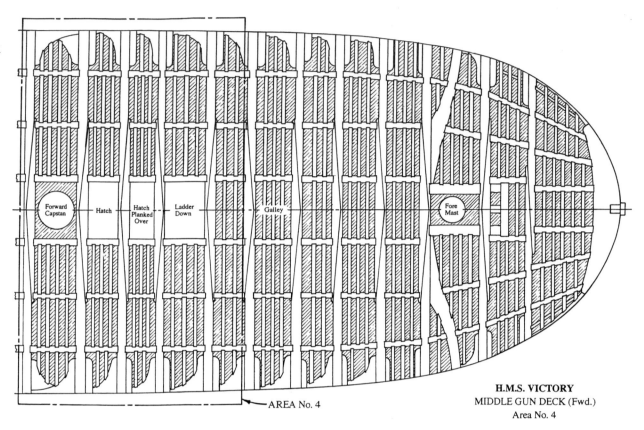

H.M.S. VICTORY
MIDDLE GUN DECK (Fwd.)
Area No. 4

─AREA No. 4

Annex 1f

Fore End and Amidships Restoration Milestones Achieved

Gammoning of Bowsprit	August 1989	Complete Rigging Fore Mast	May 1990
Complete Fit Beak Structure	October 1989	Complete Renewal of Wales Port Side Stem to No 46 Timber approx	November 1991
Remove Cover from Figurehead	March 1990		
		Fo'c's'le Only Caulked	September 1990

Annex 2

Labour distribution chart

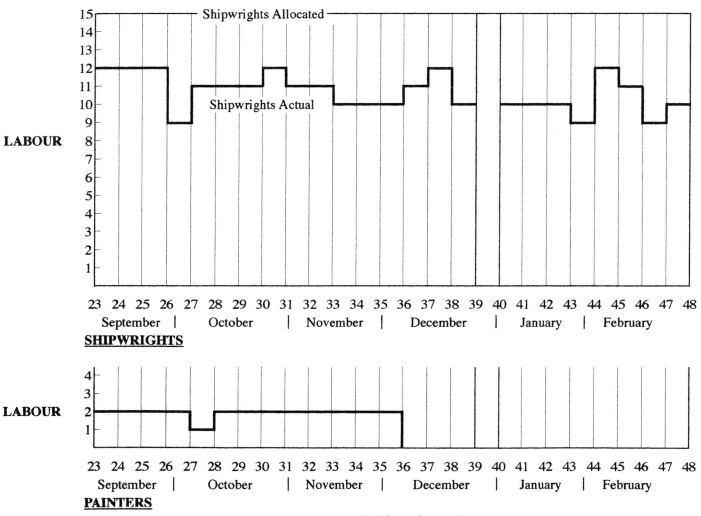

SHIPWRIGHTS

PAINTERS

H.M.S. VICTORY
LABOUR DISTRIBUTION CHART
Production Week Numbers, 1991 to 1992

Annex 3

Breakage Readings

22 October 1991 Readings

Station	Upper Deck	Middle Gundeck
5	−28	+ 30
9	−6	+ 9.5
13	+ 0.5	+ 11
16	−21.5	+ 8
20	−15.5	+ 16.5
24	−2.5	−4.5
28	−43.5	N/A
30	−47.5	+ 19

19 December 1991 Readings

Station	Upper Deck	Middle Gundeck
5	−35.0	+ 33.0
9	−13.5	+ 17.5
13	−6.0	+ 19.0
16	−27.0	+ 16.0
20	−20.5	+ 22.0
24	−8.5	+ 0.5
28	−51.0	N/A
30	−53.5	+ 21.5

31 January 1992 Readings

Station	Upper Deck	Middle Gundeck
5	−25	+ 28
9	−7	+ 11
13	+ 1	+ 11
16	−24	+ 11
20	−15	+ 15
24	−4	−2
28	−47	N/A
30	−51	+ 23

Note: -ve readings for the Upper Gundeck and +ve readings for the Middle Gundeck indicate deck has dropped. Measurements and changes of less than 2mm are disregarded

Annex 4

Pictorial guide of the restoration, forward end showing the extent of new planking and timbers fitted outboard

Legend

O	Remaining old timbers and planking	
A	Planking and timbers renewed between	
		1964–1973
B		1983–Jan 1984
C		Jan 1984–Aug 1984
D		Sept 1984–Feb 1985
E		Feb 1985–Aug 1985
F		Sept 1985–Feb 1986
G		Feb 1986–Aug 1986
H		Sept 1986–Jan 1987
J		Feb 1987–Aug 1987
K		Sept 1987–Feb 1988
L		Mar 1988–Aug 1988
M		Sept 1988–Feb 1989
N		Mar 1989–Aug 1989
P		Sept 1989–Feb 1990
R		Mar 1990–Aug 1990
S		Sept 1990–Feb 1991
T		Mar 1991–Aug 1991
U		Sept 1991–Feb 1992

Annex 4a

Starboard side
outboard (detail)

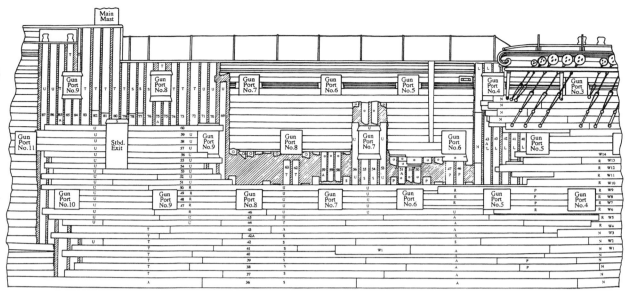

H.M.S. VICTORY
STARBOARD SIDE - OUTBOARD

Annex 4b

Area No 6 port
side outboard

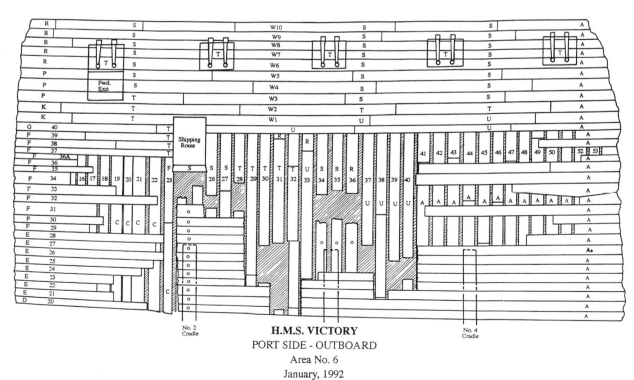

H.M.S. VICTORY
PORT SIDE - OUTBOARD
Area No. 6
January, 1992

Annex 6
Sheet 2 of 2

(Annex 5, Port Futtocks, has 2 sheets with similar layout).
Example page showing futtocks replaced

Starboard Futtocks

Stn	Length	Width	Depth	No of futtocks in length	Material removed	Material replaced	Remarks
53	10'-0"	Top 11¾" Bot 11¾	Top 8" Bot 10"	1st to Top Timber	Oak	Teak	Top fitted to a level of the beam shelf on the M.G.D. Bottom fitted to a level of the beam shelf on the L.G.D. after face recessed to house lintel and sill of the No 7 gunport on M.G.D.
56	14'-1"	Top 12" Bot 12"	Top 8" Bot 11"	1st to Top Timber	Oak	Teak	Top fitted to a level of the beam shelf on M.G.D. Bottom fitted to a level above the 2nd strake of spirketting on the L.G.D. fwd face recessed to house lintel and sill of No 7 gunport on the M.G.D.
69	13'-11½"	Top 11⅞"	Top 5"	Top Timber	Oak	Teak	Top fitted to the underside of the Double Block on the underside of the Plank Sheer. Bottom fitted to the beam shelf on the L.G.D. Recessed on the after face to house the lintel and sill to No 9 gunport M.G.D.
70	8'-10"	Top 12"	Top 4"	Top Timber	Oak	Teak	Top fitted to the underside of the Plank Sheer. Bottom fitted above lintel to No 9 gunport M.G.D. Recessed on the fwd face to house the Double Sheave Block.

Annex 7

Sheet 4 of 4

(Annex 8, Port Outer Planking has 1 sheet with similar layout).
Example page showing planking renewed

Starboard Outer Planking

Strake	No of laminates	Length	Width	Thickness	Material Removed	Material Replaced	Stations	Remarks
55	3	7'-5¾"	Fwd 8⅜" Aft 8⅝"	5⅛"	Teak	Iroko	81 timber 86 timber	Fitted Jan 1992
56	3	10'-8¾"	Fwd 9" Aft 8¾"	5"	Teak	Iroko	69/70 tbr 78 timber	Fitted Jan 1992
56	3	8'-7¾"	Fwd 8¾" Aft 8½"	5"	Teak	Iroko	81 timber 87 timber	Fitted Feb 1992
57	3	8'-9½"	Fwd 10½" Aft 10½"	4¾"	Teak	Iroko	72 timber 78 timber	Fitted Jan 1992
57	3	9'-4¼"	Fwd 10½" Aft 10½"	4¾"	Teak	Iroko	81 timber 87/88 tbr	Fitted Feb 1992
58	2	8'-9½"	Fwd 11¾" Aft 12"	4½"	Teak	Iroko	72 timber 78 timber	Fitted Jan 1992
58	2	9'-4¼"	Fwd 12" Aft 11⅞"	4½"	Teak	Iroko	81 timber 87/88 tbr	Fitted Feb 1992
59	2	8'-9½"	Fwd 9⅜" Aft 9⅜"	4¼"	Teak	Iroko	72 timber 78 timber	Fitted Jan 1992
59	2	9'-4¼"	Fwd 9½" Aft 9½"	4¼"	Teak	Iroko	81 timber 87/88 tbr	Fitted Feb 1992
60	2	12'-9"	Fwd 8⅞" Aft 8⅞"	4"	Teak	Iroko	69 timber 78 timber	Fitted Jan 1992
60	2	8'-5¼"	Fwd 9" Aft 9"	4"	Teak	Iroko	81 timber 86 timber	Fitted Feb 1992

Annex 9

Sheet 7 of 7

Example page of monthly readings

HMS *Victory* – Maintenance of form height between deck underside of beam

*R = Repairs in hand

Readings taken monthly 1991 – 1992

Gunter Position	Beam	Sept	Oct	Nov	Dec	Jan	Feb
Orlop Deck							
Port	3	*R	*R	*R	*R	*R	*R
Middle Line	4	5'-0¹⁵⁄₁₆"	5'-1"	5'-1"	5'-1"	5'-1"	5'-1"
Stbd	3	*R	*R	*R	*R	*R	*R
Port	7	4'-11¹¹⁄₁₆"	4'-11¾"	4'-11¾"	4'-11¾"	4'-11¾"	4'-11¾"
Middle Port	7	5'-0⁹⁄₁₆"	5'-0⁹⁄₁₆"	5'-0⅝"	5'-0⅝"	5'-0⅝"	5'-0⅝"
Stbd	7	5'-0⅝"	5'-0¹¹⁄₁₆"	5'-0¹¹⁄₁₆"	5'-0¹¹⁄₁₆"	5'-0¹¹⁄₁₆"	5'-0¹¹⁄₁₆"
Port	15	5'-4⅜"	5'-4⅜"	5'-4⅜"	5'-4⅜"	5'-4⅜"	5'-4⁷⁄₁₆"
Middle Line	15	5'-1"	5'-1"	5'-1"	5'-1"	5'-1"	5'-1"
Stbd	15	5'-4⅝"	5'-4⅝"	5'-4⅝"	5'-4⅝"	5'-4⅝"	5'-4⅝"
Port	21	5'-1⅝"	5'-1⅝"	5'-1⅝"	5'-1⅝"	5'-1⅝"	5'-1⅝"
Middle Line	21	5'-2¹⁄₁₆"	5'-2¹⁄₁₆"	5'-2¹⁄₁₆"	5'-2¹⁄₁₆"	5'-2¹⁄₁₆"	5'-2¹⁄₁₆"
Stbd	21	5'-0⅝"	5'-0⅝"	5'-0⅝"	5'-0⅝"	5'-0⅝"	5'-0⅝"
Port	27	5'-1¹¹⁄₁₆"	5'-1¹¹⁄₁₆"	5'-1¹¹⁄₁₆"	5'-1¹¹⁄₁₆"	5'-1¹¹⁄₁₆"	5'-1¹¹⁄₁₆"
Stbd	27	4'-11¾"	4'-11¾"	4'-11¾"	4'-11¾"	4'-11¾"	4'-11¾"
Hold to Orlop							
Middle Line	1	*R	*R	*R	*R	*R	*R
Port	4	*R	*R	*R	*R	*R	*R
Middle Line	4	9'-11½"	9'-1½"	9'-1½"	9'-1½"	9'-1½"	9'-1½"
Stbd	4	*R	*R	*R	*R	*R	*R
Port	9	10'-1⅝"	10'-1⅝"	10'-1⅝"	10'-1⁹⁄₁₆"	10'-1⁹⁄₁₆"	10'-1⁹⁄₁₆"
Middle Line	9	10'-0⅞"	10'-0⅞"	10'-0¹⁵⁄₁₆"	10'-0⅞"	10'-0⅞"	10'-0⅞"
Stbd	9	10'-3⅛"	10'-3⅛"	10'-3⅛"	10'-3⅛"	10'-3⅛"	10'-3⅛"
Port	13	10'-10¾"	10'-10¾"	10'-10¾"	10'-10¾"	10'-10¾"	10'-10¾"
Middle Line	13	10'-2⅛"	10'-2⅛"	10'-2⅛"	10'-2⅛"	10'-2⅛"	10'-2⅛"
Stbd	13	10'-9⅛"	10'-9⅛"	10'-9⅛"	10'-9⅛"	10'-9⅛"	10'-9⅛"
Port	17	10'-7⁵⁄₁₆"	10'-7⁵⁄₁₆"	10'-7⁵⁄₁₆"	10'-7⁵⁄₁₆"	10'-7⅜"	10'-7⅜"
Middle Line	17	10'-6³⁄₁₆"	10'-6³⁄₁₆"	10'-6³⁄₁₆"	10'-6³⁄₁₆"	10'-6¼"	10'-6¼"
Stbd	17	10'-7⁵⁄₁₆"	10'-7¼"	10'-7¼"	10'-7¼"	10'-7¼"	10'-7¼"
Middle Line	26	9'-3⅝"	9'-3¹¹⁄₁₆"	9'-3¹¹⁄₁₆"	9'-3⅝"	9'-3¹¹⁄₁₆"	9'-3¹¹⁄₁₆"

Annex 10

Sheet 2 of 5

Example page Load Tests

Load Test of Decks   Date: 11/11/91

Cycle Time	Test area	Deck Position	Datum S No	Load Test	Area	Before Test	Deflection Under load	After test	Perm set
1 Year	Upper Gundeck Fwd Port Test Area Number 26	Beam No.10	115	64 Cwt	24' x 5'	5'–10¼"	5'–10¼"	5' - 10¼"	Nil
		Beam No.11	116			5'–9¼"	5'–9¼"	5'–9¼"	Nil
		Beam No. 12	117			5'–10⁷⁄₁₆"	5'–10⁷⁄₁₆"	5'–10⁷⁄₁₆	Nil
1 Year	Upper Gundeck Fwd Stbd Test Area Number 25	Beam No.10	160	64 Cwt	24' x 5'	5'–11³⁄₁₆"	5'–11³⁄₁₆"	5'–11³⁄₁₆"	Nil
		Beam No.11	161			5'–10⅛	5'–10⅛"	5'–10⅛"	Nil
		Beam No. 12	162			5'–10¾	5'–10¾"	5'–10¾"	Nil
1 Year	Upper Gundeck Mid Port Test Area Number 6	Carling	118	64 Cwt	24' x 5'	6'–2⁹⁄₁₆"	6'–2½"	6'–2⁹⁄₁₆"	Nil
		Beam No.15	119			5'–8⅝"	5'–8⁹⁄₁₆"	5'–8⅝"	Nil
		Carling	120			6'–1⅞"	6'–1¾"	6'–1⅞"	Nil
		Beam No.16	121			5'–9⁵⁄₁₆"	5'–9¼"	5'–9⁵⁄₁₆"	Nil
1 Year	Upper Gundeck Mid Stbd Test Area Number 7	Carling	163	64 Cwt	24' x 5'	6'–3³⁄₁₆"	6'–3³⁄₁₆"	6'–3³⁄₁₆"	Nil
		Beam No.15	164			5'–9⁵⁄₁₆"	5'–9⁵⁄₁₆"	5'–9⁵⁄₁₆"	Nil
		Carling	165			6'–2½"	6'–2⁷⁄₁₆"	6'–2½"	Nil
		Beam No.16	166			5'–10¹⁄₁₆"	5'–10¹⁄₁₆"	5'–10¹⁄₁₆"	Nil
5 Years	Upper Gundeck Aft Stbd Test Area Number 5	Beam No. 22	122	54 Cwt	20' x 5'	Next test due Nov 1993	Next test due Nov 1993	Next test due Nov 1993	
		Beam No.23	123						
		Beam No. 24	124						
5 Years	Upper Gundeck Aft ML Test Area Number 4	Beam No. 26	125	58 Cwt	18' x 6'	Next test due Nov 1993	Next test due Nov 1993	Next test due Nov 1993	
		Beam No. 27	126						

Annex 11

PROCUREMENT EXECUTIVE
MINISTRY OF DEFENCE
DIRECTORATE GENERAL OF DEFENCE
QUALITY ASSURANCE
TECHNICAL SUPPORT DIRECTORATE
ROYAL ARSENAL EAST, WOOLWICH,
LONDON SE18 6TD

Mr P Meyer
Scientific Services Officer
DRA Laboratory
PP16
HM Naval Base
Portsmouth

February 1992

Dear Mr Meyer

Identification of Suspect Fungus from HMS *Victory*

Introduction

The piece of material was received by the Microbiology Laboratory on 28/1/92 and was subsequently examined using light microscopy. This showed that it was of fungal origin and so small pieces of the sample were used to innoculate various types of agar to enable identification of the fungus.

Results

The fungus was brought into pure culture and was identified as *Penicillium spinulosum*.

Conclusions and Recommendations

This is a commonly occurring fungus usually found in soil. Although it is not a fungus traditionally associated with wood rot, under the right conditions it is capable of degrading wood. It is therefore unlikely to spread to other areas of the ship unless the conditions that it was found in are common throughout. The growth of the fungus should not recur once the waterlogged timber is removed and adequate drainage is ensured.

W SYMONDS
Microbiology Laboratory

Annex 12

AREA FIRE PREVENTION OFFICER
DEFENCE FIRE SERVICE

Room 5109
Frigate Office Block (PP67)
HM Naval Base, Portsmouth PO1 4SE
23 October 1991

Hosereel Inspection – HMS *Victory*

Reference:

A. Telecon FPO(S)/MA HMS *VICTORY* dated 22 October 1991

1. As requested at Reference A, fire staff carried out an inspection of subject installation with the following results:

a. **Upper Gundeck.**

	FWD		*AFT*
Reel:	Serviceable	Reel:	Serviceable
Hose:	Unserviceable	Hose:	Unserviceable
Nozzle:	Serviceable	Nozzle:	Unserviceable
Valve:	Serviceable	Valve:	Serviceable

b. **Middle Gundeck.**

	FWD		*AFT*
Reel:	Unserviceable	Reel:	Serviceable
Hose:	,,	Hose:	Unserviceable
Nozzle:	,,	Nozzle:	,,
Valve:	,,	Valve:	,,

c. **Lower Gundeck.**

	FWD		*AFT*
Reel:	Unserviceable	Reel:	Unserviceable
Hose:	,,	Hose:	,,
Nozzle:	,,	Nozzle:	,,
Valve:	,,	Valve:	,,

d. **Hold.**

	FWD		*AFT*
Reel:	Serviceable	Reel:	Serviceable
Hose:	,,	Hose:	,,
Nozzle:	,,	Nozzle:	,,
Valve:	,,	Valve:	,,

e. **Orlop Deck.**

	FWD		*AFT*
Reel:	Serviceable	Reel:	Serviceable
Hose:	,,	Hose:	,,
Nozzle:	,,	Nozzle:	,,
Valve:	,,	Valve:	,,

2. The Inspecting Officer was very concerned at the demise of the firefighting capabilities with this ship. To this end, it is recommended that this letter be used as authority for demand of defective items. It is suggested that this demand be actioned at 04 Priority.

3. All defective items are available under Crown Supplies, independently. Stock numbers are repeated below for ease of reference:

a. Hose Reel Drum – Code No 70.05.0114

b. Hose – Code No 70.05.0231

Note: Hose reel drums are of Mark III type, and hoses are of 19mm internal bore and come complete with nozzle, coupling, and operating instructions. It should also be noted that each new and existing drum will be fitted with One x 45m hose.

4. It would assist fire staff greatly if a monthly progress report is made in respect of these recommendations. On completions, fire staff will undertake to inspect the completed works.

5. Any further assistance in bringing about a speedy conclusion to this matter should be staffed through AFPO Portsmouth office.

B G J EDNEY
FSOII
for Area Fire Prevention Officer

15. THE VICTORY ADVISORY TECHNICAL COMMITTEE[8]

Reference has already been made to the composition and work of the Society for Nautical Research's Technical Committee, formed in 1922 under the chairmanship of Sir Philip Watts, a former Director of Naval Construction. On the completion of the 1920s restoration it was invited by the Board of Admiralty to continue in an advisory capacity, Admiral Sir George P W Hope having succeeded as chairman following the death of Sir Philip Watts. It is not clear how often the committee met thereafter. Its views were certainly sought on the plans for the *Victory* museum in 1936, but it is evident that no further work of significance was carried out on the ship before the Second World War made a very low priority of all but the barest maintenance.

Victory was later in receiving attention in the post-war years than might have been good for her. In the event it probably made little difference in the long term. The delay was caused by a number of factors: the Commander-in-Chief's use of the ship – the Great Cabin and probably Hardy's cabin – as his headquarters office until 1949, the Royal Navy's preoccupation with the transition to peace-time organisation, inevitably more bureaucratic and bound by red tape than the relative freedom from such restraints in wartime, and perhaps the absence of any reminder from the advisory body. The latter seems to have arisen from a well meant but injudicious decision by Sir Geoffrey Callender in 1938, compounded by his untimely death in 1946. The former Professor of History at the Royal Naval College Greenwich had been appointed Director of the newly created National Maritime Museum in 1933 and was later knighted for his services. He had also been, it will be remembered, perhaps the most knowledgeable and certainly the most energetic member of the committee that had advised on the restoration of the 1920s.

In 1938 Callender proposed that the VATC be dis-

charged from its duties and its function transferred to the Trustees of the Museum, on the grounds that all the latter were members of the Society for Nautical Research. The Admiralty Board, with other more urgent concerns on its mind agreed. In 1946 Callender was succeeded as Director by F G G Carr, also a member of the SNR. Carr, new to the museum world though not to maritime matters, had to play himself in as Director and it was two years before the subject of *Victory* was raised. In 1948 Carr suggested that a panel of experts be nominated by the museum trustees. This proposal was accepted by the Admiralty, but the panel met only once, on 14 July 1949. Its subsequent report was sent to the Admiral Superintendent the following year, together with the Constructive Department's survey. As a result, the Admiralty agreed that the decayed structure should gradually be replaced, the whole made watertight and everything possible done to improve the circulation of air. It seemed that all would now be well.

Unfortunately, the advisory panel did not meet again to follow up the results. Perhaps it was felt that to do so would be an impertinence and seen as a check upon the dockyard authorities. At all events no more was heard from it until 1954 when, as a matter of courtesy, the Admiral Superintendent copied to Carr a proposed scheme of work that included the intention to deck over the skid beams in the waist as part of the plan to exclude rainwater. Alarmed, Carr copied the correspondence to other members of the panel with the result that a letter was sent to the Admiral Superintendent, protesting that the proposal would substantially alter the appearance of the weather deck from its Trafalgar form. He also wrote to Sir John Lang, Secretary to the Board of Admiralty raising the question of 'the responsibilities and interests of the various persons concerned directly or in an advisory capacity with regard to the *Victory*' and pointing out that 'apart from the Admiralty whose position is paramount, nobody is clear what responsibilities, if any, are borne by other people'.

---

8. PRO ADM 1/27660 for all the correspondence, minutes of meetings and Admiralty signals concerning the reconstitution of the VATC.

This led to an interesting exchange of letters between Sir John Lang and the C-in-C Portsmouth, Admiral Sir George Creasy. It was determined that there should be one single body to whom the Admiral Superintendent should turn for advice concerning *Victory*'s restoration and repair, but that the existing arrangement was less than satisfactory. Mindful of the vital part played by the Society of Nautical Research, first in *Victory*'s preservation, then in funding much of the restoration and still administering a fund raised by the Society for that purpose, both Sir John and the C-in-C were concerned that the Society had no formal representation on the panel, nor was it seen to play a part in any deliberations about the ship. Sir George recommended that a meeting be convened with representatives from the Admiralty, the Admiral Superintendent, the National Maritime Museum and the Society for Nautical Research, the last two to be represented specifically and not by anyone wearing two hats.

In the event, the meeting convened at 11am, 11 February 1955 in the Permanent Secretary's room at the Admiralty consisted of the following. For the Admiralty: Sir John Lang GCB (in the chair), Sir Victor Shepheard KCB, Director of Naval Construction, Vice-Admiral JSC Salter CB, DSO, Admiral Superintendent Portsmouth, Mr J E King CBE Manager, Constructive Department, Portsmouth. For the NMM: The Rt Hon The Earl Stanhope KG, DSO, MC, (Chairman of the Trustees), Mr F G G Carr CBE Director of the Museum. For the SNR: Dr R C Anderson, FSA, President of the Society, Professor Michael Lewis CBE Chairman of the Society. For the Advisory Panel: Professor A E Richardson, PRA, FSA, member of the panel.

Sir John summarised the history of the advisory body and the background to the current state of affairs, adding that whatever solution was reached, the Admiralty would wish to deal with a single body. He then sought the views of those represented and from the discussion that ensued, it is clear that there was no seriously contrary view. Finally it was agreed that the *Victory* Advisory Technical Committee should be formally reconstituted. The Admiralty would invite nominations from the Society for Nautical Research and the National Maritime Museum, while reserving for itself the right to add to its own nominees when necessary. In the minutes of the meeting, paragraph 18, the second under the heading 'Conclusions' begins;

The Admiralty would be responsible for circulating information to the members of the committee and for summoning the committee to meet. It would also provide facilities for holding the meetings, either in the ship or in London. The committee would be consulted directly from Portsmouth although it might at times be necessary for the Admiralty itself to consult the committee. The committee would select its own chairman, but this would not be one of the Admiralty representatives on it.

The Board of Admiralty approved the arrangement, and on 19 May 1955 a signal was sent to the C-in-C Portsmouth announcing that their Lordships had 'decided to reconstitute the *Victory* Advisory Technical Committee' with the following membership: –

a. Admiralty representatives: Director of Naval Construction, Admiral Superintendent, Portsmouth, Manager, Constructive Department, Portsmouth, and R C Fisher Esq. PhD, Forest Products Research Laboratory.

b. Members nominated by the National Maritime Museum: A J Villiers Esq. DSC, FRCS, Professor A E Richardson PRA, J N Robertson Esq. Lloyds Register of Shipping, F G G Carr Esq. OBE National Maritime Museum

c. Members nominated by the Society for Nautical Research: R C Anderson Litt.D., FSA, Professor Michael A Lewis, E H B Boulton Esq. MA, Lieut. Cdr. G P B Naish RNVR.

The secretary of the committee was to be the secretary to the Admiral Superintendent, Portsmouth. The committee later selected Professor Richardson as its chairman.

The first meeting of the committee was on 30 June

1955 and it has met formally twice yearly ever since, in the Spring and Autumn, when it receives a six-monthly report from the Constructive Department of the dockyard.[9] Extraordinary meetings are convened as necessary. There is also a Timber Sub-Committee and an Interpretation Sub-Committee. The membership of the committee has of course changed, but the representation is broadly the same. On the Admiralty side, titles have changed but the only additions made have been the Commanding Officer of *Victory* and more recently, a representative of the Procurement Executive responsible for the provision of the timber. This latter addition was deemed helpful because of the problems resulting from the need to use sustainable resources from politically acceptable regimes.

The representation of the Society for Nautical Research and the National Maritime Museum has been slightly re-arranged. In 1985, with the approval of the Chairman and the Director respectively, it was decided that as nominees of the SNR and NMM retired from the committee, they need not necessarily be replaced provided that the range and quality of advice available to the Naval Base authorities was not compromised. The Chairman and the Director each reserved the right to revert to the 1955 representation at his discretion.

Currently, the Society has two representatives, one of whom retired from the Museum as a department head. The Museum has one representative who is also a member of the SNR Council. The chairman of the committee is a retired senior officer of the Museum and is also a Vice President of the Society. Happily, contentious issues are rare. The nominees of the Society and the Museum offer guidance over historical accuracy and interpretation, but are also mindful of the various practical problems that face the Constructive Department in its work.

There has however, been a major change in the dockyard. In 1995 it was decided that work for the Ministry of Defence (Navy) should be in the hands of an agency, having the effect of privatisation. After protracted negotiations and a long period of preparation, tenders were invited and that of Fleet Support Limited was accepted, Vesting Day being 3 January 1998.

Oversight of all work is the responsibility of the Superintendent Ships, an office held by a Captain RN, but the organisation and execution of the work falls to FSL under contract. The workforce remains largely the same at the moment but its members are no longer employed by the MoD (N). Two representatives of FSL are on the *Victory* Advisory Technical Committee and there is every reason to suppose that the meetings will continue to be as harmonious and effective as has been the case since its reconstitution in 1955.

---

9. Later from the Director, Fleet Maintenance and Repairs Organisation and now from the Managing Director, Fleet Support Limited. The report reproduced on page 103 was from the Director FMRO.

The Drawings

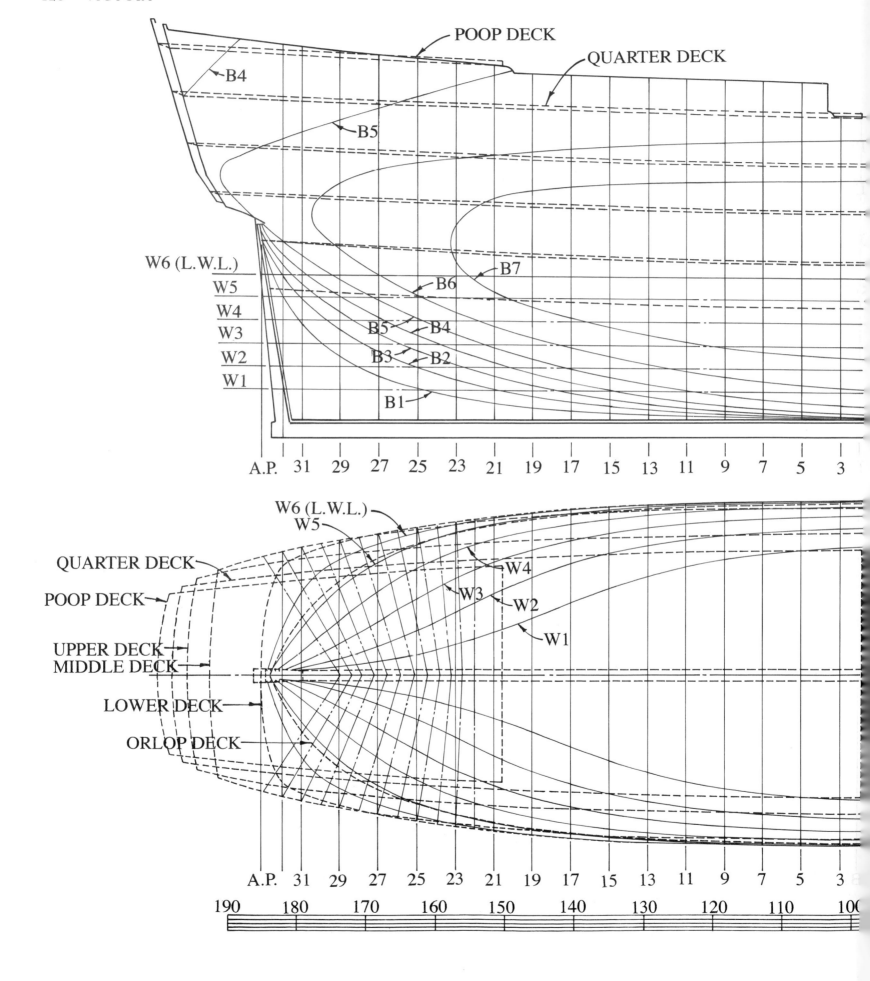

POOP DECK

QUARTER DECK

B4

B5

W6 (L.W.L.)

W5

W4

W3

W2

W1

B7

B6

B5 B4

B3 B2

B1

A.P. 31 29 27 25 23 21 19 17 15 13 11 9 7 5 3

W6 (L.W.L.)
W5

QUARTER DECK

POOP DECK

UPPER DECK
MIDDLE DECK

LOWER DECK

ORLOP DECK

W4

W3 W2

W1

A.P. 31 29 27 25 23 21 19 17 15 13 11 9 7 5 3

190 180 170 160 150 140 130 120 110 100

The sheer and lines plans. The sheer plan shows the same contours as the body plan (p130) but in a side elevation, while the lines plan shows them in true plan form.

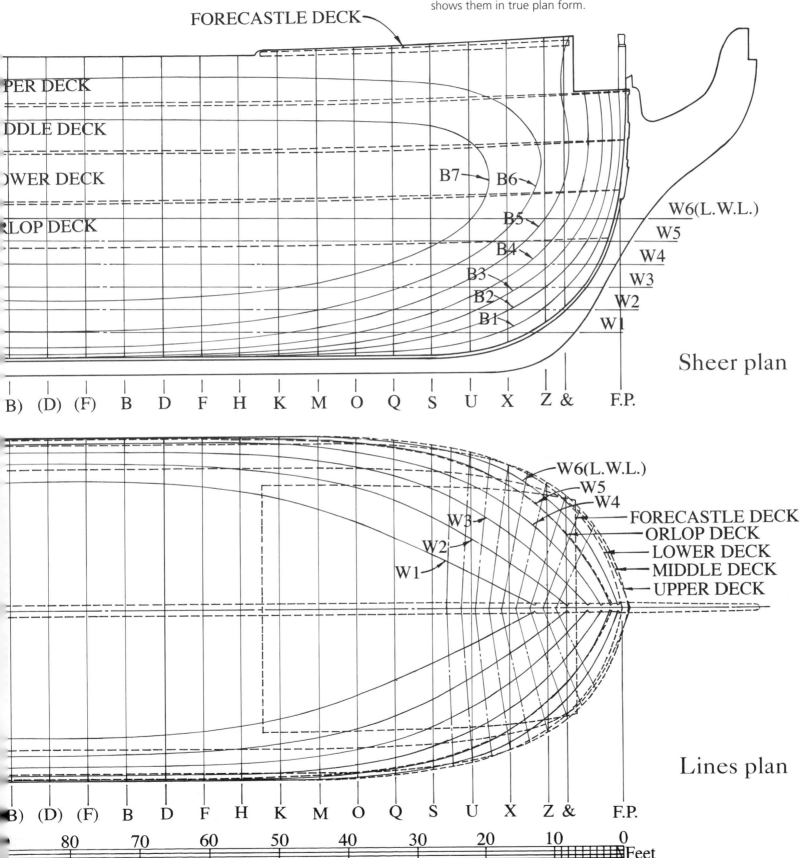

FORECASTLE DECK

PER DECK

DDLE DECK

OWER DECK

RLOP DECK

B7 B6

B5

B4

B3

B2

B1

W6(L.W.L.)

W5

W4

W3

W2

W1

Sheer plan

B) (D) (F) B D F H K M O Q S U X Z & F.P.

W6(L.W.L.)
W5
W4
W3
W2
W1

FORECASTLE DECK
ORLOP DECK
LOWER DECK
MIDDLE DECK
UPPER DECK

Lines plan

B) (D) (F) B D F H K M O Q S U X Z & F.P.

80 70 60 50 40 30 20 10 0 Feet

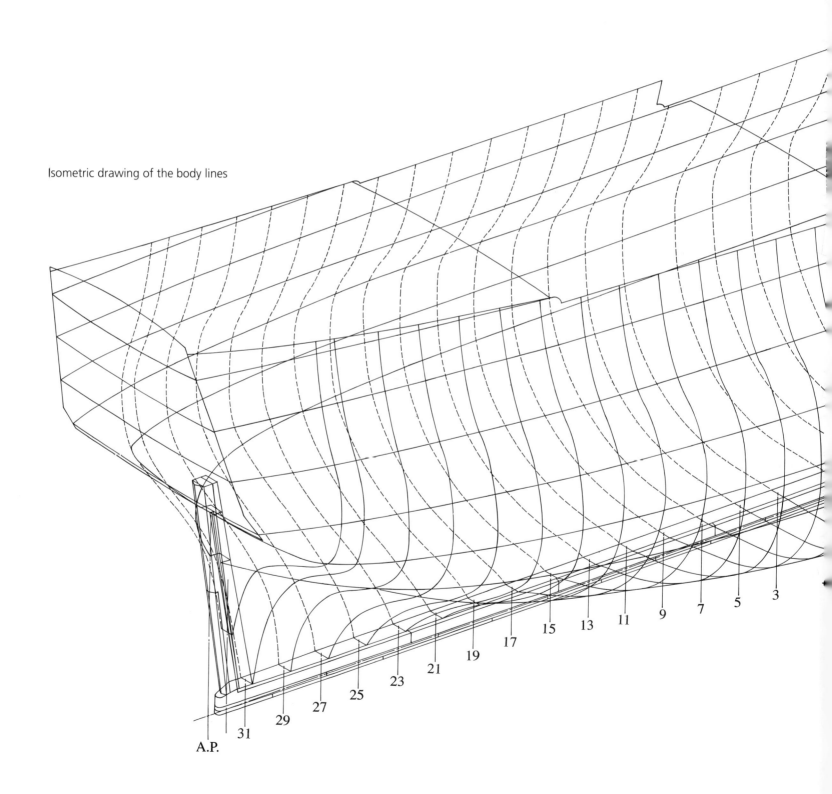

Isometric drawing of the body lines

A.P.

31

29

27

25

23

21

19

17

15

13

11

9

7

5

3

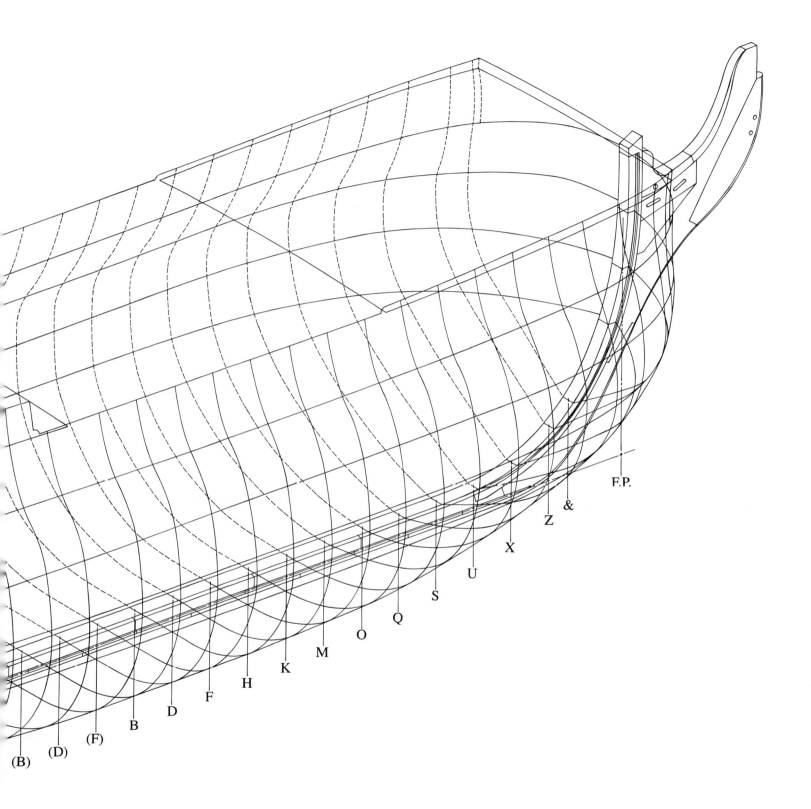

Body lines

Body plan

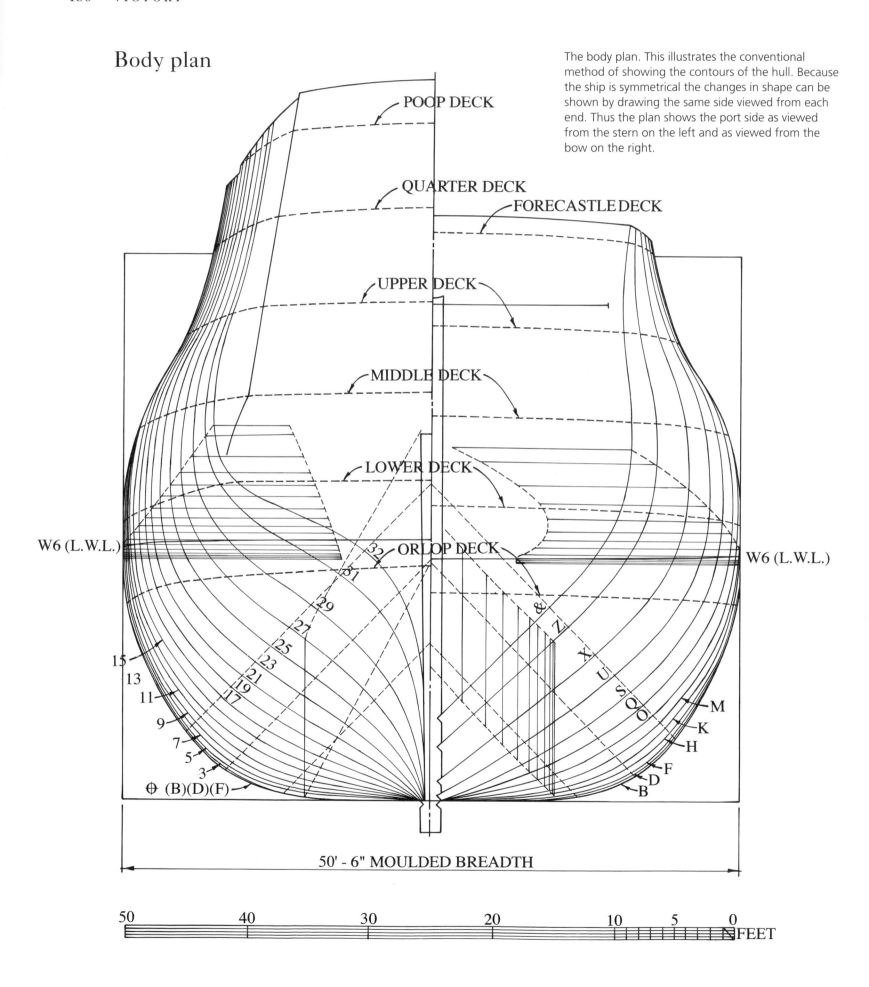

The body plan. This illustrates the conventional method of showing the contours of the hull. Because the ship is symmetrical the changes in shape can be shown by drawing the same side viewed from each end. Thus the plan shows the port side as viewed from the stern on the left and as viewed from the bow on the right.

POOP DECK

QUARTER DECK

FORECASTLE DECK

UPPER DECK

MIDDLE DECK

LOWER DECK

W6 (L.W.L.)   ORLOP DECK   W6 (L.W.L.)

50' - 6" MOULDED BREADTH

50   40   30   20   10   5   0
FEET

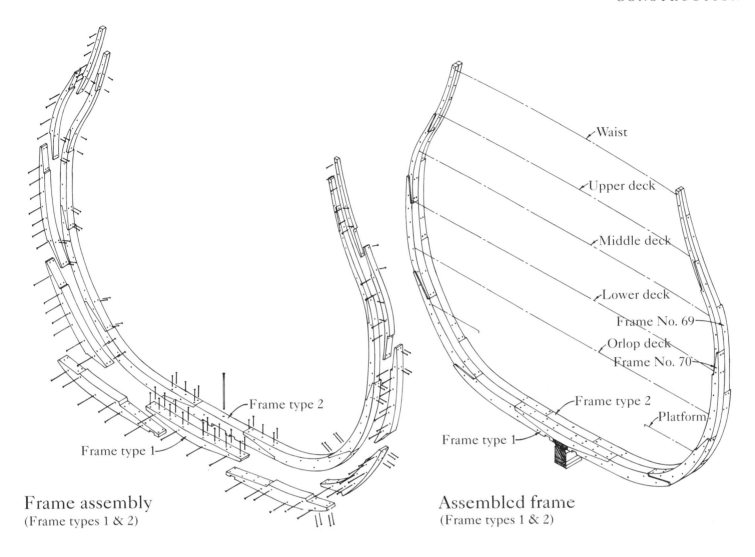

Frame assembly
(Frame types 1 & 2)

Frame type 1

Frame type 2

Assembled frame
(Frame types 1 & 2)

Waist

Upper deck

Middle deck

Lower deck

Frame No. 69

Orlop deck

Frame No. 70

Frame type 2

Frame type 1

Platform

The frame construction details. These drawings show the two parts of a framed bend and illustrate the complexity of the construction.

It should also be remembered that nearly every piece of timber shown weighs several hundredweight.

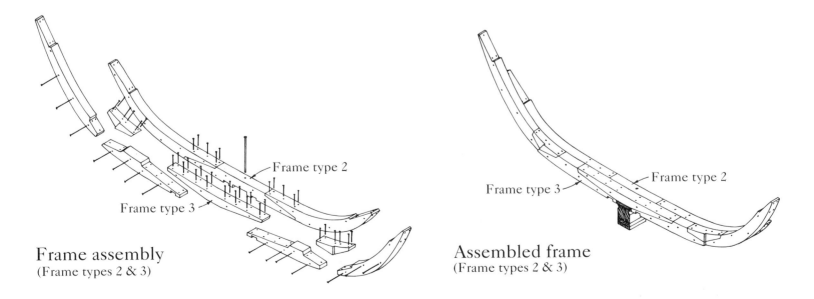

Frame assembly
(Frame types 2 & 3)

Frame type 2

Frame type 3

Assembled frame
(Frame types 2 & 3)

Frame type 2

Frame type 3

Rider construction details. The largest riders are sided 15in with the moulded width hardly less.

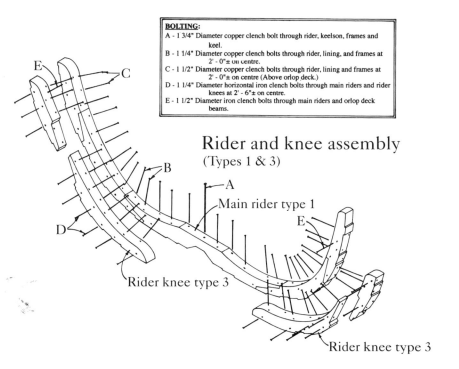

BOLTING:
A - 1 3/4" Diameter copper clench bolt through rider, keelson, frames and keel.
B - 1 1/4" Diameter copper clench bolts through rider, lining, and frames at 2' - 0"± on centre.
C - 1 1/2" Diameter copper clench bolts through rider, lining and frames at 2' - 0"± on centre (Above orlop deck.)
D - 1 1/4" Diameter horizontal iron clench bolts through main riders and rider knees at 2' - 6"± on centre.
E - 1 1/2" Diameter iron clench bolts through main riders and orlop deck beams.

Rider and knee assembly
(Types 1 & 3)

Main rider type 1

Rider knee type 3

Rider knee type 3

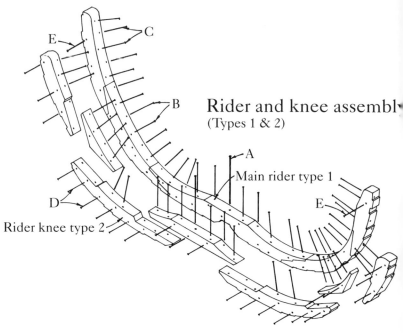

Rider and knee assembl~
(Types 1 & 2)

Main rider type 1

Rider knee type 2

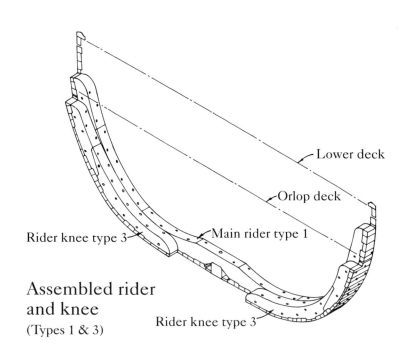

Lower deck

Orlop deck

Rider knee type 3

Main rider type 1

Assembled rider and knee
(Types 1 & 3)

Rider knee type 3

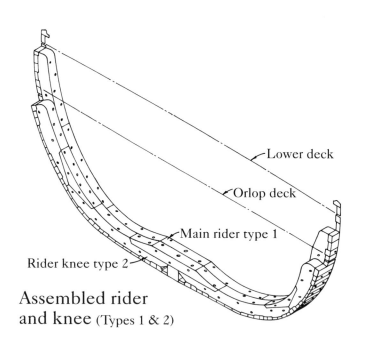

Lower deck

Orlop deck

Main rider type 1

Rider knee type 2

Assembled rider and knee (Types 1 & 2)

Beam construction details. The lightest beams are those for the poop deck and are approximately 6in deep and 8in wide. Those for the lower gundeck, which have to carry so much more weight, are approximately 16in deep and 15in wide.

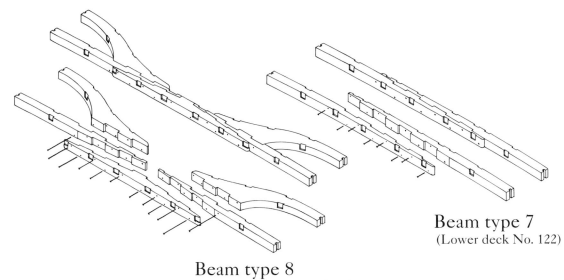

Beam type 7
(Lower deck No. 122)

Beam type 8
(Lower deck No.'s 80 & 85)

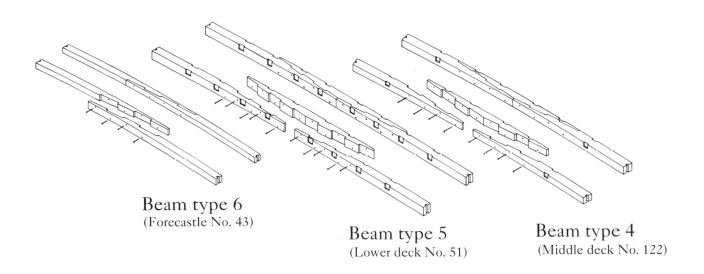

Beam type 6
(Forecastle No. 43)

Beam type 5
(Lower deck No. 51)

Beam type 4
(Middle deck No. 122)

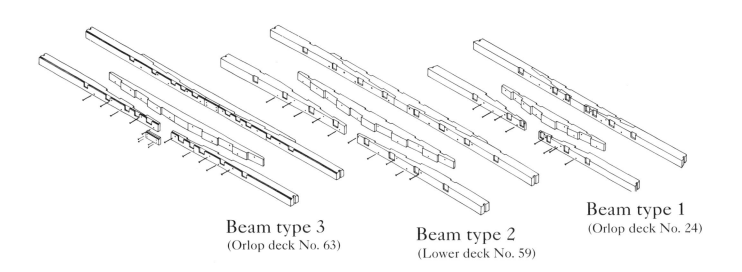

Beam type 3
(Orlop deck No. 63)

Beam type 2
(Lower deck No. 59)

Beam type 1
(Orlop deck No. 24)

The stern

The stern. Until late in the nineteenth century, First Rates had open stern galleries on the upper and middle gun decks. *Victory*'s stern was enclosed during the Great Repair completed in 1803. Here we see the windows of Hardy's cabin, Nelson's cabin and the wardroom. On the lower gun deck below the wardroom is the gunroom where the midshipmen and the most junior officers lived. Throughout the ship there is about 5ft 6ins between the deck and the underside of the beams (except on the orlop where it is rather less). In the gunroom the available height is reduced still further by the tiller arm that sweeps round just below the beams.

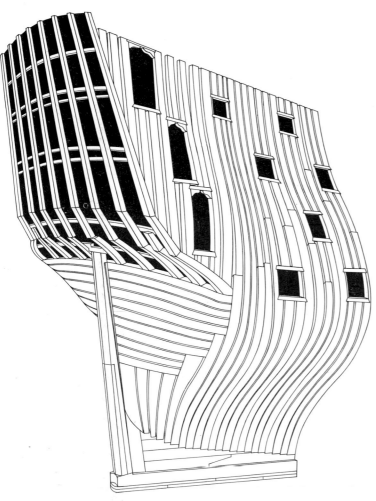

The major structural strength of the stern lies in the sternpost and the horizontal timbers which are the transoms. Ideally, each one was a single piece of timber and in the case of the topmost, the wing transom, it is 14in deep, 28in moulded width and 35ft long. The sternpost, originally also one piece, had to be a minimum of 26in square at the top and roughly 40ft in length.

The bow framing. The hawse holes adjacent to the beak give the name to the vertical timbers on either side of the stem – the hawse timbers.

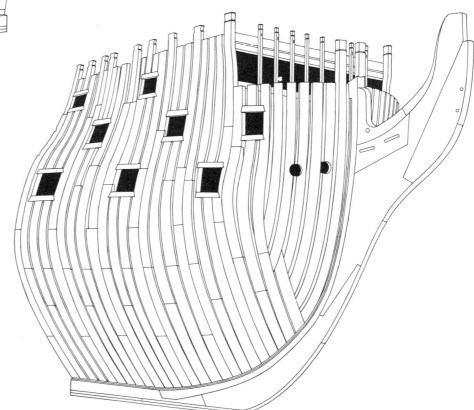

The planking (above the waterline) and framing (below).

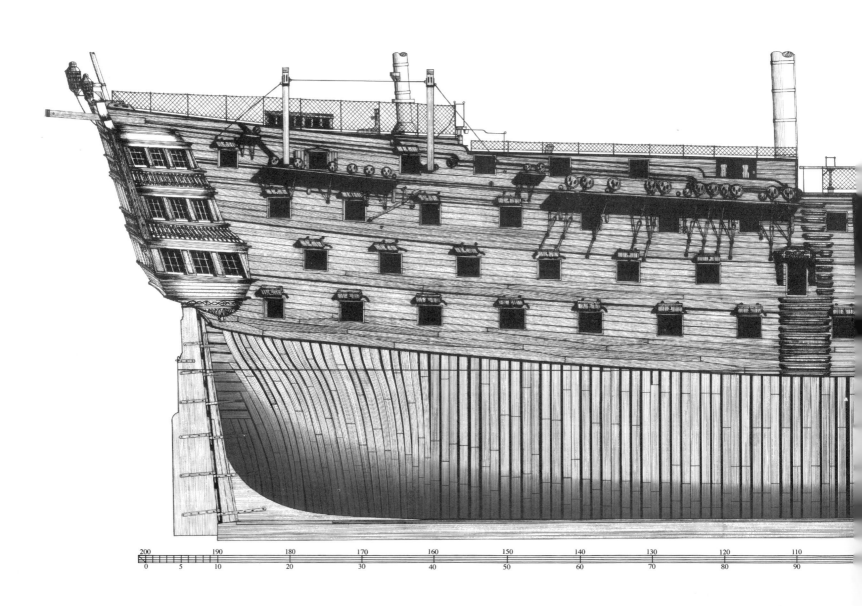

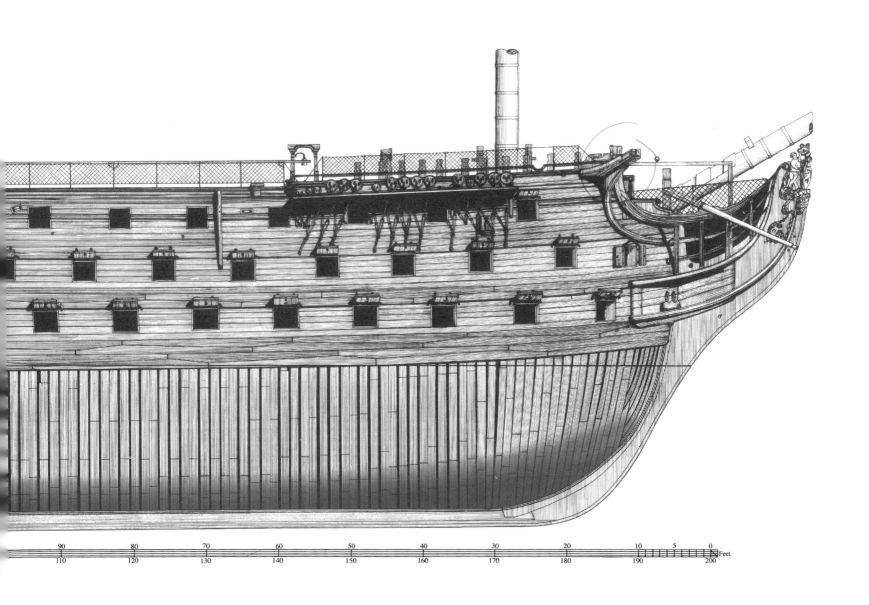

The plank expansion plan. The distortion is caused by the 'flattening out' of the underwater curve rather in the way that the Mercator projection distorts the map of the world. However the plank expansion plan enables the shipwright to see every plank that goes into the hull. It also shows clearly the important shift of butts, the practice of never having plank joins (butts) above each other on adjoining strakes, so avoiding building an inherent weakness into the structure.

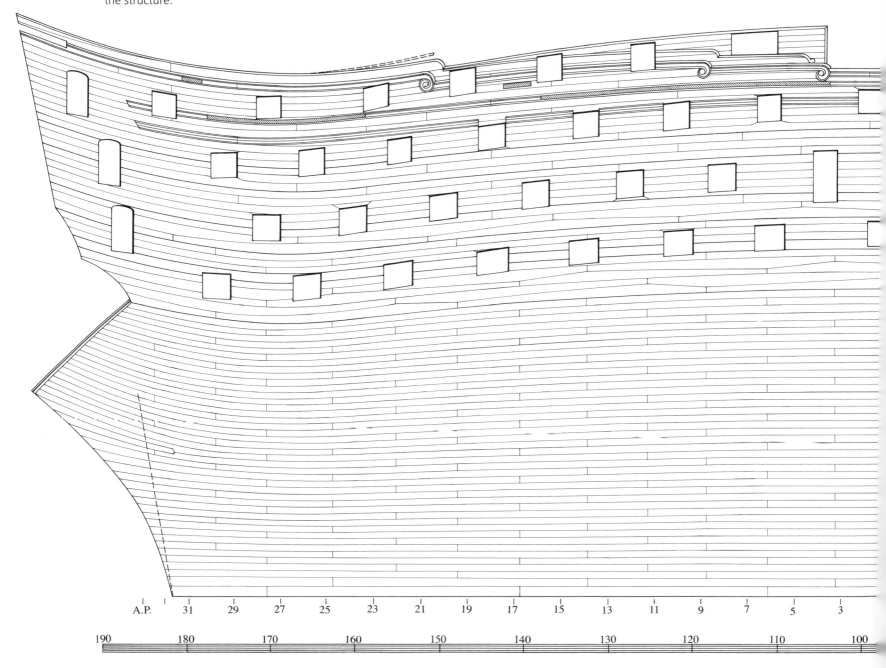

Plank expansion plan

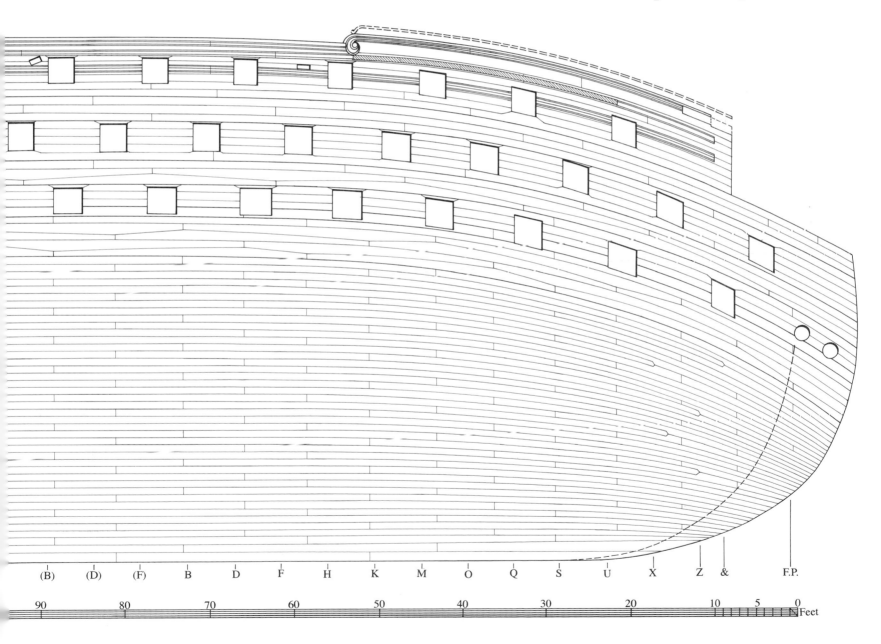

(B) (D) (F) B D F H K M O Q S U X Z & F.P.

90 80 70 60 50 40 30 20 10 5 0 Feet

Copper sheathing. The copper sheathing was necessary to protect
the hull planking and timbers from the depredations of the
shipworm and the gribble and also to inhibit the marine growth
that could adversely affect the ship's sailing qualities. Note the close
spacing of the fastenings.

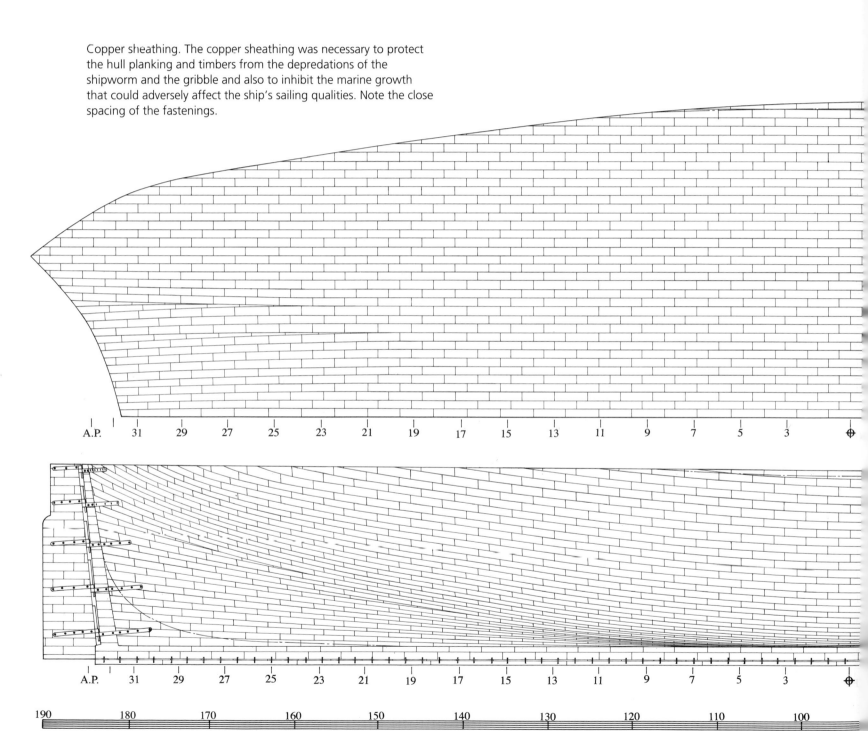

Expansion plan: copper sheathing

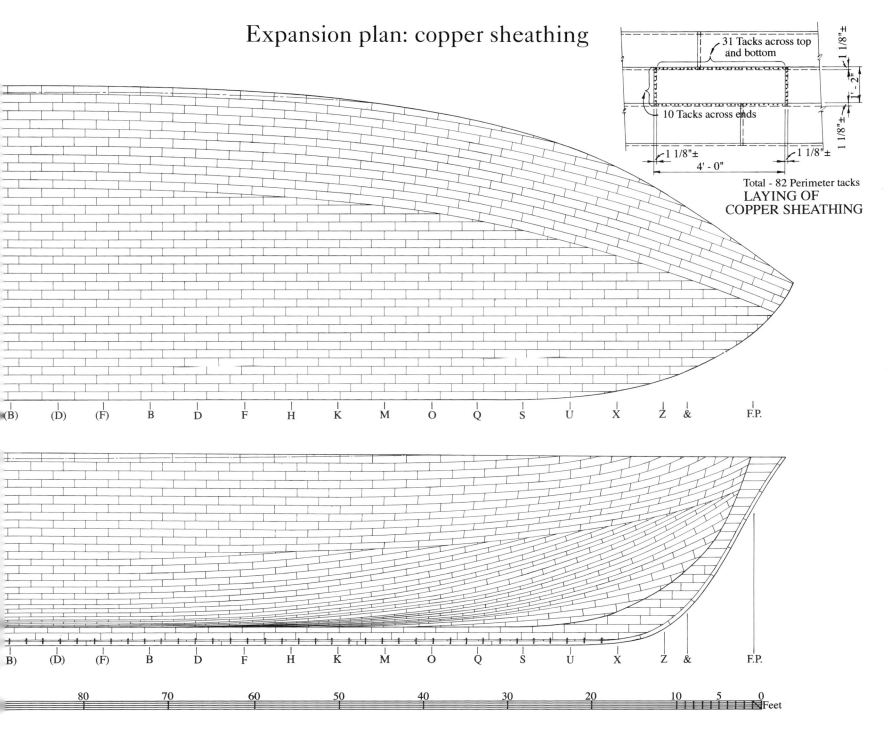

31 Tacks across top and bottom

1 1/8"±

2"

10 Tacks across ends

1 1/8"±

1 1/8"±   1 1/8"±
4' - 0"

Total - 82 Perimeter tacks
LAYING OF COPPER SHEATHING

(B)   (D)   (F)   B   D   F   H   K   M   O   Q   S   U   X   Z   &   F.P.

(B)   (D)   (F)   B   D   F   H   K   M   O   Q   S   U   X   Z   &   F.P.

80   70   60   50   40   30   20   10   5   0
Feet

Outboard profile: copper sheathing

Inboard. It was important for the health of the ship as well as for the crew to circulate as much air as possible below decks, hence the large number of gratings. Fresh air, rarely less than bracing in other than tropical waters, was fed in from the waist and from the gunports that were opened whenever the weather permitted. Even when the ports were closed, their scuttles (see p200) could provide fresh air in all but the wildest weather.

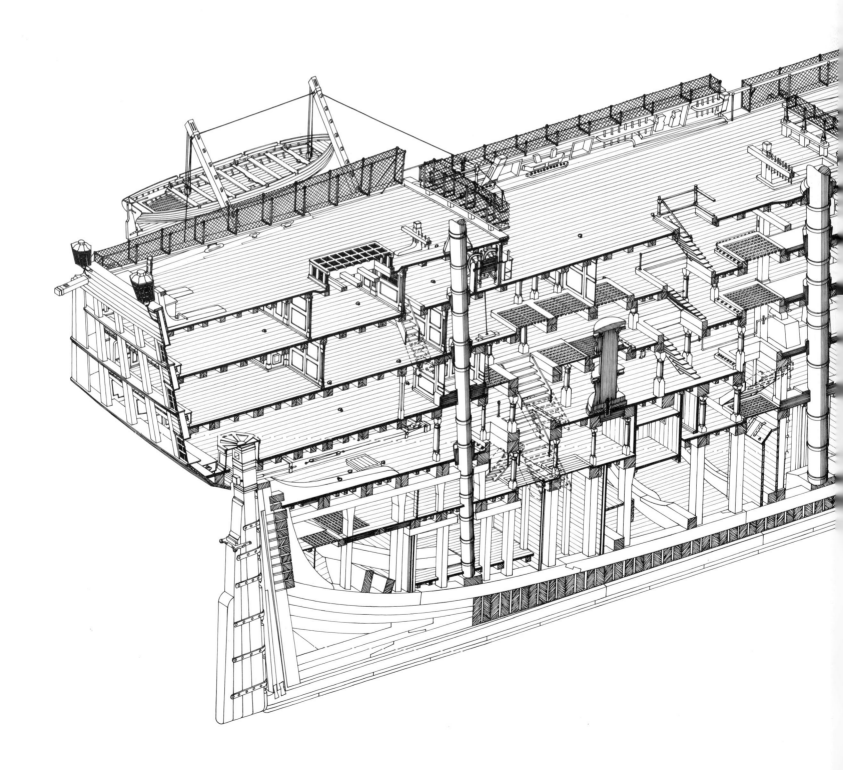

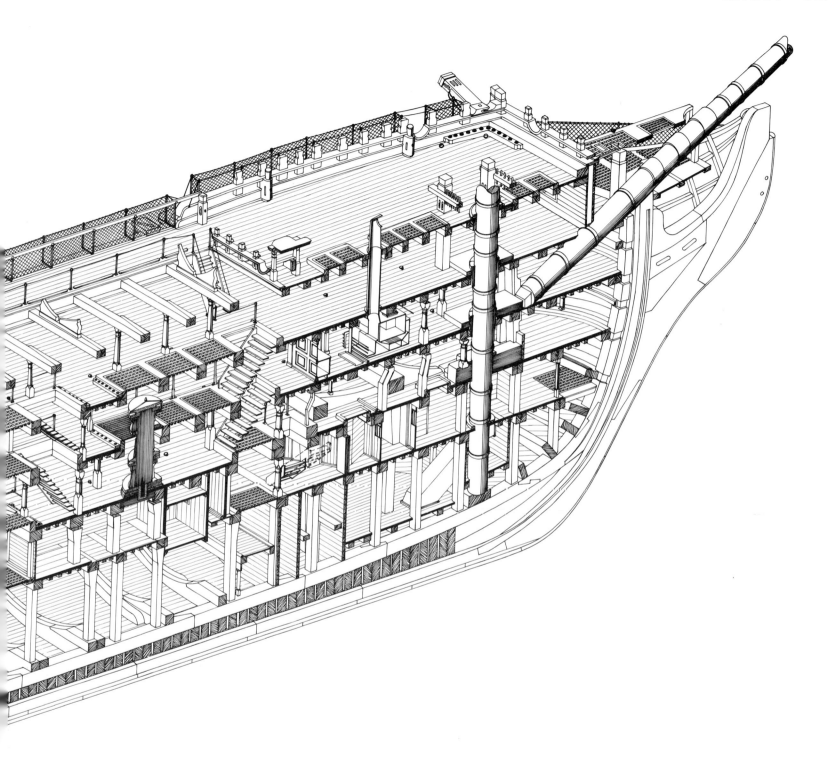

This inboard profile gives some notion of the warren-like arrangement that greeted the inexperienced newcomer, especially with 800 or so men busy about the daily routine. Ships of the line were all generally similar in their layout.

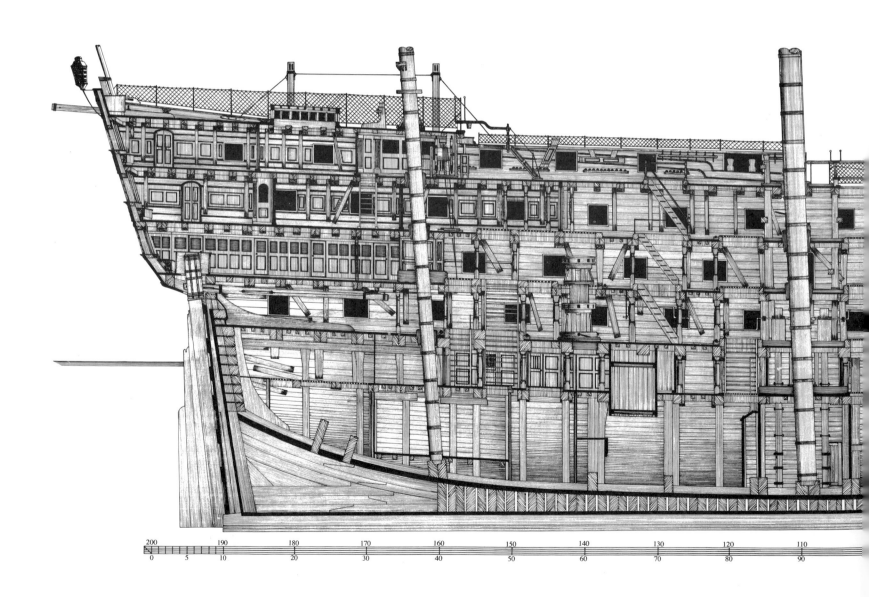

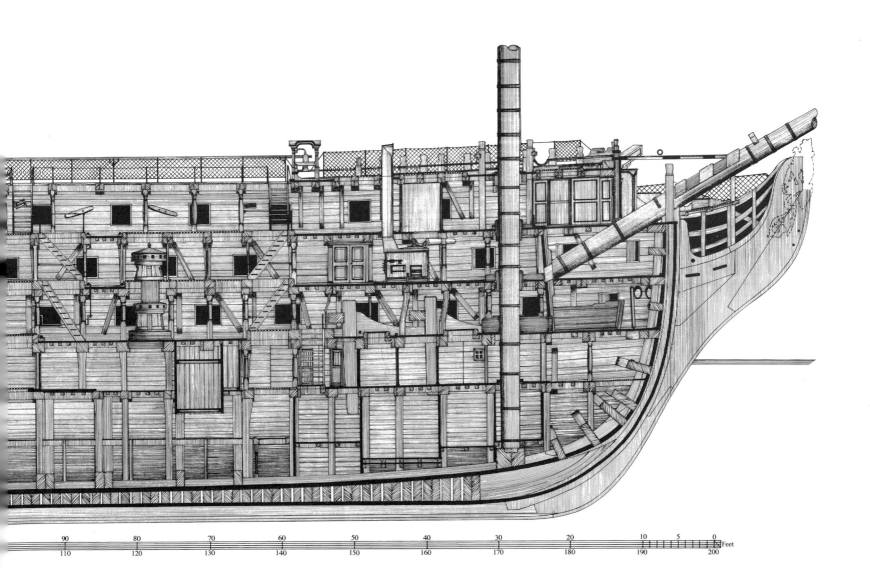

The juxtaposition of the decks in this single drawing shows their relationship to each other and how their various functions made logical the layout of the whole.

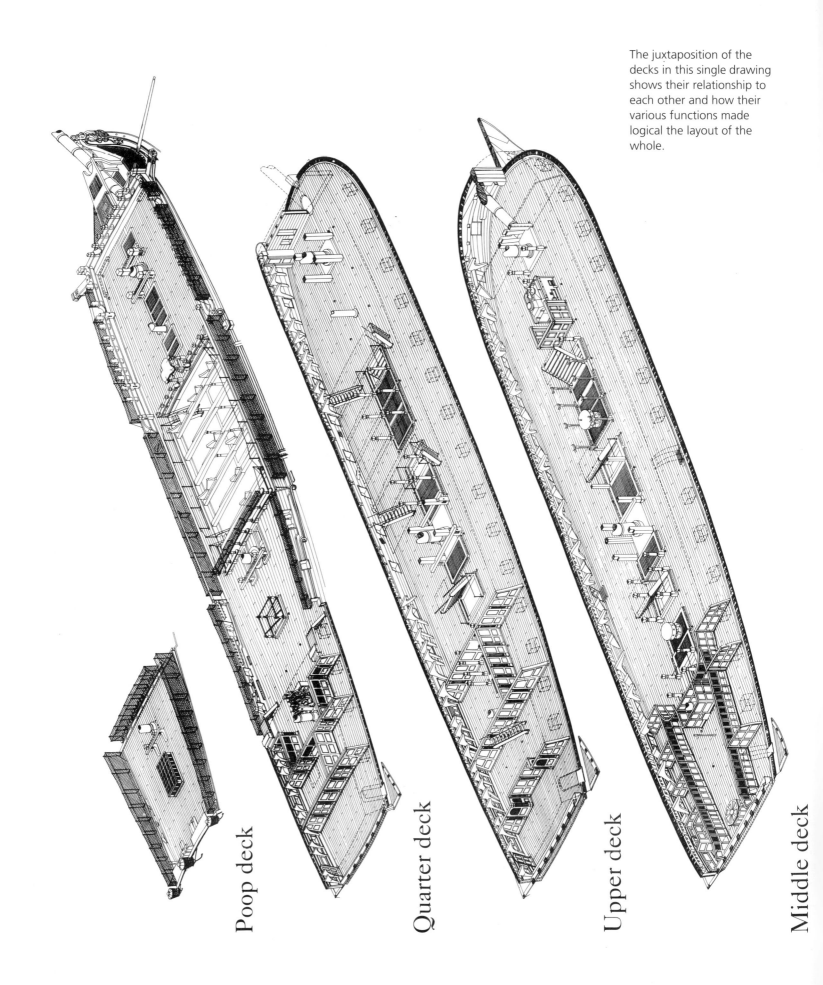

Poop deck

Quarter deck

Upper deck

Middle deck

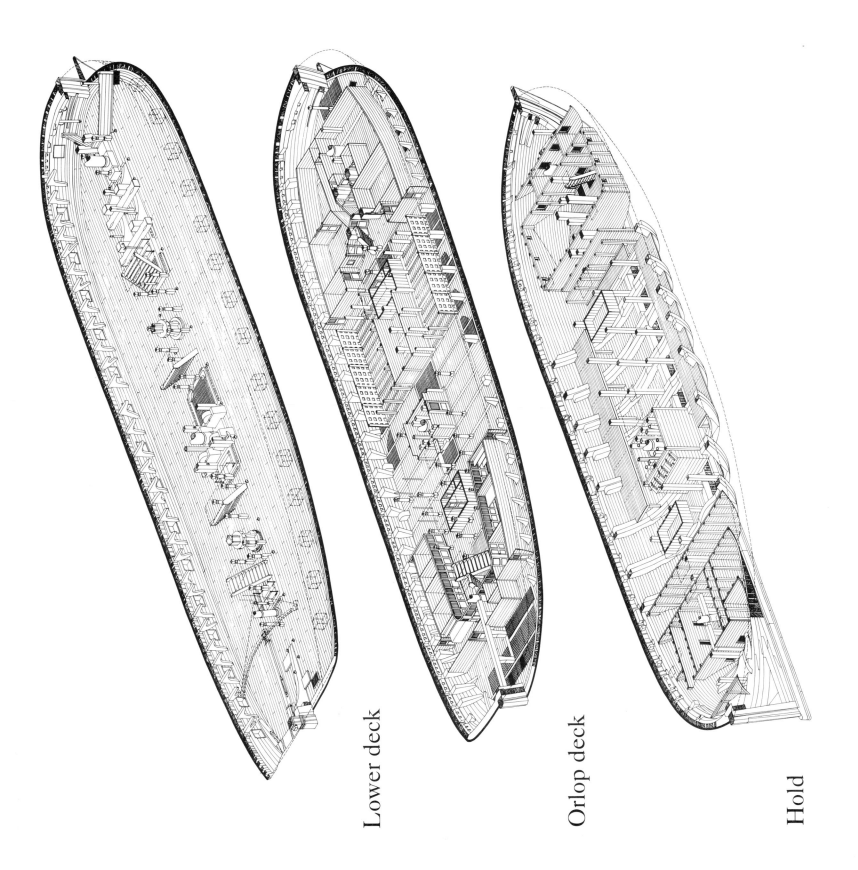

Lower deck

Orlop deck

Hold

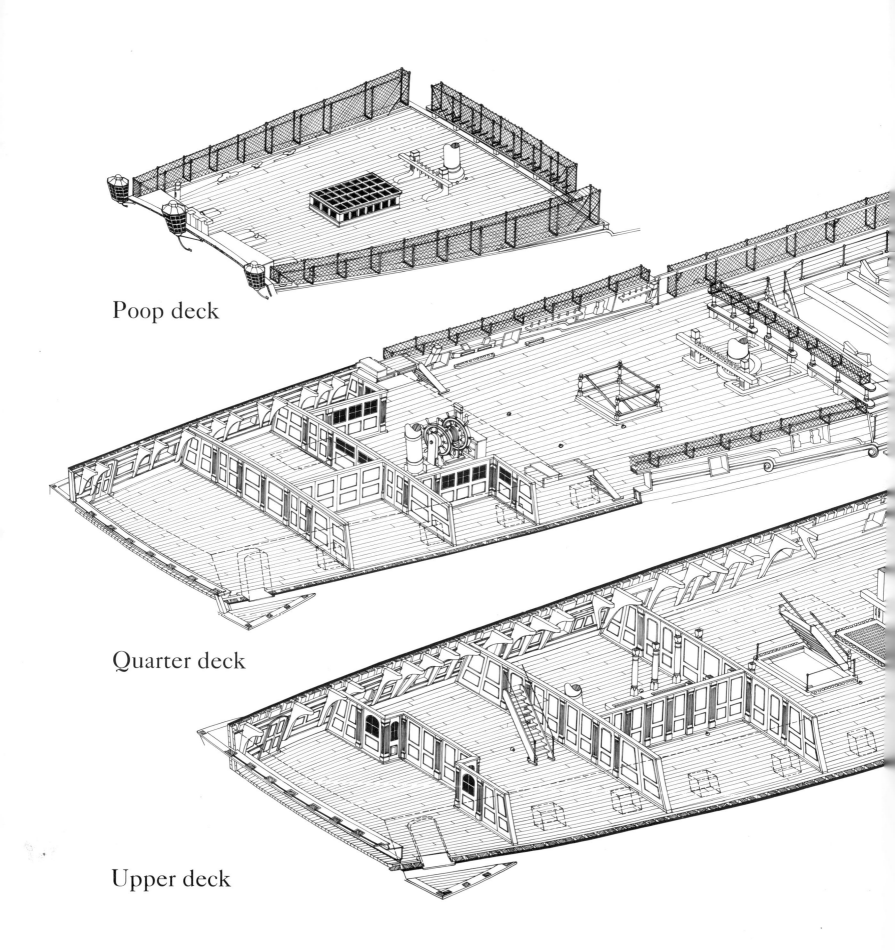

Poop deck

Quarter deck

Upper deck

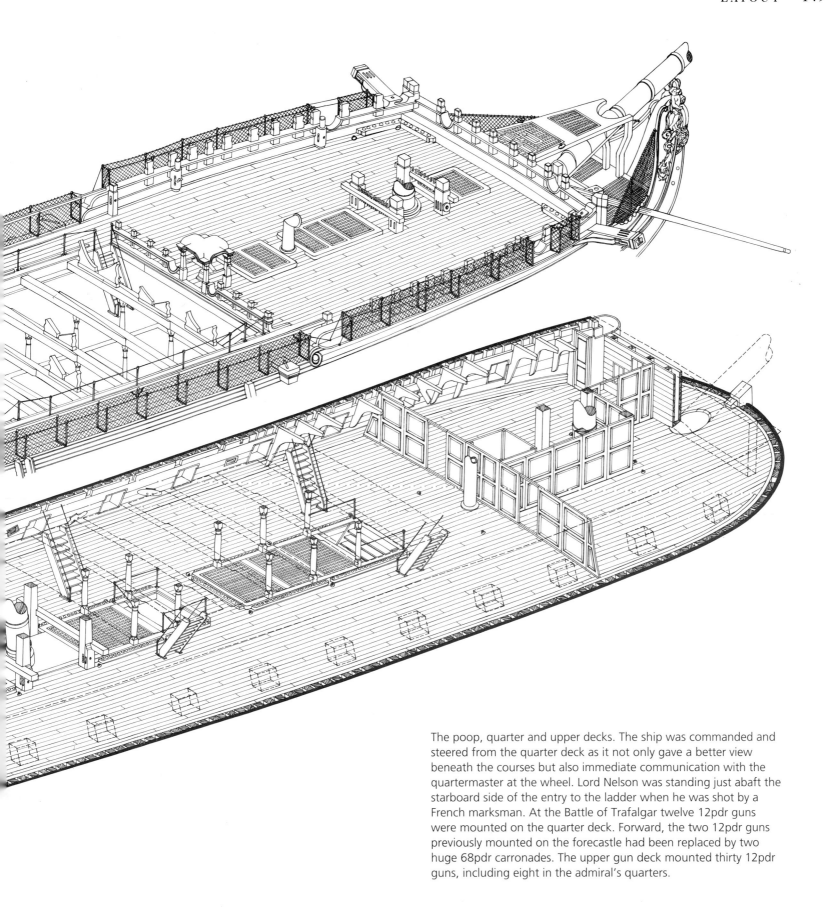

The poop, quarter and upper decks. The ship was commanded and steered from the quarter deck as it not only gave a better view beneath the courses but also immediate communication with the quartermaster at the wheel. Lord Nelson was standing just abaft the starboard side of the entry to the ladder when he was shot by a French marksman. At the Battle of Trafalgar twelve 12pdr guns were mounted on the quarter deck. Forward, the two 12pdr guns previously mounted on the forecastle had been replaced by two huge 68pdr carronades. The upper gun deck mounted thirty 12pdr guns, including eight in the admiral's quarters.

The middle and lower decks. The large enclosed area at the after
end of the middle gun deck is the wardroom where the bulk of the
officers lived. The middle gun deck mounted twenty-eight 24pdr
guns. The lower gun deck mounted thirty of the heaviest guns,
sometimes 42pdr guns but often 32pdrs which Nelson preferred
because of their faster rate of fire.

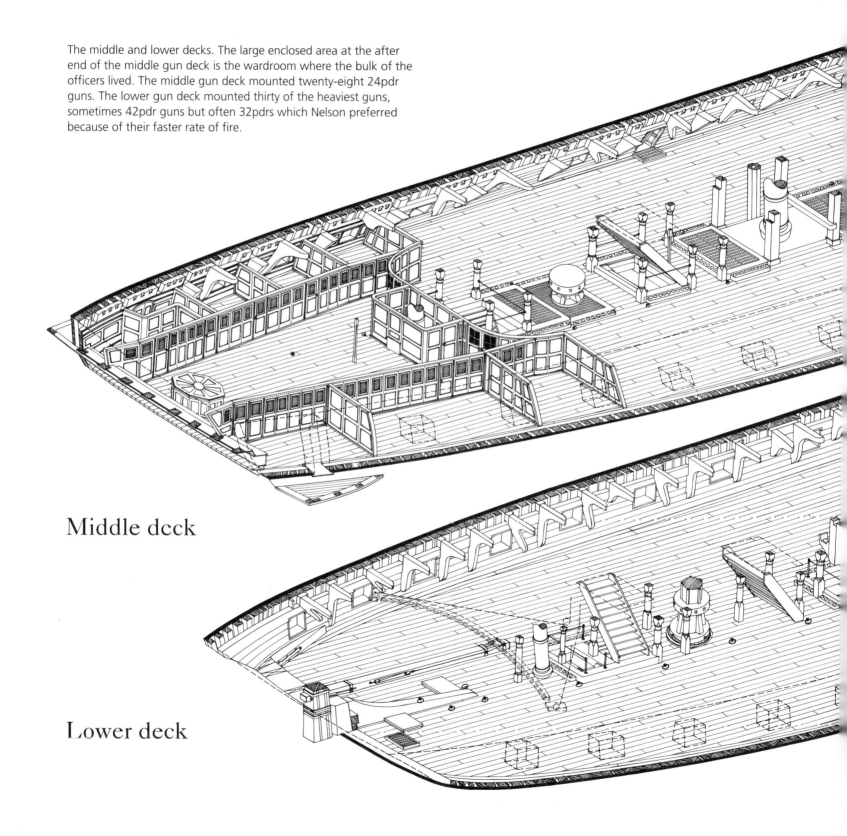

Middle deck

Lower deck

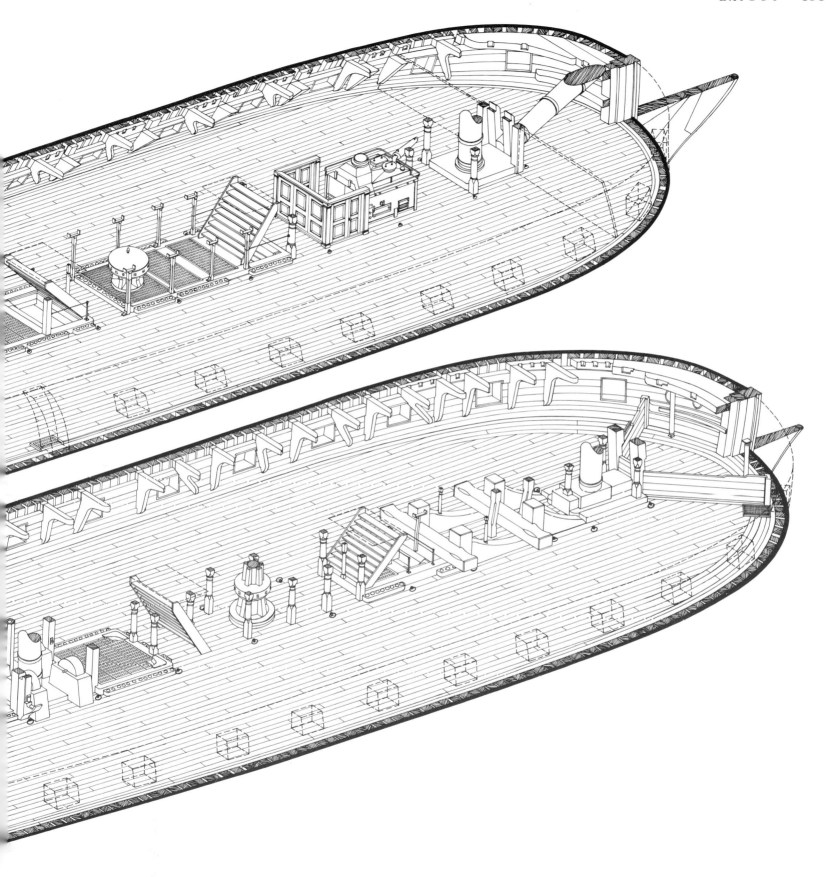

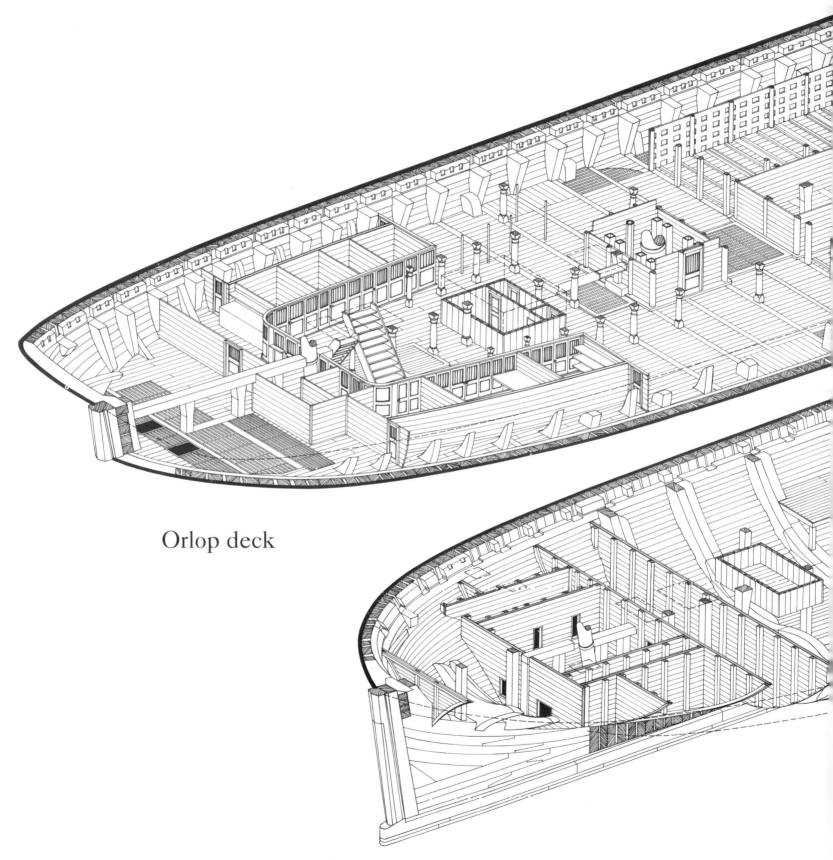

Orlop deck

Hold

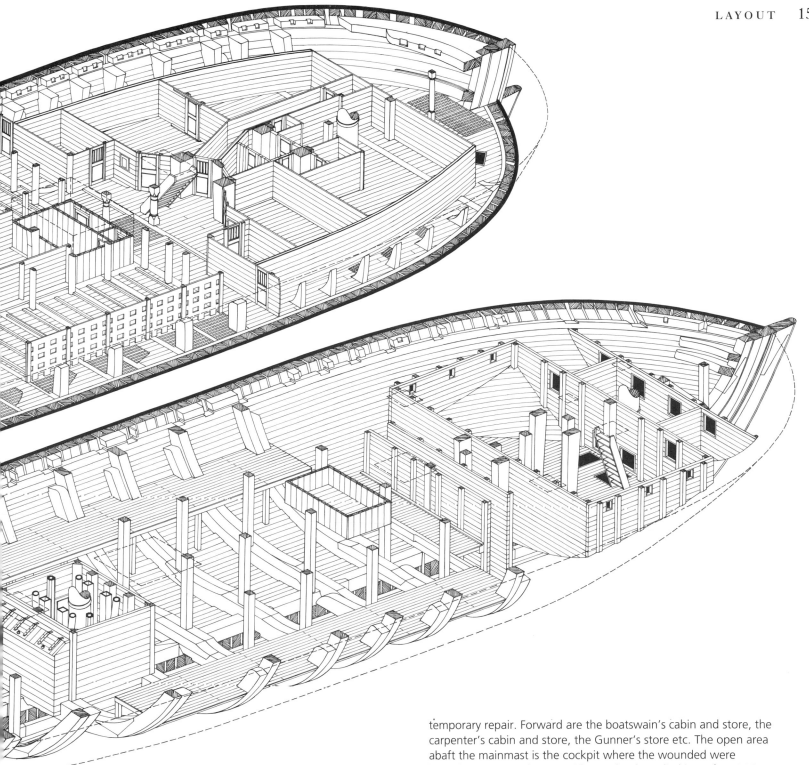

The orlop and hold. Strictly speaking, there is no such thing as the orlop deck because the term itself, originally 'overlope', includes deck by definition. The 'overlope' was the name given to the first continuous deck. On the orlop, the narrow passages between the bulkheads and the ship's side are all part of the carpenter's walk, giving access to the hull for inspection and when necessary,

temporary repair. Forward are the boatswain's cabin and store, the carpenter's cabin and store, the Gunner's store etc. The open area abaft the mainmast is the cockpit where the wounded were brought. Here, on the port side, Lord Nelson died just after 4.30pm on 21 October 1805. Forward in the hold is the grand magazine, illuminated solely by borrowed light through a window in the adjacent light room. Anyone entering the grand magazine had to wear felt slippers to avoid the possibility of a spark. At the stern are various storerooms: flour stowage, spirit room, after powder room. The well bulkhead contains the pumps on each side of the mainmast; on its after side is the shot locker. Between the shot locker and the main transverse bulkhead is the hanging magazine.

The poop, quarter deck, waist and forecastle. This view gives a
good indication of the tumblehome as well as the storage of boats
and anchors.

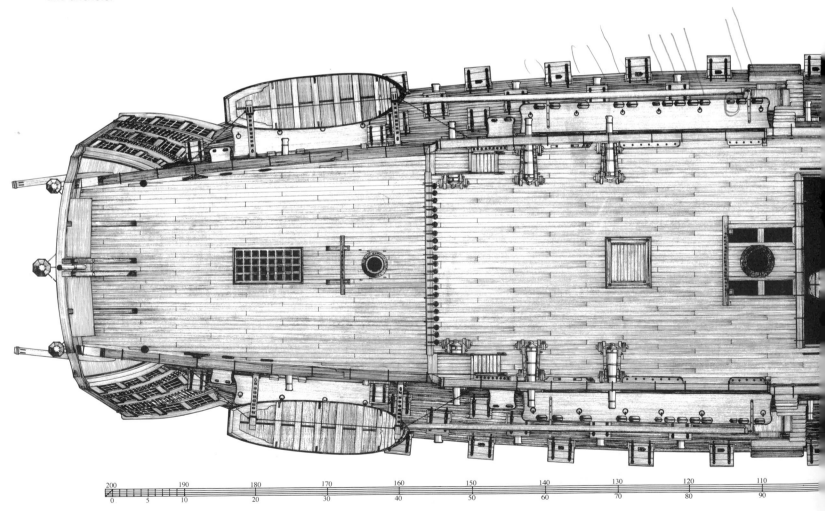

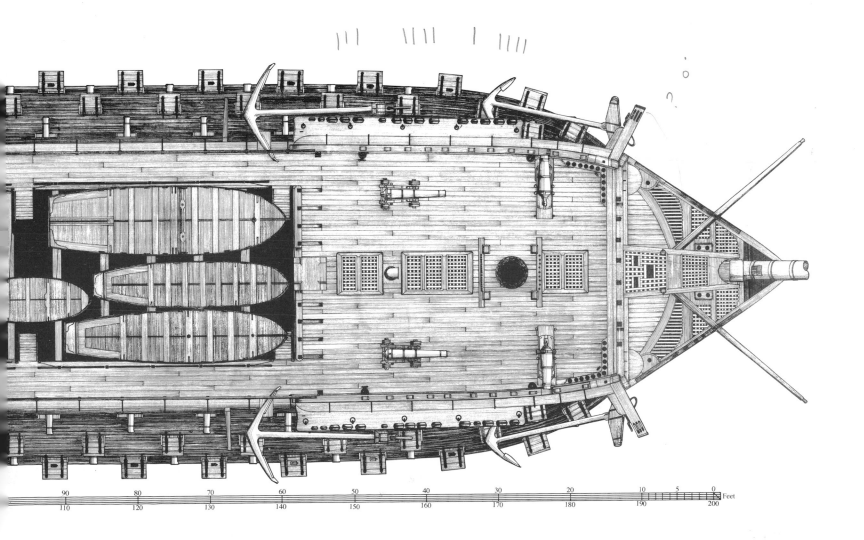

90   80   70   60   50   40   30   20   10   5   0   Feet
110   120   130   140   150   160   170   180   190   200

The fore and aft sails. This drawing shows how the masts support each other by means of the stays and how the loss of any one mast could have disastrous consequences. It also demonstrates how the stays have been utilised to carry the staysails, the main fore and aft canvas on a square-rigged ship.

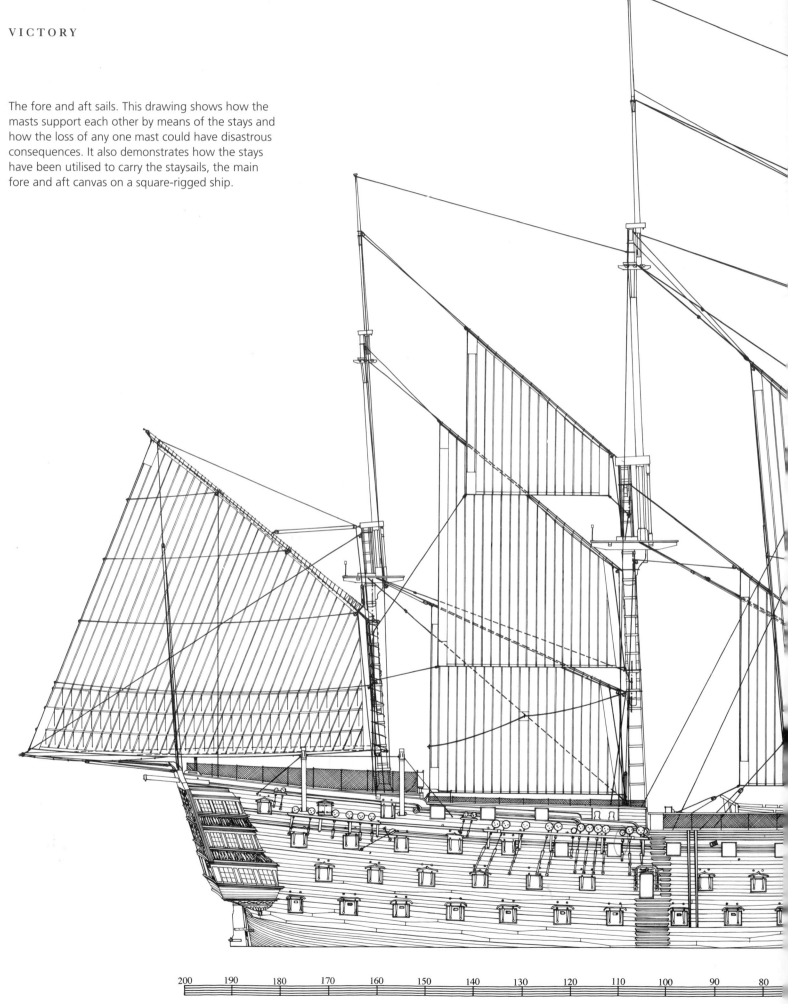

200   190   180   170   160   150   140   130   120   110   100   90   80

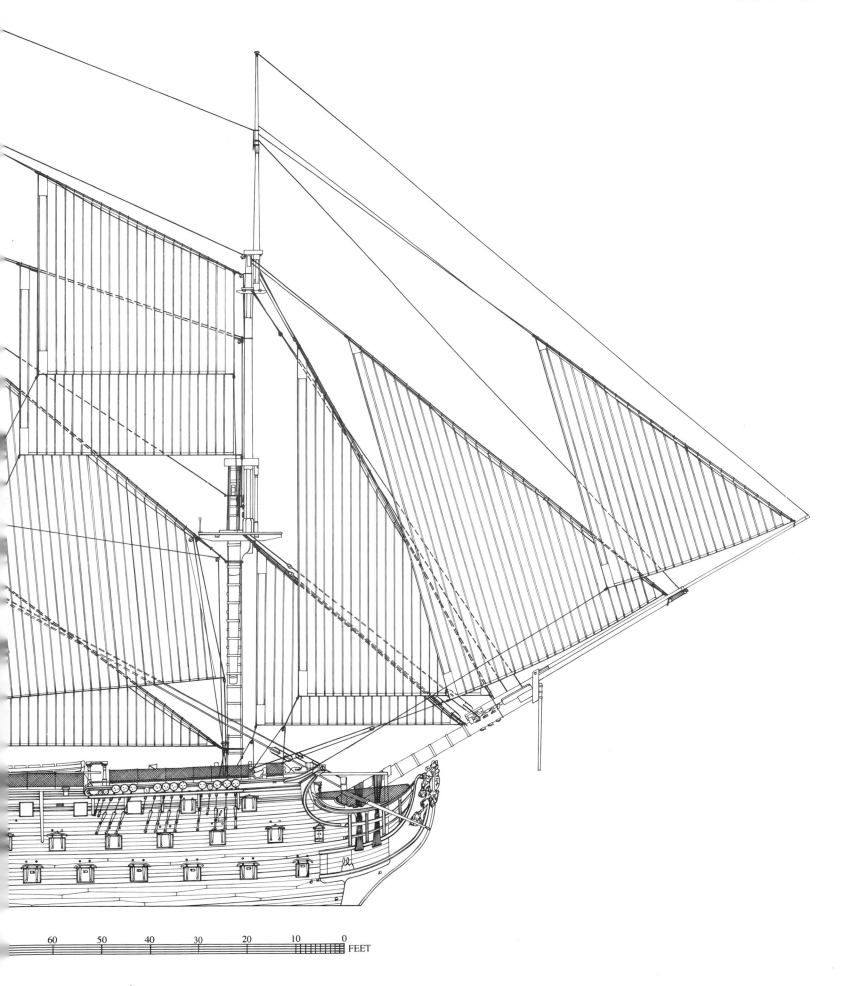

The square sails and spanker or driver (on the mizzen).

200   190   180   170   160   150   140   130   120   110   100   90   80

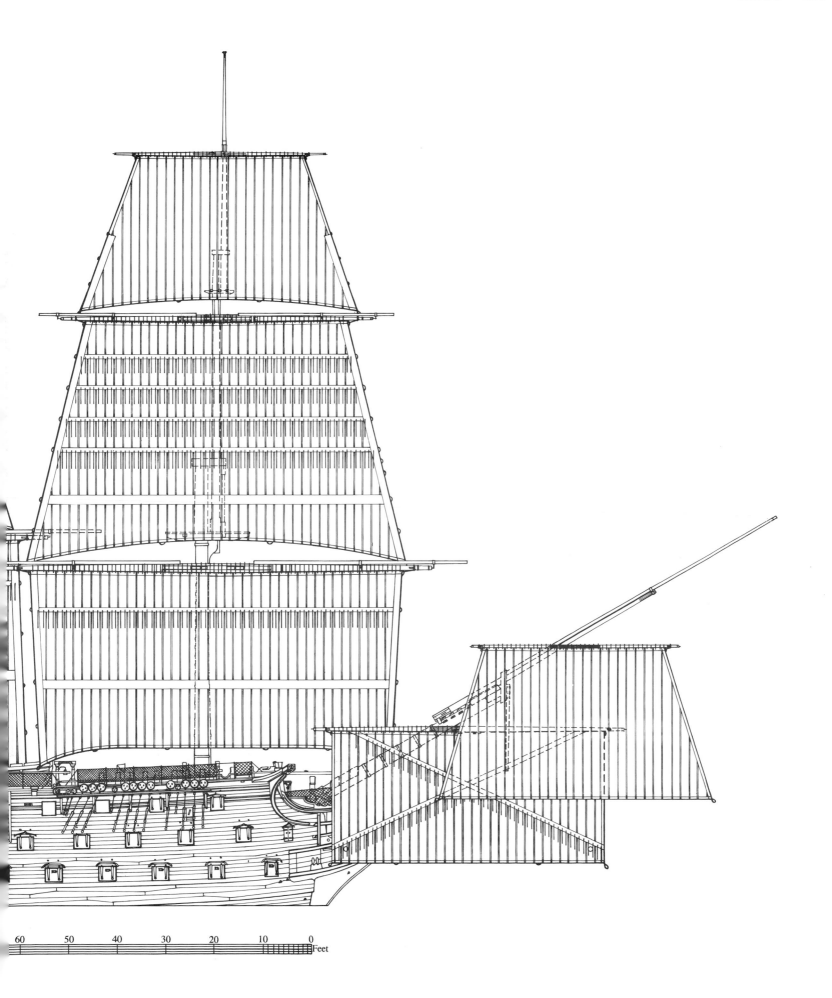

60   50   40   30   20   10   0
Feet

The suit of square sails, including studdingsails (pronounced stuns'ls).

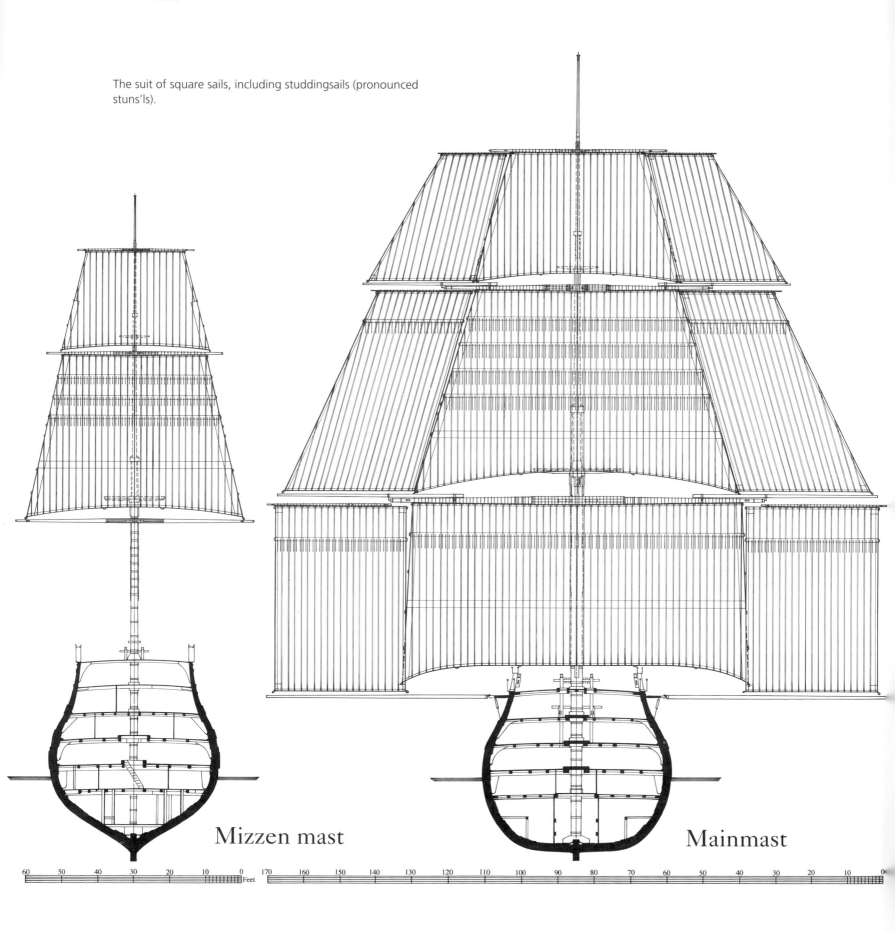

Mizzen mast

Mainmast

60   50   40   30   20   10   0   Feet   170   160   150   140   130   120   110   100   90   80   70   60   50   40   30   20   10   0

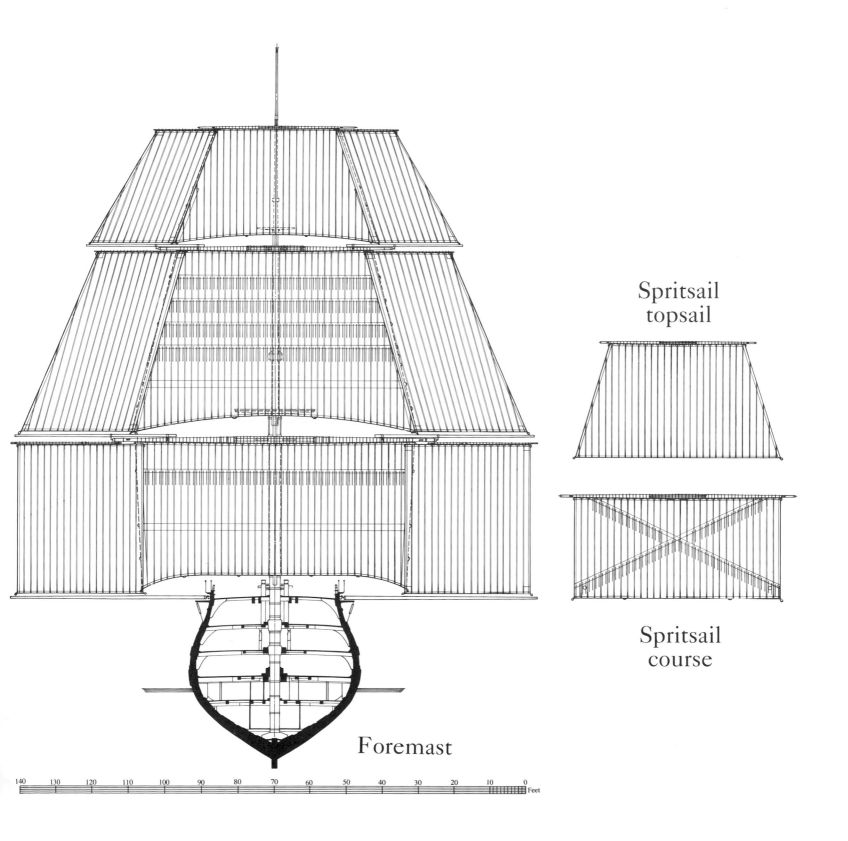

Spritsail
topsail

Spritsail
course

Foremast

140 130 120 110 100 90 80 70 60 50 40 30 20 10 0 Feet

The bowsprit standing rigging. The bowsprit is really only a mast set at an angle. Just as the bowsprit is supported by the bobstay that runs down to the stem, so the dolphin striker was rigged to support the jibboom. Introduced with the jibboom in 1794, it was originally called the martingale but with the wide acceptance of the vernacular and descriptive term "dolphin striker", the term martingale came to be used solely for its stays.

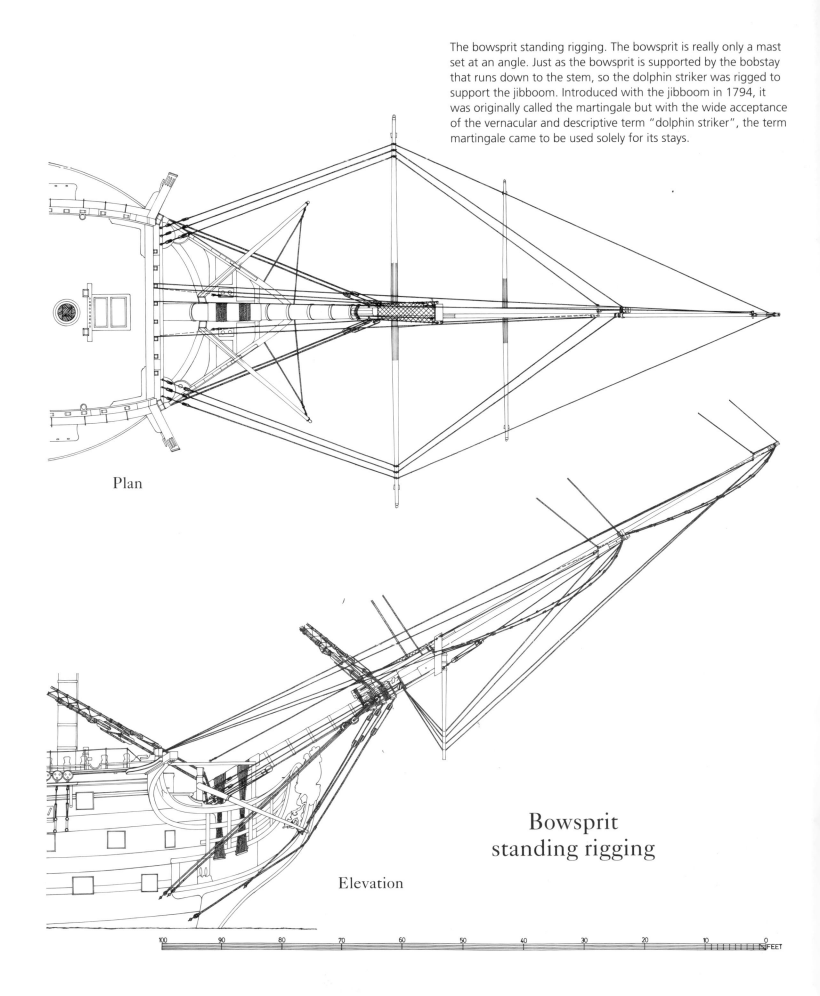

Plan

Elevation

Bowsprit
standing rigging

100 90 80 70 60 50 40 30 20 10 0 FEET

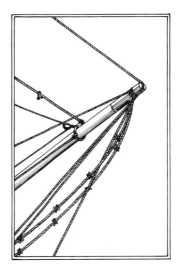

Flying jibboom

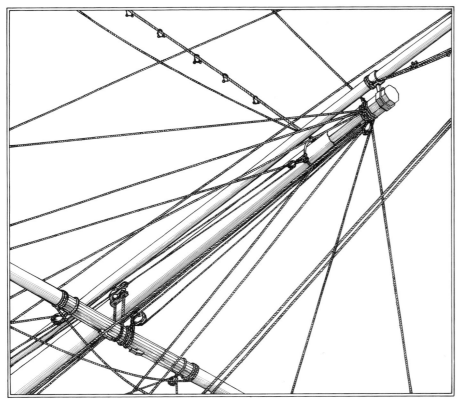

Jibboom

Details of the bowsprit cap with the dolphin striker and the spritsail yard; the jibboom with the yard for the spritsail topsail; and the jibboom.

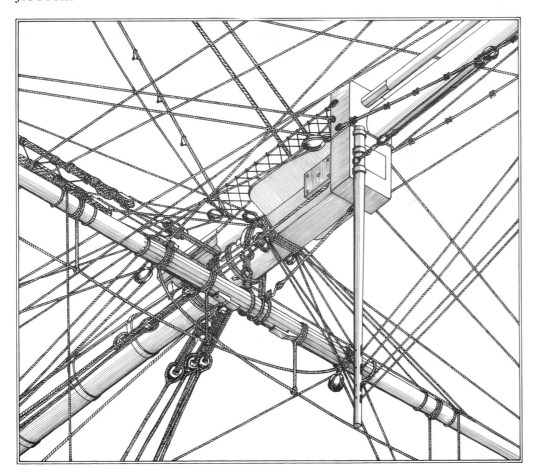

Bowsprit cap

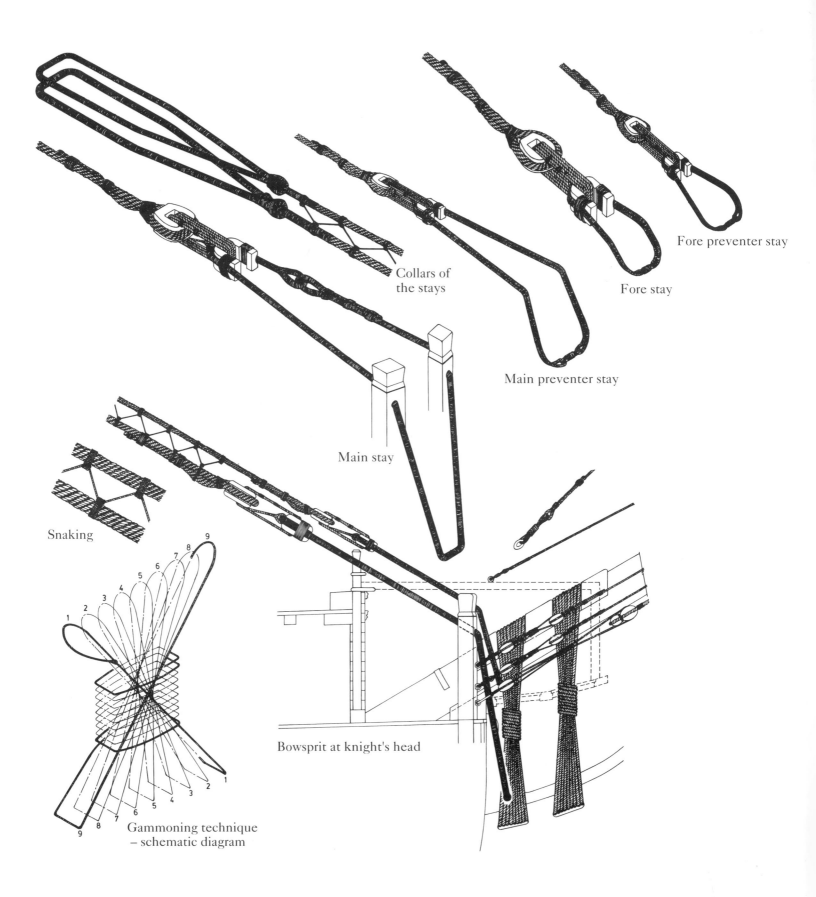

Collars of
the stays

Main preventer stay

Fore stay

Fore preventer stay

Main stay

Snaking

Gammoning technique
– schematic diagram

Bowsprit at knight's head

Bowsprit standing rigging details

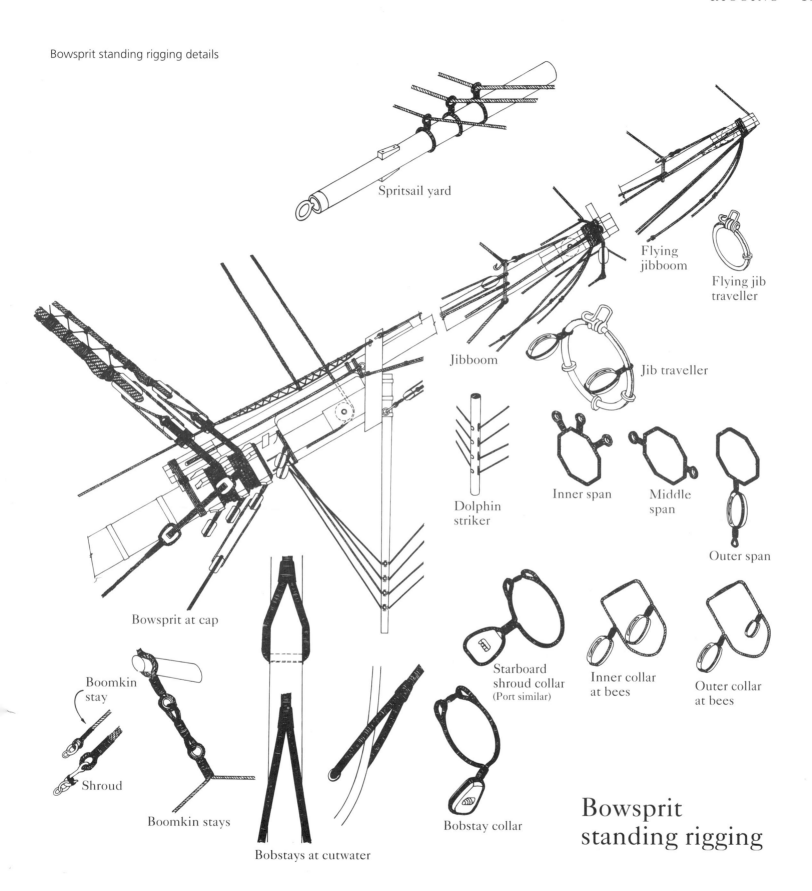

Spritsail yard

Flying jibboom

Flying jib traveller

Jibboom

Jib traveller

Dolphin striker

Inner span

Middle span

Outer span

Bowsprit at cap

Boomkin stay

Shroud

Boomkin stays

Bobstays at cutwater

Bobstay collar

Starboard shroud collar (Port similar)

Inner collar at bees

Outer collar at bees

Bowsprit standing rigging

The bowsprit assmbly and the two spritsail yards.

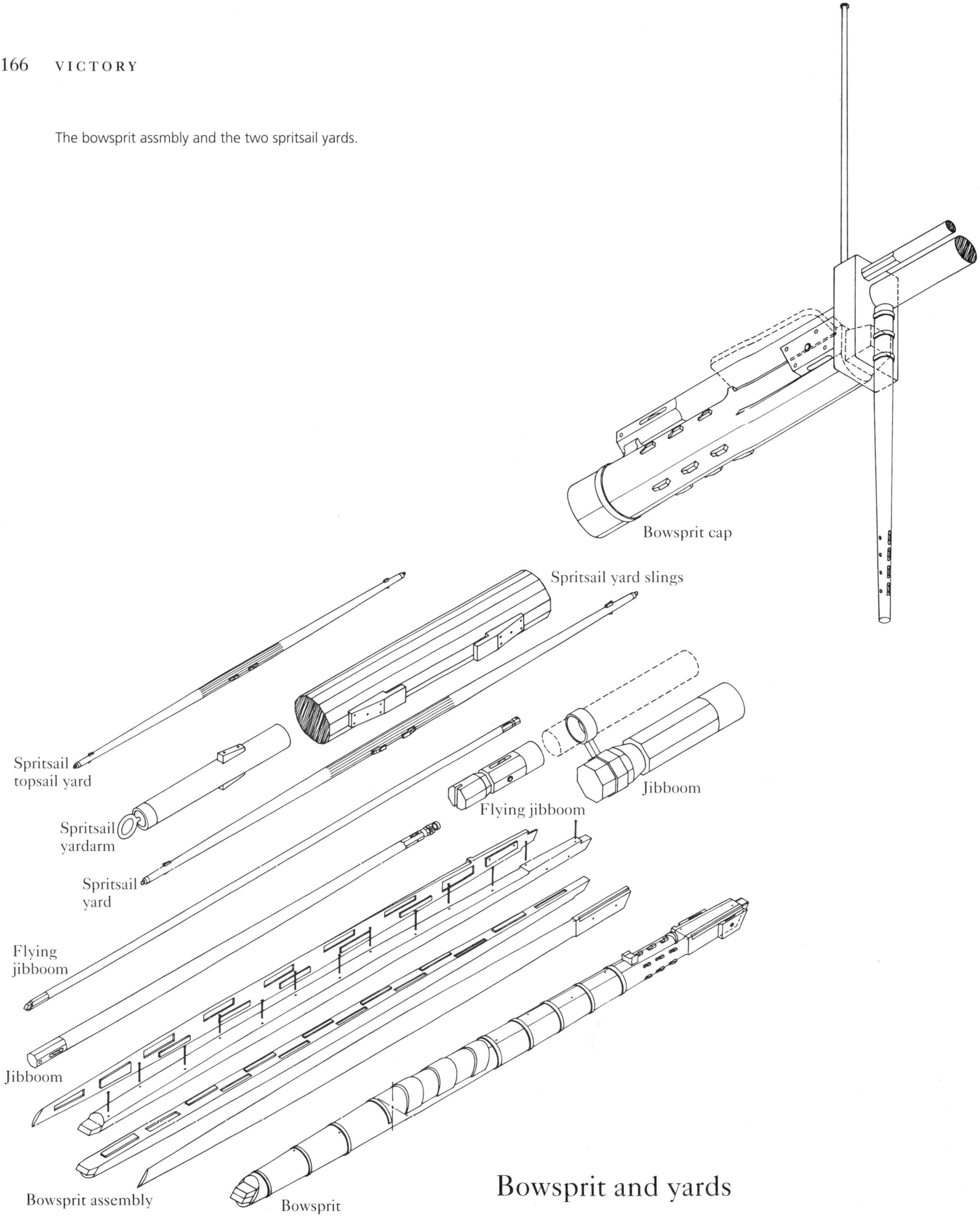

Bowsprit cap

Spritsail yard slings

Spritsail
topsail yard

Spritsail
yardarm

Spritsail
yard

Flying jibboom

Jibboom

Flying
jibboom

Jibboom

Bowsprit assembly

Bowsprit

Bowsprit and yards

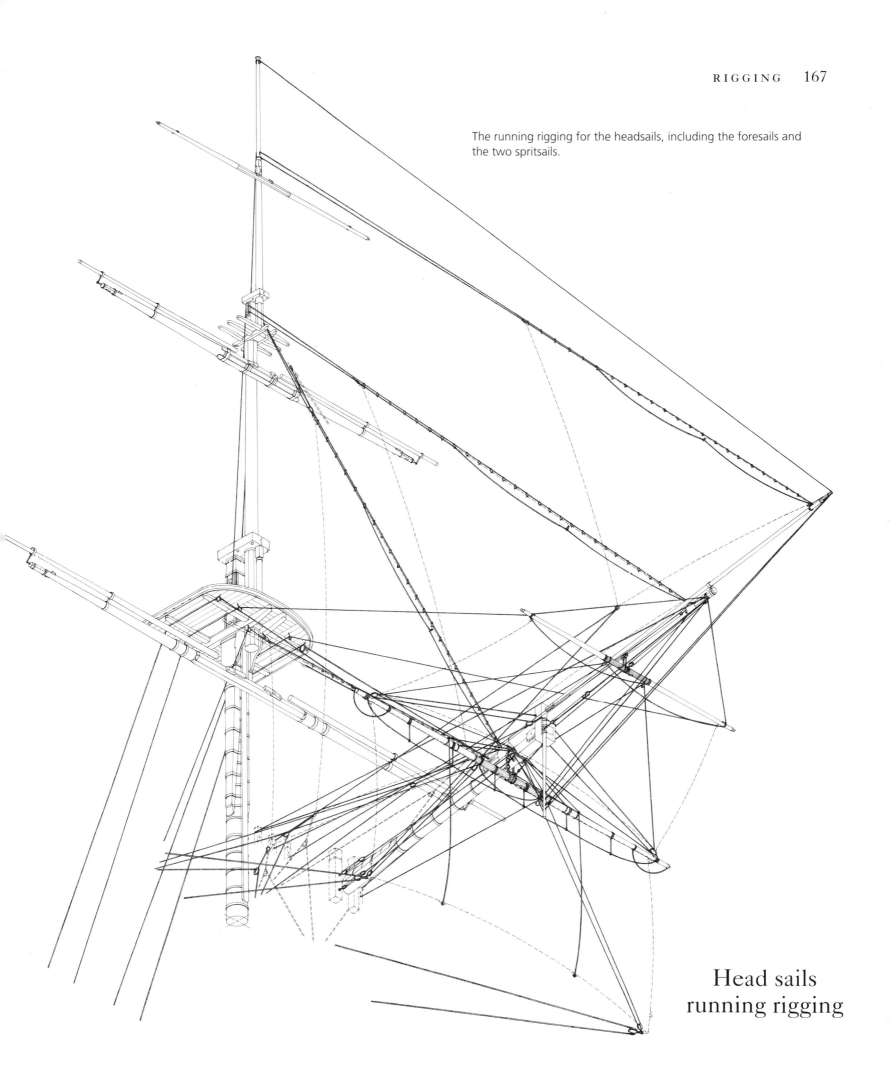

The running rigging for the headsails, including the foresails and the two spritsails.

Head sails
running rigging

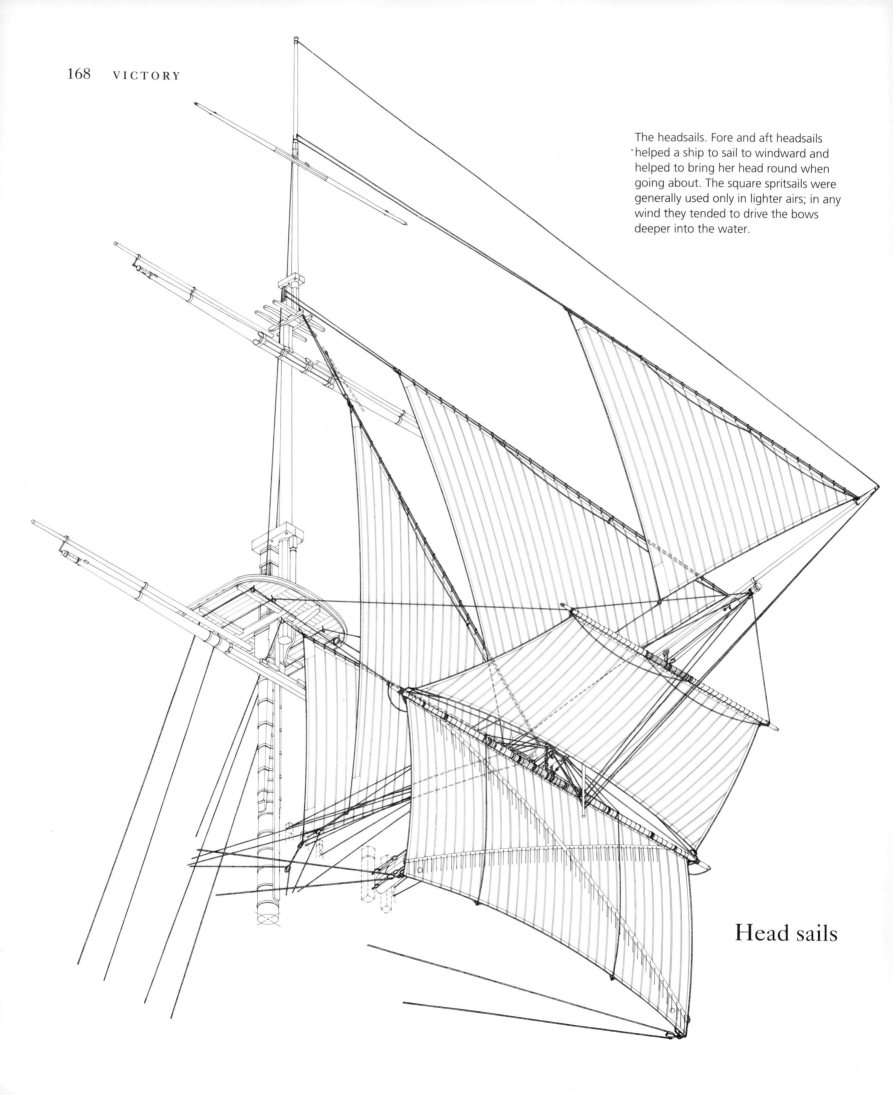

The headsails. Fore and aft headsails
helped a ship to sail to windward and
helped to bring her head round when
going about. The square spritsails were
generally used only in lighter airs; in any
wind they tended to drive the bows
deeper into the water.

Head sails

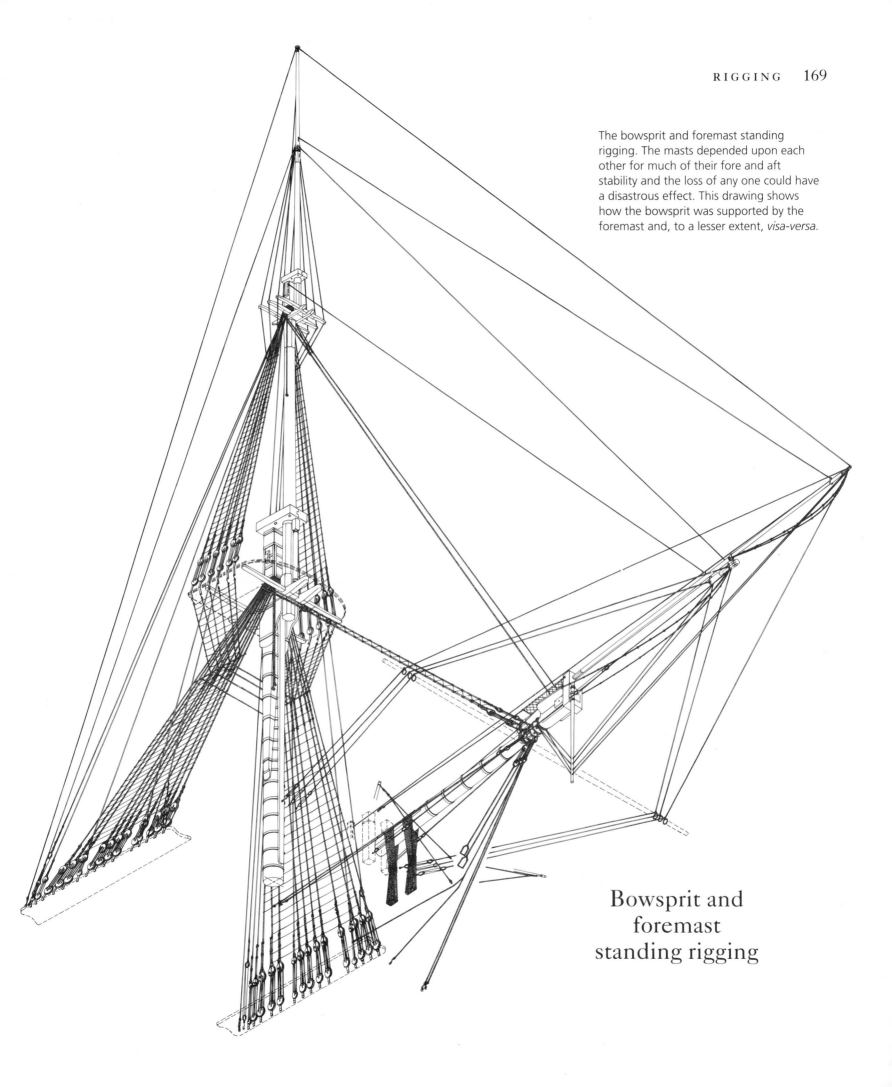

The bowsprit and foremast standing rigging. The masts depended upon each other for much of their fore and aft stability and the loss of any one could have a disastrous effect. This drawing shows how the bowsprit was supported by the foremast and, to a lesser extent, *visa-versa*.

Bowsprit and
foremast
standing rigging

Foremast
standing rigging

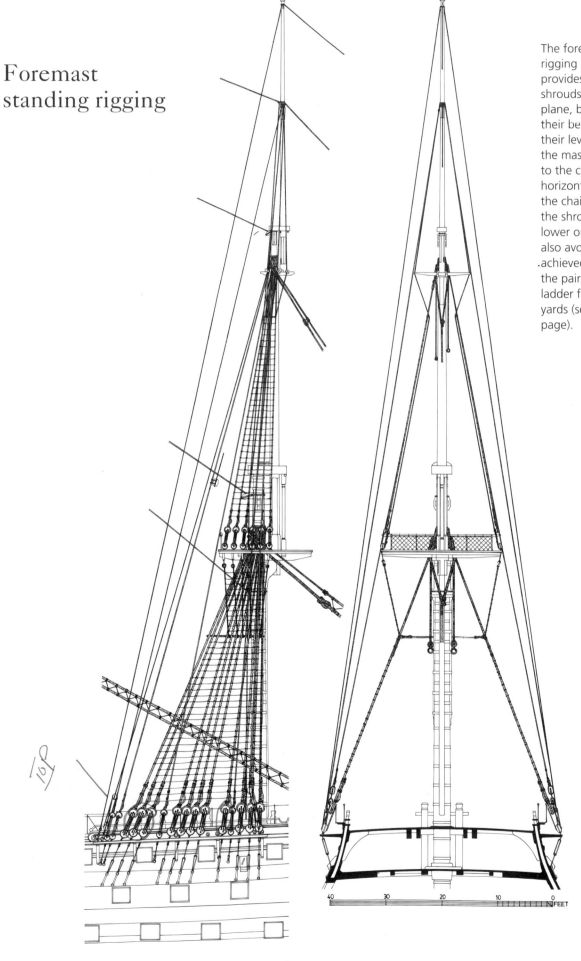

The foremast standing rigging. Standing rigging in the form of shrouds and stays provides the fixed support for the masts. The shrouds support them principally in a lateral plane, but also to a degree longitudinally by their being led aft of the mast. To improve their leverage, the angle is increased between the mast and the shrouds by leading them out to the chainwale, a broad thick plank bolted horizontally to the ship's side. By this means, the chain plates securing the bottom end of the shrouds have a more secure fastening lower on the ship's side; the risk of chafing is also avoided. The tension on the shrouds is achieved by means of the lanyards between the pairs of deadeyes. The ratlines create a ladder for access to the tops and so to the yards (see also the drawing on the previous page).

40   30   20   10   0
N FEET

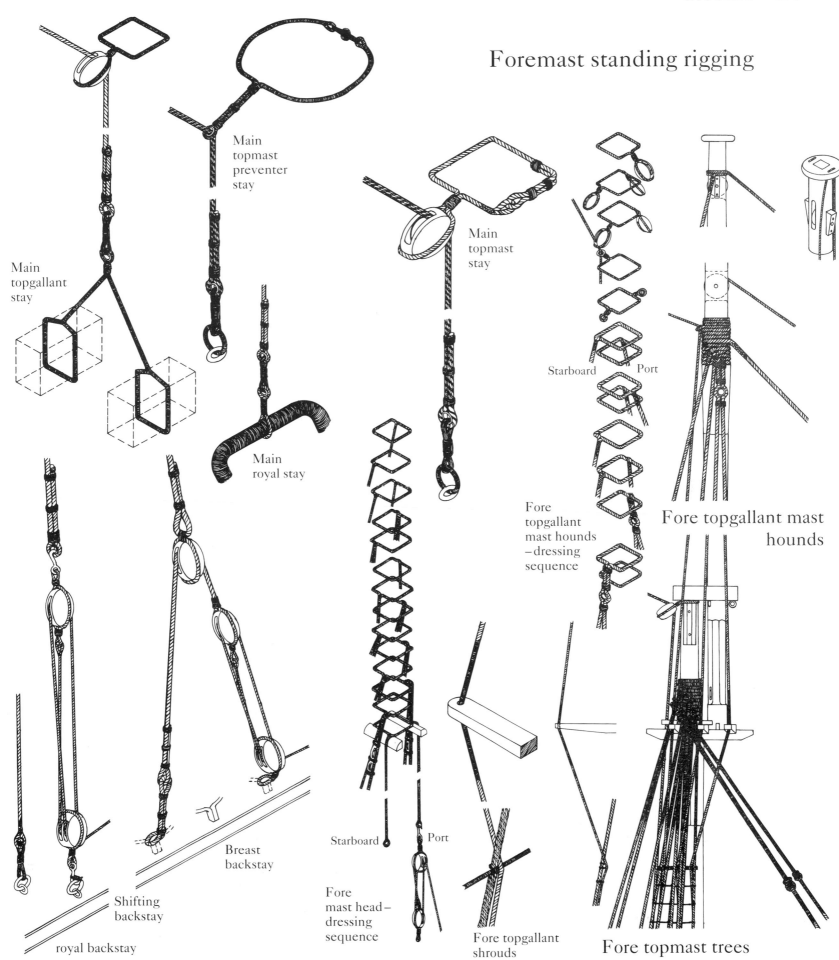

Foremast standing rigging

Main topmast preventer stay

Main topgallant stay

Main royal stay

Main topmast stay

Starboard   Port

Fore topgallant mast hounds –dressing sequence

Fore topgallant mast hounds

Breast backstay

Shifting backstay

royal backstay

Starboard   Port

Fore mast head – dressing sequence

Fore topgallant shrouds

Fore topmast trees

Foremast standing rigging

The foremast standing rigging details (pp 171-173). At the head of the lower mast, the longitudinal trestle trees with their athwartship crosstrees, support the platform of the top, the main function of which is to spread the shrouds of the topmast above. The top also provides easy access to the lower yard. There is no platform to create a top on the trees at the head of the topmast in order to avoid excess weight and windage high up. Instead, the topmen use the trees themselves to reach the yard and the trees also spread the shrouds of the topgallant mast. There are no ratlines on the topgallant shrouds. When the topgallant mast was rigged the men reached the yard by means of a single rope ladder attached to the mast (Jacob's ladder). (see also p174 and p189).

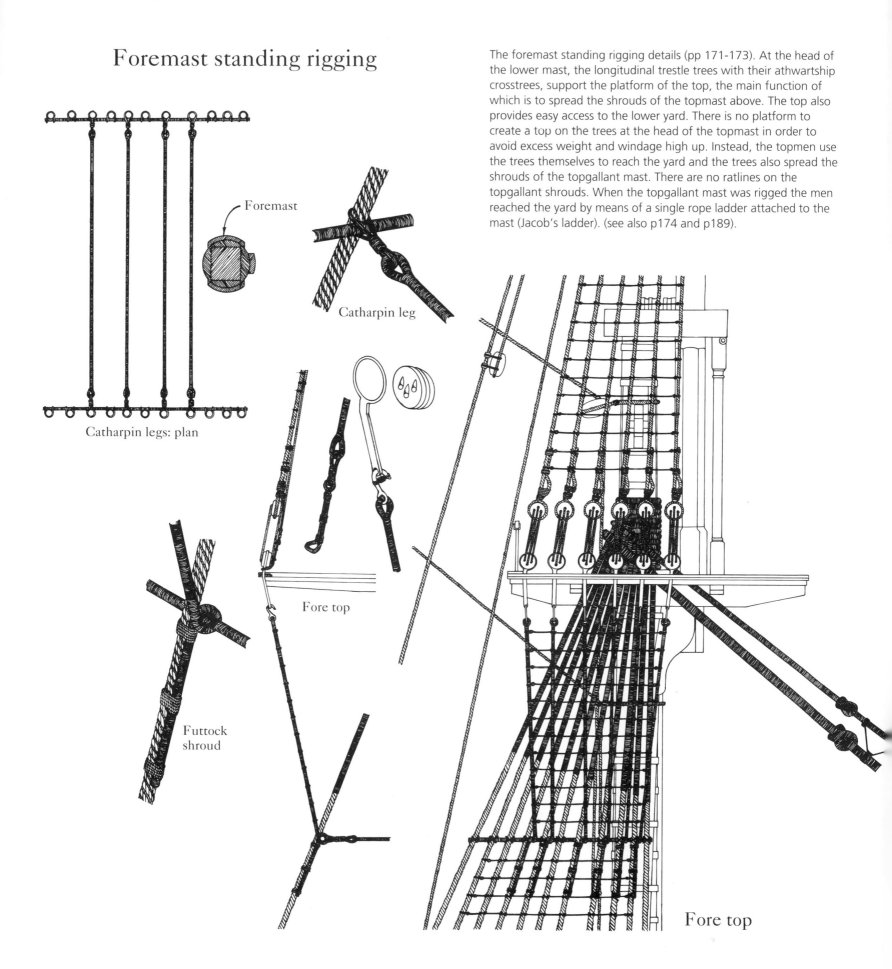

Foremast

Catharpin leg

Catharpin legs: plan

Fore top

Futtock shroud

Fore top

Foremast standing rigging

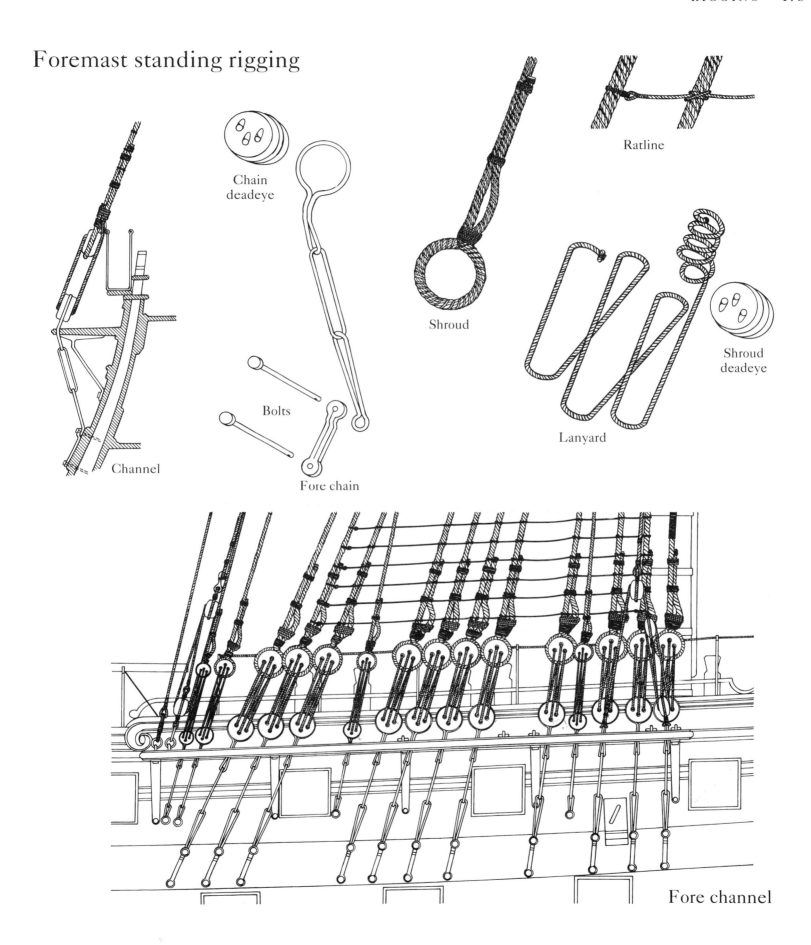

Chain
deadeye

Ratline

Shroud

Channel

Bolts

Fore chain

Lanyard

Shroud
deadeye

Fore channel

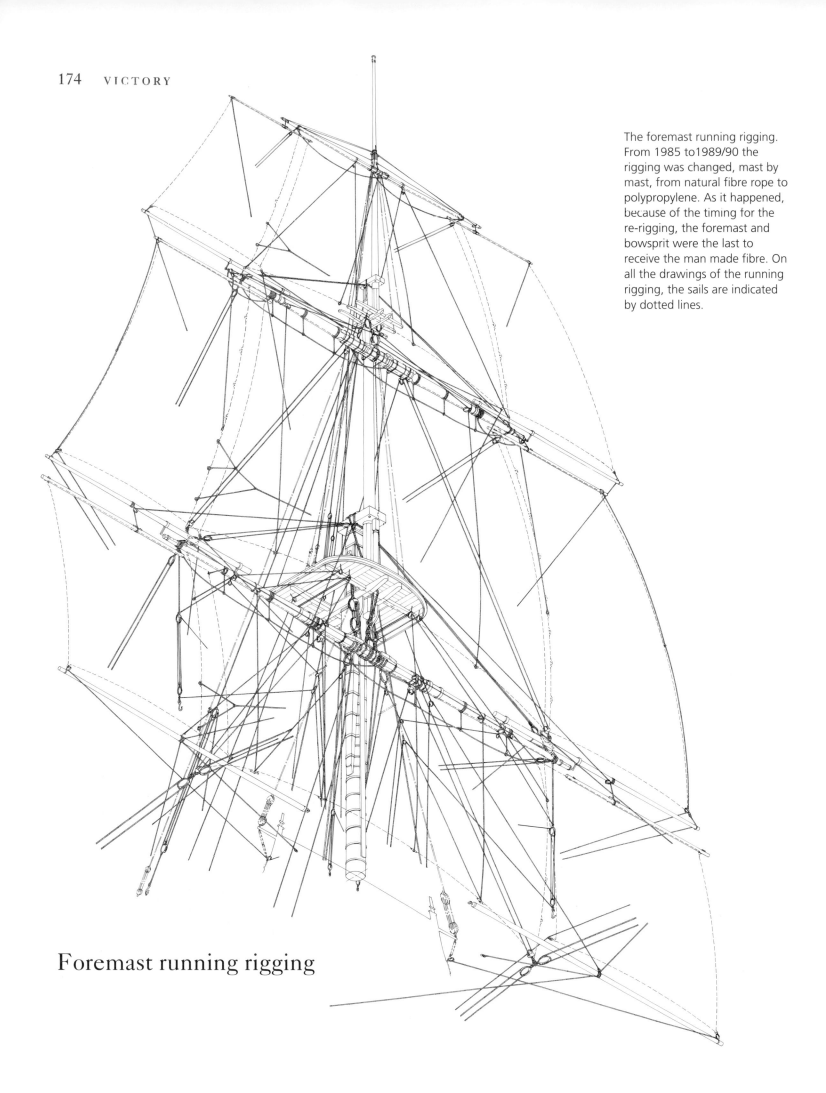

The foremast running rigging. From 1985 to1989/90 the rigging was changed, mast by mast, from natural fibre rope to polypropylene. As it happened, because of the timing for the re-rigging, the foremast and bowsprit were the last to receive the man made fibre. On all the drawings of the running rigging, the sails are indicated by dotted lines.

Foremast running rigging

The foremast square sails. In the centre of the drawing is the fore topsail, and the battle torn Trafalgar topsail still exists at Portsmouth. The fore topsail and topgallantsail tend to lift the bow and reduce resistance (see also p161).

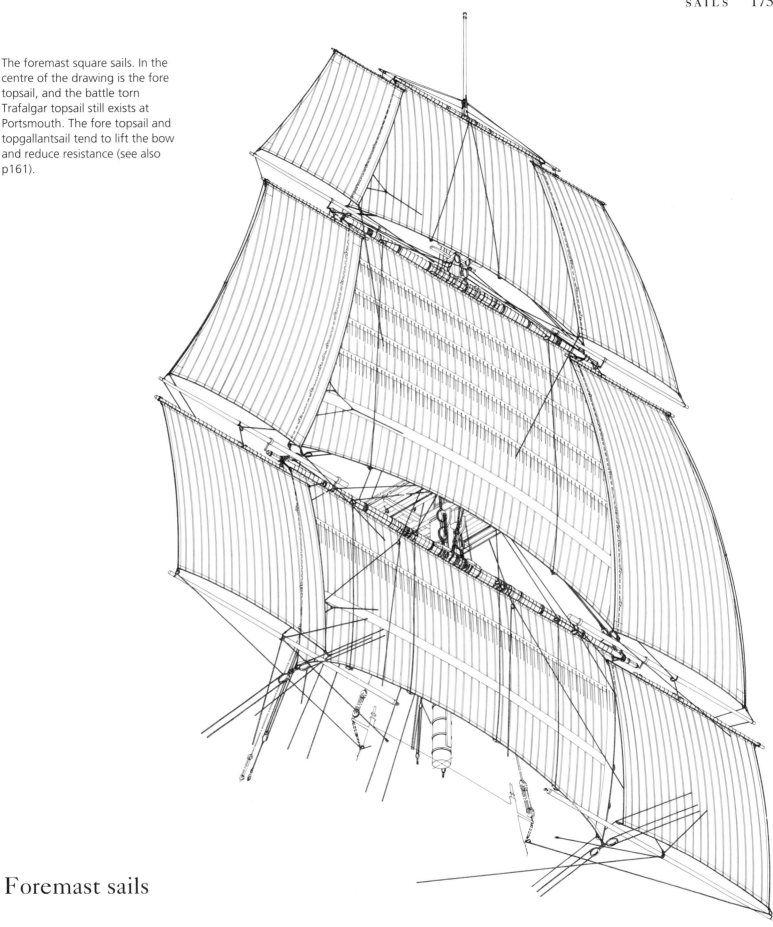

Foremast sails

The mainmast standing rigging. This illustrates in more detail the importance of the stays. The tackle shown rigged to the main preventer stay was used to assist in lifting the boats stowed in the waist. The topmen, those who worked aloft, were the prime seamen. They climbed to the top using the ratlines and then actually ran along the lower yard or the topsail yard before dropping to their place on the footrope hanging below the yard. In harbour, or at sea when there was little or no breeze the shrouds on each side were used. In any sort of wind, the men used the weather (windward) shrouds only, so that they were pushed towards the shrouds rather than away from them.

Mainmast standing rigging

The mainmast running rigging. Unlike the standing rigging, the running rigging was not tarred. Although this meant that the running rigging had a shorter life, the tar would have caused the blocks to run less easily. Polypropylene running rigging, with the colour and finish of natural fibre is now used, but, prone to deterioration from ultra-violet light, it does not have the lasting qualities of the natural fibre.

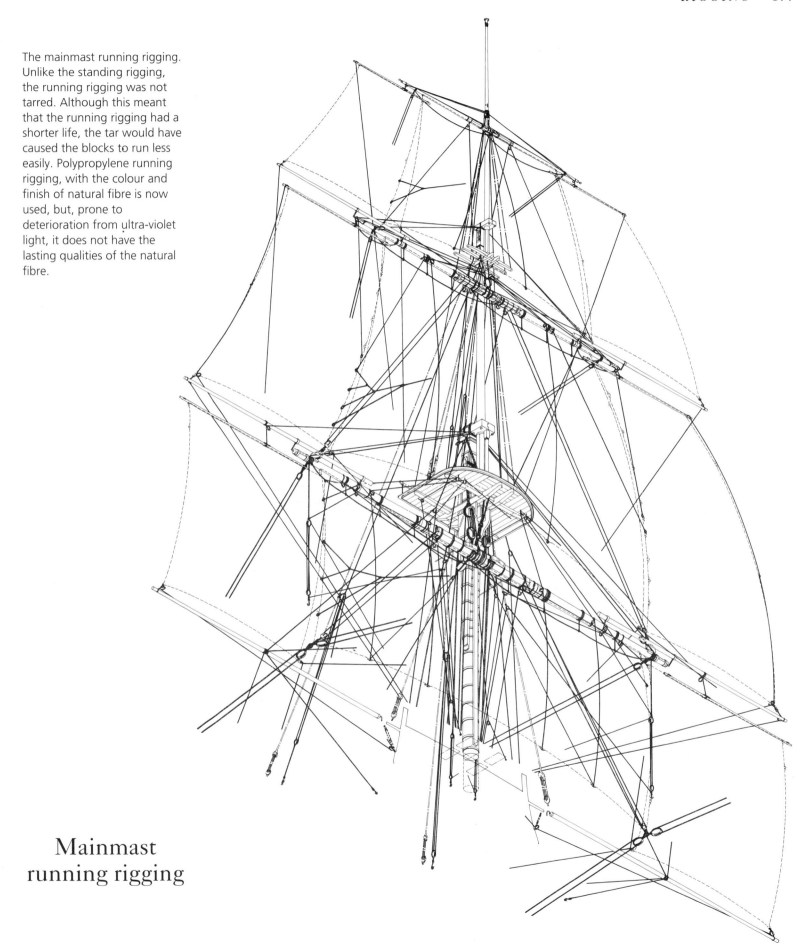

Mainmast running rigging

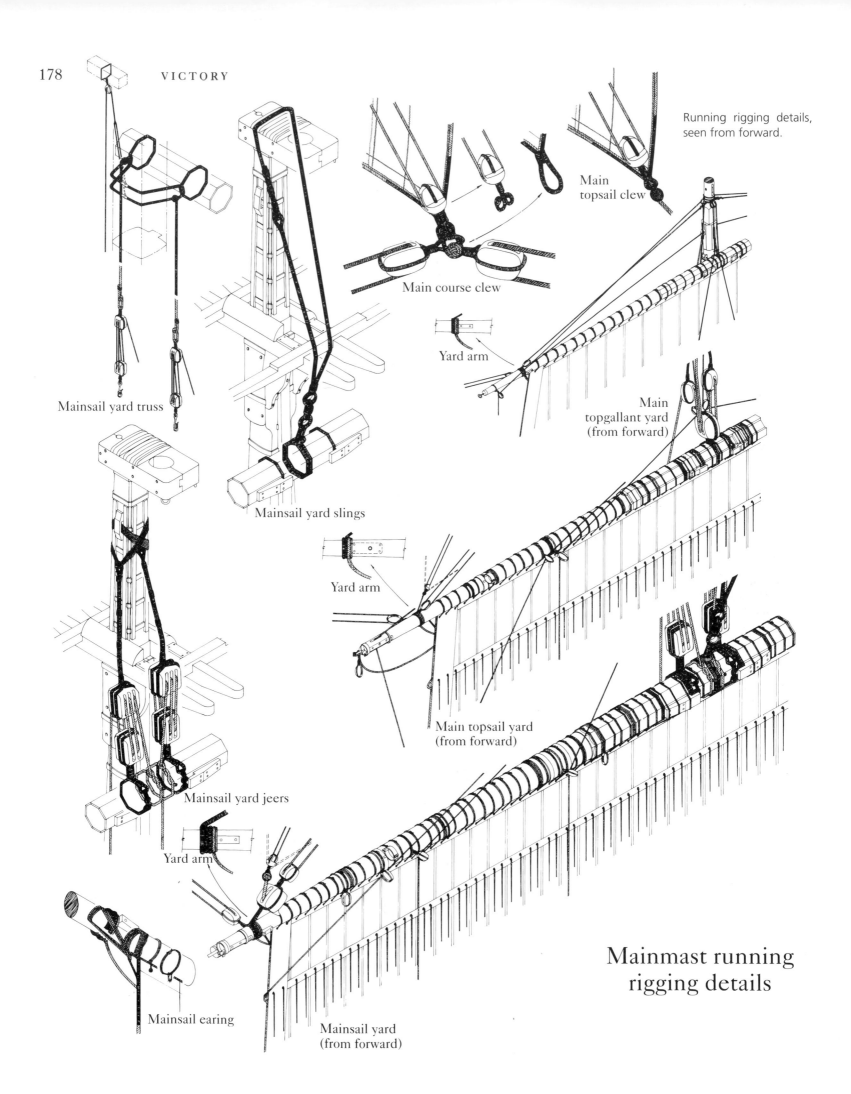

Running rigging details,
seen from forward.

Main
topsail clew

Main course clew

Yard arm

Main
topgallant yard
(from forward)

Yard arm

Main topsail yard
(from forward)

Mainsail yard truss

Mainsail yard slings

Mainsail yard jeers

Yard arm

Mainsail earing

Mainsail yard
(from forward)

Mainmast running
rigging details

Running rigging details, seen from aft.

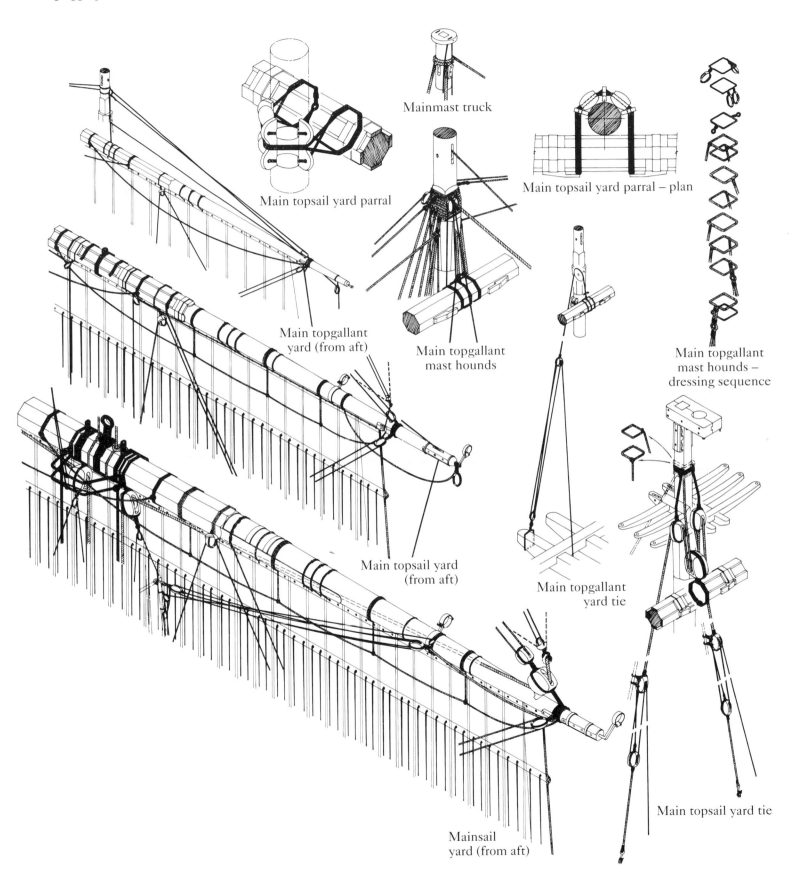

Mainmast truck

Main topsail yard parral

Main topsail yard parral – plan

Main topgallant
yard (from aft)

Main topgallant
mast hounds

Main topgallant
mast hounds –
dressing sequence

Main topsail yard
(from aft)

Main topgallant
yard tie

Main topsail yard tie

Mainsail
yard (from aft)

The mainmast sails. Square sails
provide the main power that
drives the ship forward. Reef
points are carried on the main
course and the topsail as well as
the studding sails. The smaller
topgallants were never reefed,
but simply taken in.

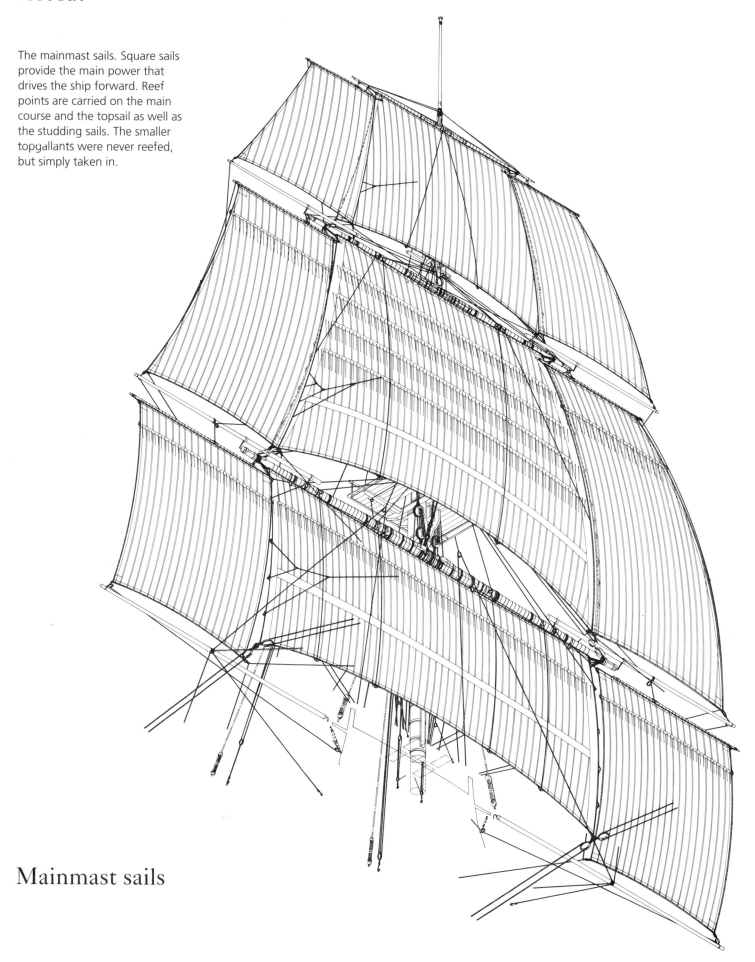

Mainmast sails

The mainmast staysails. From the top: main topgallant staysail, middle staysail, main topmast staysail, main staysail. These fore and aft sails provide some power and may also help to keep the ship's head up to the wind. Opinions varied as to their effectiveness and they were little used by the navy after about 1830.

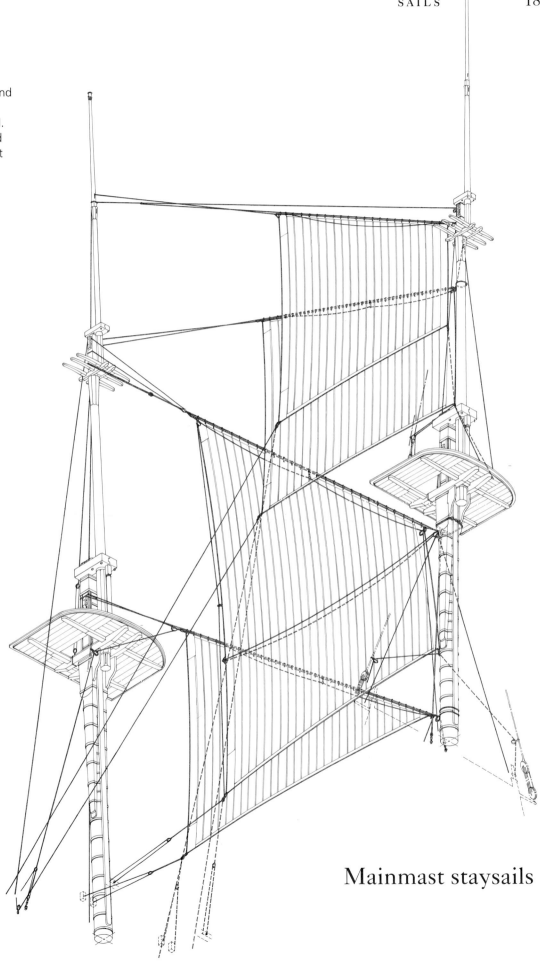

Mainmast staysails

The mainmast

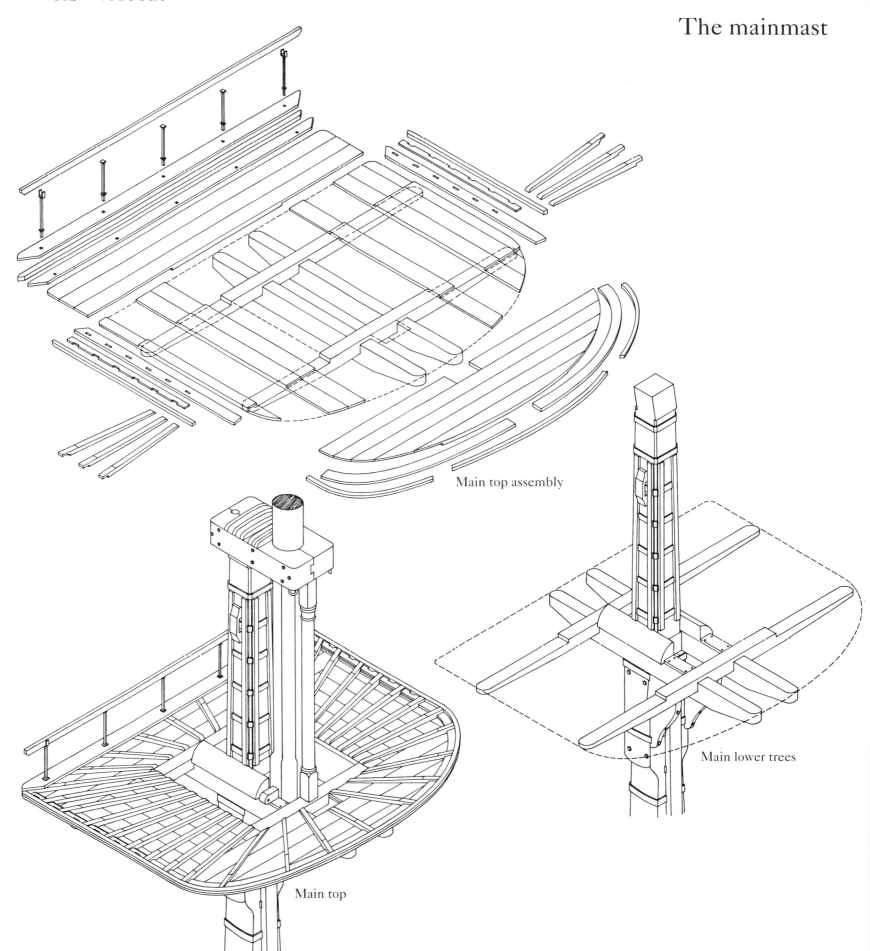

Main top assembly

Main lower trees

Main top

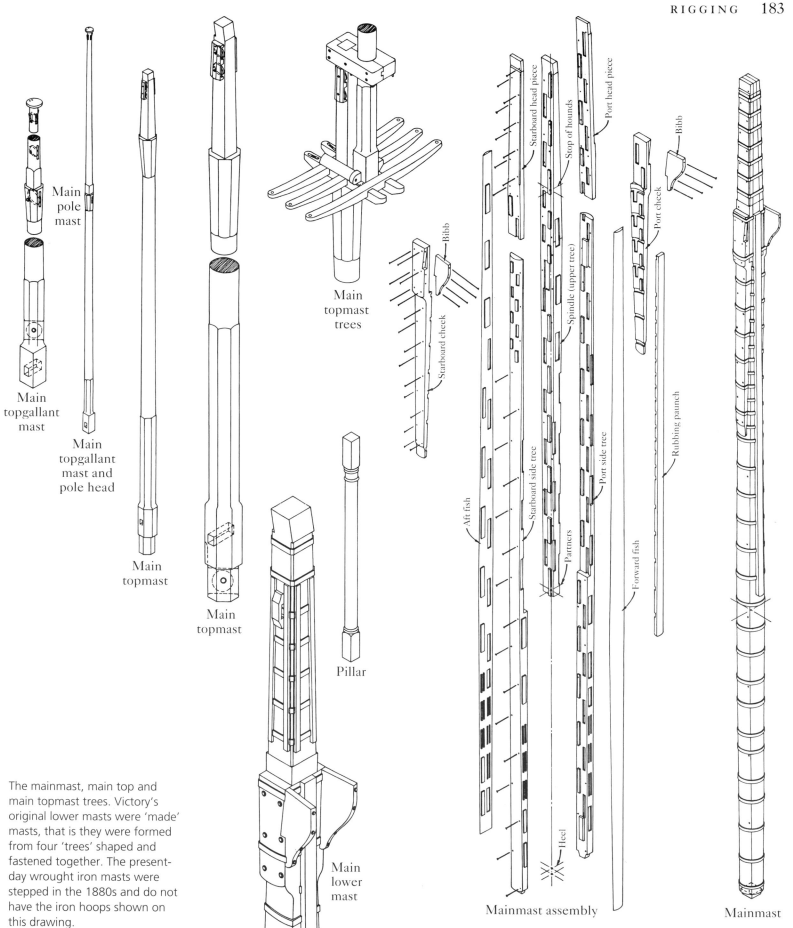

Main pole mast

Main topgallant mast

Main topgallant mast and pole head

Main topmast

Main topmast

Main topmast

Main topmast trees

Main lower mast

Pillar

Starboard check

Bibb

Aft fish

Starboard side tree

Partners

Starboard head piece

Stop of hounds

Spindle (upper tree)

Port side tree

Port head piece

Port cheek

Bibb

Forward fish

Rubbing paunch

Heel

Mainmast assembly

Mainmast

The mainmast, main top and main topmast trees. Victory's original lower masts were 'made' masts, that is they were formed from four 'trees' shaped and fastened together. The present-day wrought iron masts were stepped in the 1880s and do not have the iron hoops shown on this drawing.

The mainmast yards and their assembly.

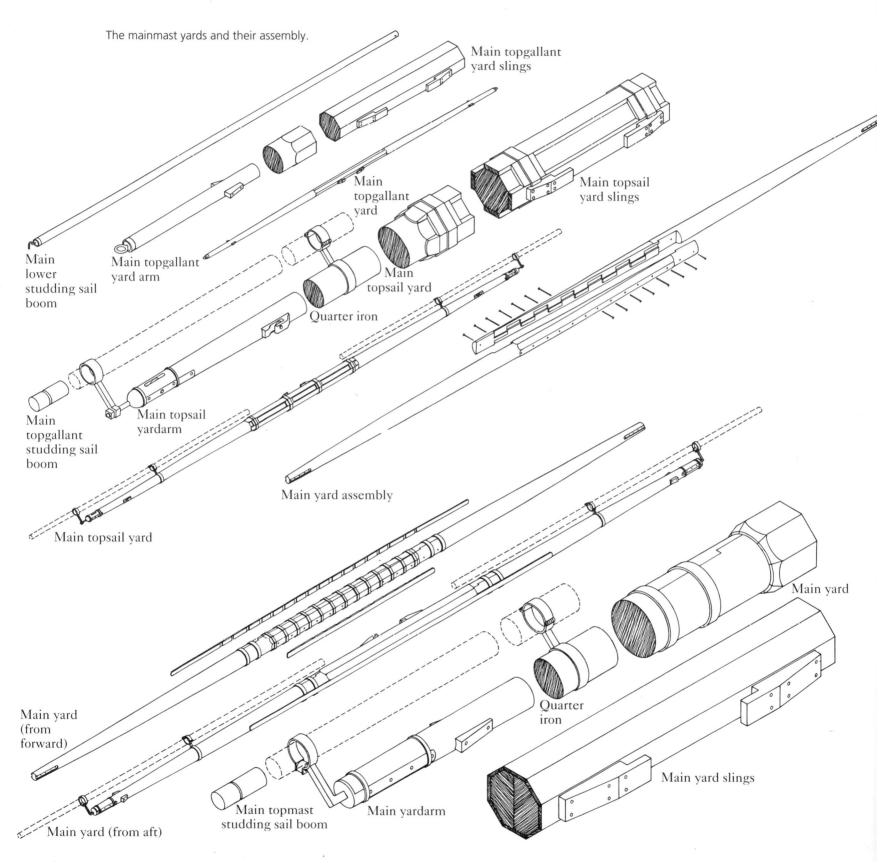

Main topgallant yard slings

Main topsail yard slings

Main topgallant yard

Main topsail yard

Quarter iron

Main lower studding sail boom

Main topgallant yard arm

Main topsail yardarm

Main topgallant studding sail boom

Main topsail yard

Main yard assembly

Main yard (from forward)

Main yard (from aft)

Main topmast studding sail boom

Main yardarm

Quarter iron

Main yard

Main yard slings

Mainmast yards

The mizzen mast standing rigging

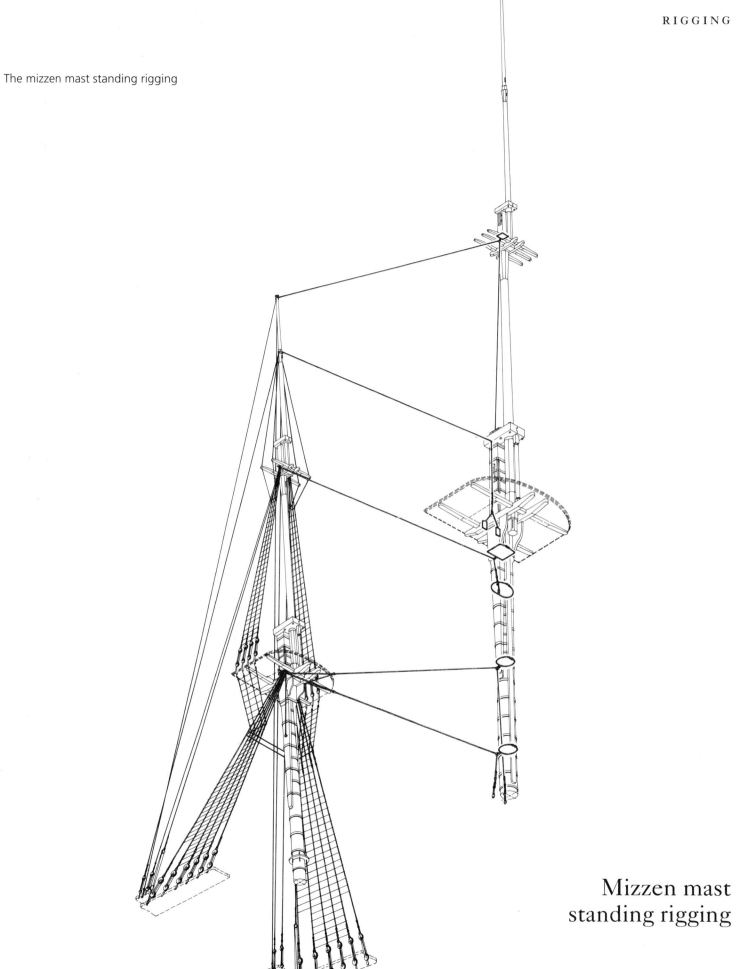

Mizzen mast
standing rigging

The mizzen mast running rigging.

Mizzen mast
running rigging

The mizzen mast sails. The lower yard on the mizzen mast is called the crossjack (cro'jack) yard and, like a boom, its purpose is to spread the foot of the topsail. Setting a square sail to it was an American practice introduced in the nineteenth century but it was never adopted by the Royal Navy

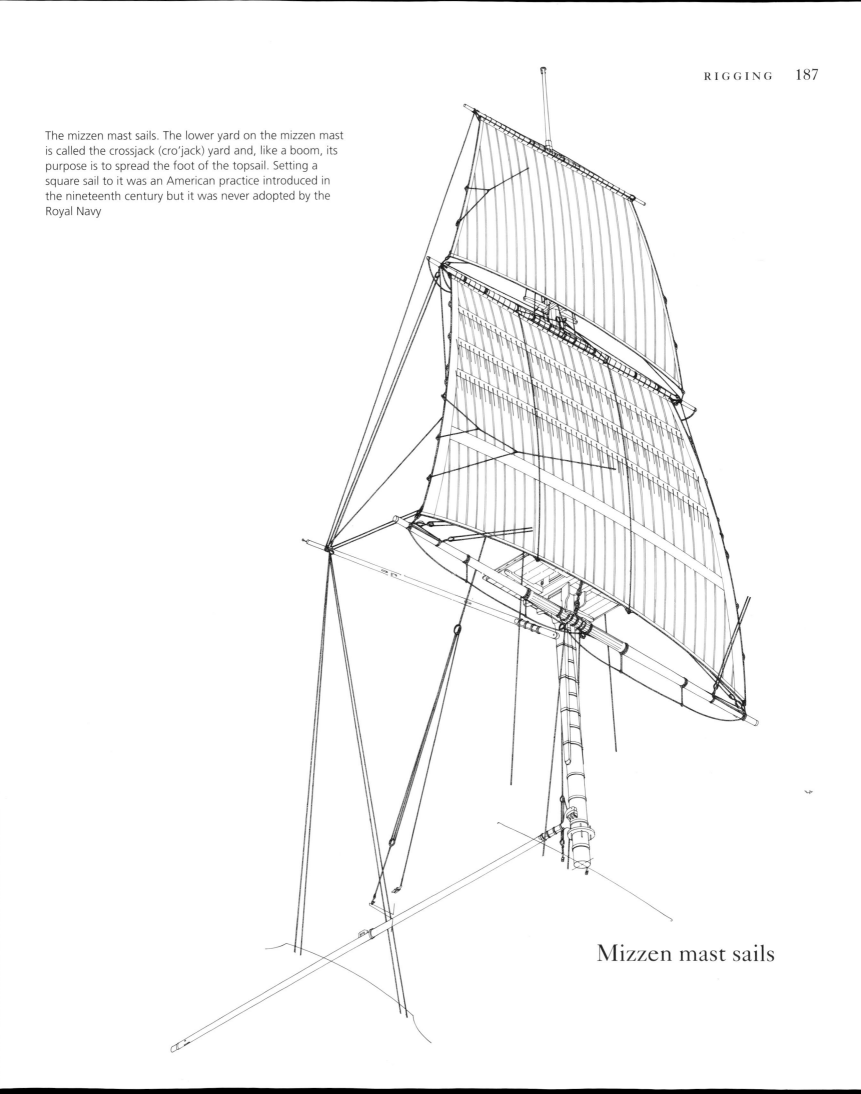

Mizzen mast sails

The mizzen staysails. Because of the enormous leverage they can exert so far aft, the mizzen course, the driver, or the spanker (they are virtually interchangeable) greatly aid the steering and were essential for keeping the ship's head up to the wind.

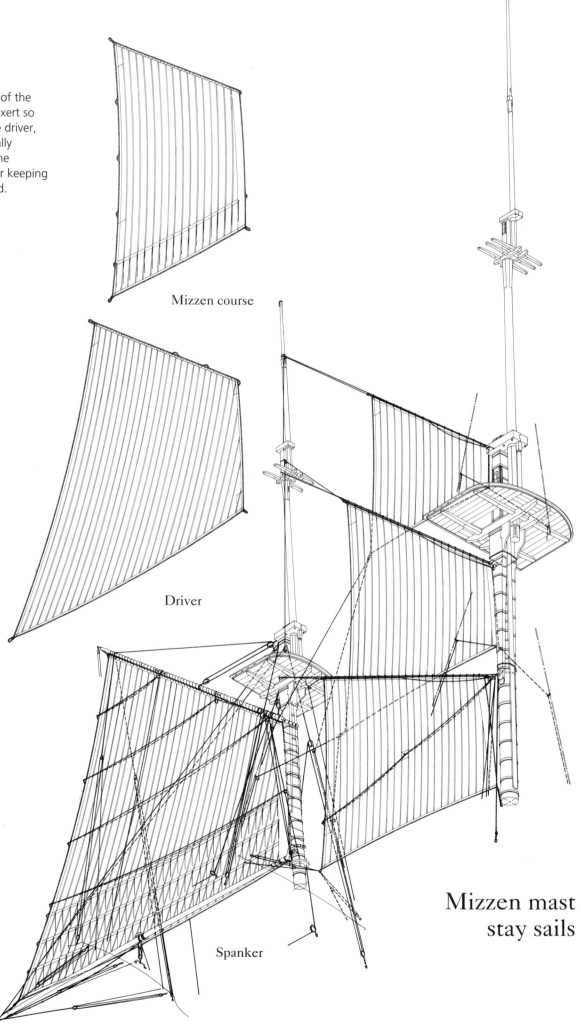

Mizzen course

Driver

Spanker

Mizzen mast
stay sails

The mizzen mast yards. The jaws on the driver gaff and boom
enable them to fit close to the mizzen mast on which they pivot.

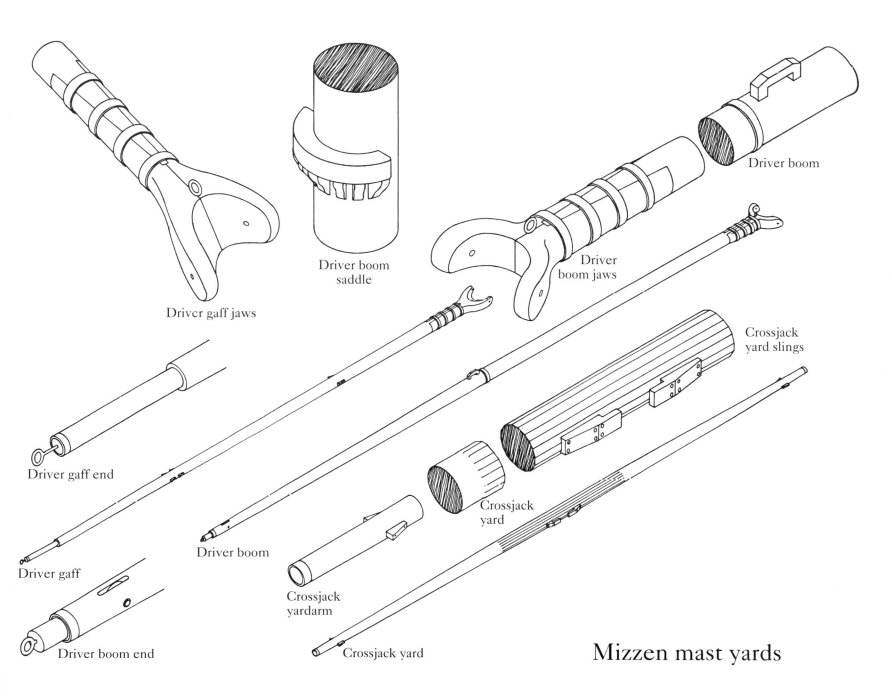

Driver gaff jaws

Driver boom
saddle

Driver boom

Driver
boom jaws

Driver gaff end

Crossjack
yard slings

Driver gaff

Driver boom

Crossjack
yard

Driver boom end

Crossjack
yardarm

Crossjack yard

Mizzen mast yards

The studding sails. The studding sails were fair weather sails set when the wind was abaft the beam. They were bent to light yards that were extensions to the yard proper and had to be sent aloft each time they were used.

Studding sails
rigging

The fore top, fore topmast trees and the fore topgallant mast hounds. In each top, the 'lubber's' hole in the centre accommodated the mast and shrouds. Any seaman who used it to reach the platform rather than going over the outside edge via the futtock shrouds, earned the undying contempt of his shipmates. Indeed, they would have denied him the dignity of the term seaman.

Fore topgallant mast hounds

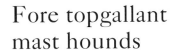

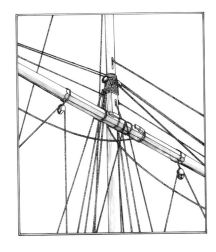

Fore top

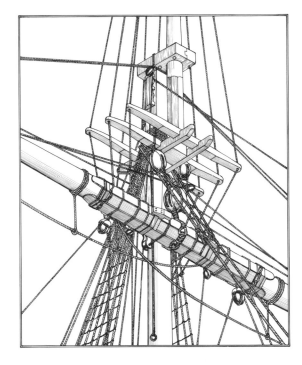

Fore top topmast trees

Anchor handling. The anchor having been weighed, it was hauled to the cathead and then fished (secured in a horizontal position). It was then secured to the cathead by a second point to prepare for sea.

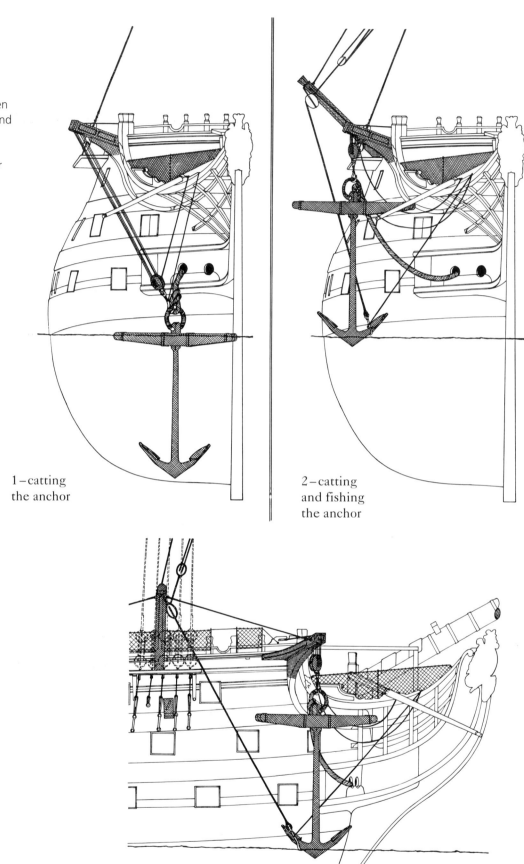

1–catting
the anchor

2–catting
and fishing
the anchor

3–catting
and fishing
the anchor

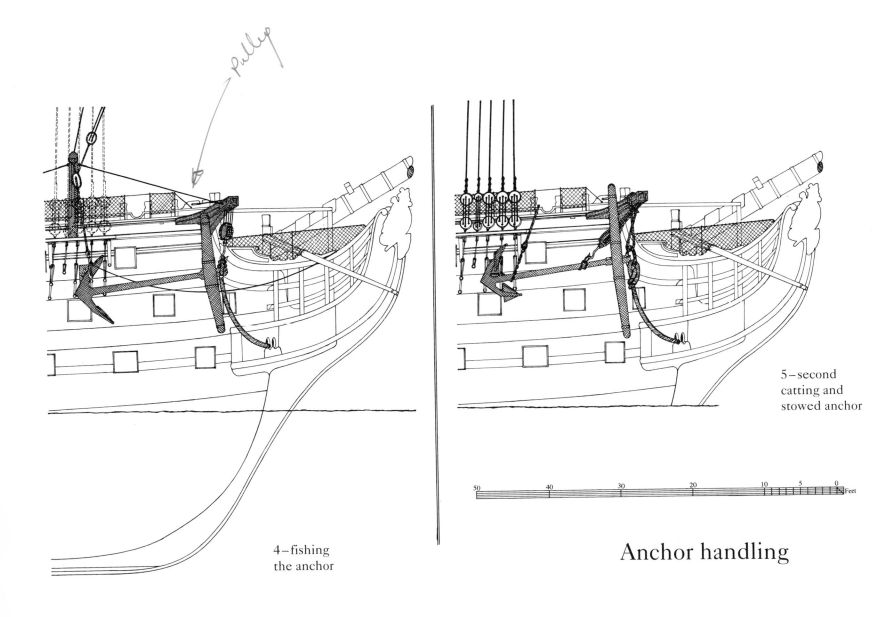

pulley

4−fishing
the anchor

5−second
catting and
stowed anchor

50   40   30   20   10   5   0
Feet

Anchor handling

Anchor handling. The enclosed area right in the bows is the
manger, with low bulkheads to contain the muck and water
scrubbed from the cable as it comes aboard. In the drawing the
starboard anchor is being worked and the cable can be seen nipped
to the traveller.

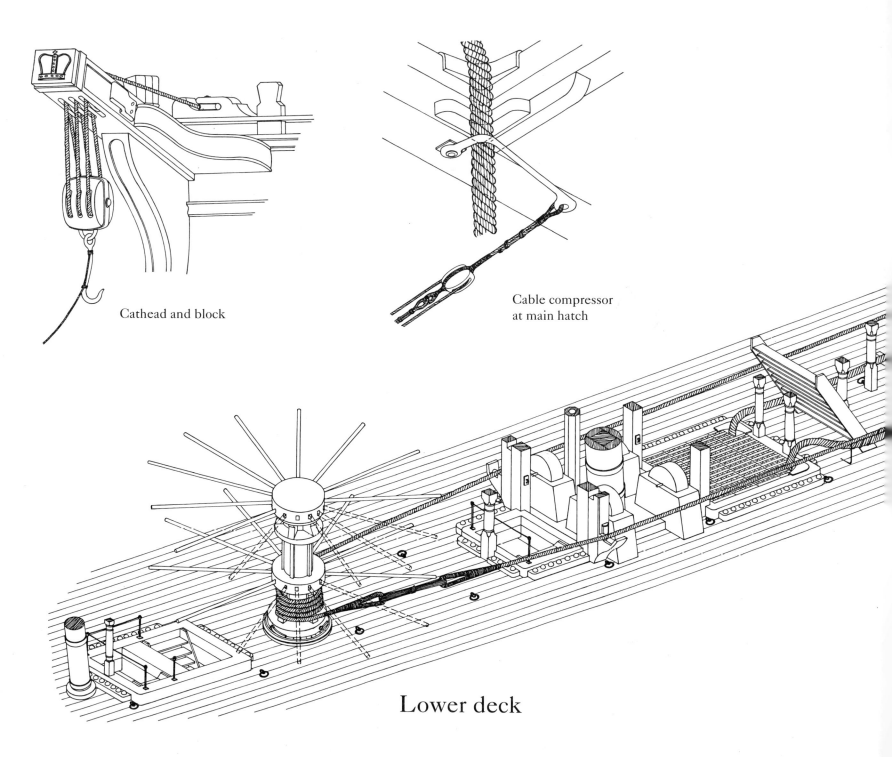

Cathead and block

Cable compressor
at main hatch

Lower deck

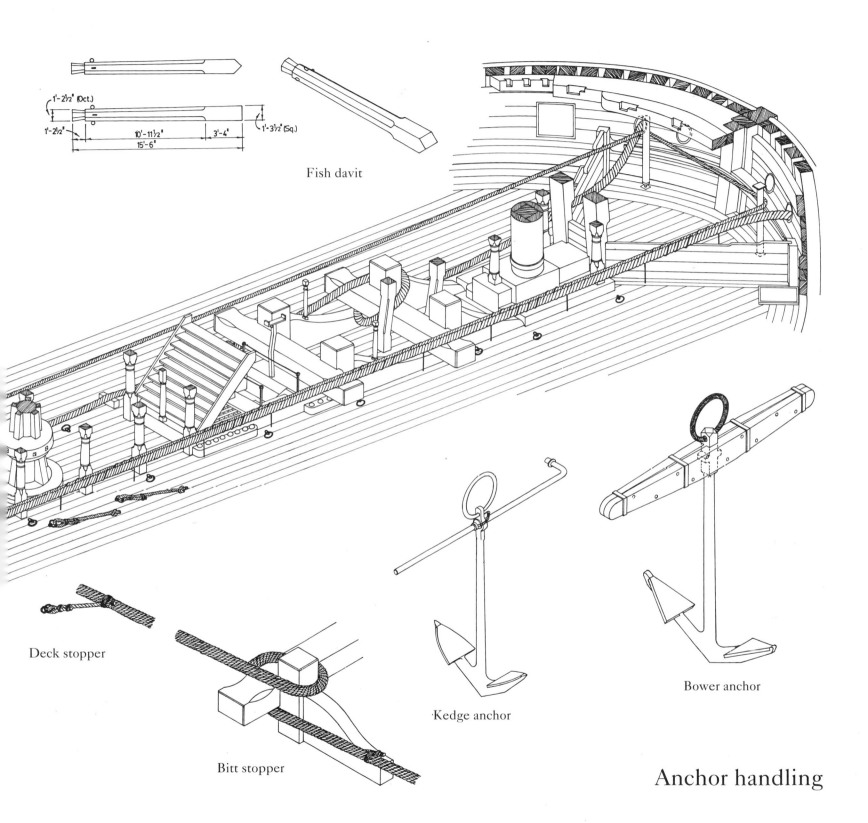

1'-2½" (Oct.)

1'-2½"

10'-11½"

3'-4'

15'-6"

1'-3½" (Sq.)

Fish davit

Deck stopper

Bitt stopper

Kedge anchor

Bower anchor

Anchor handling

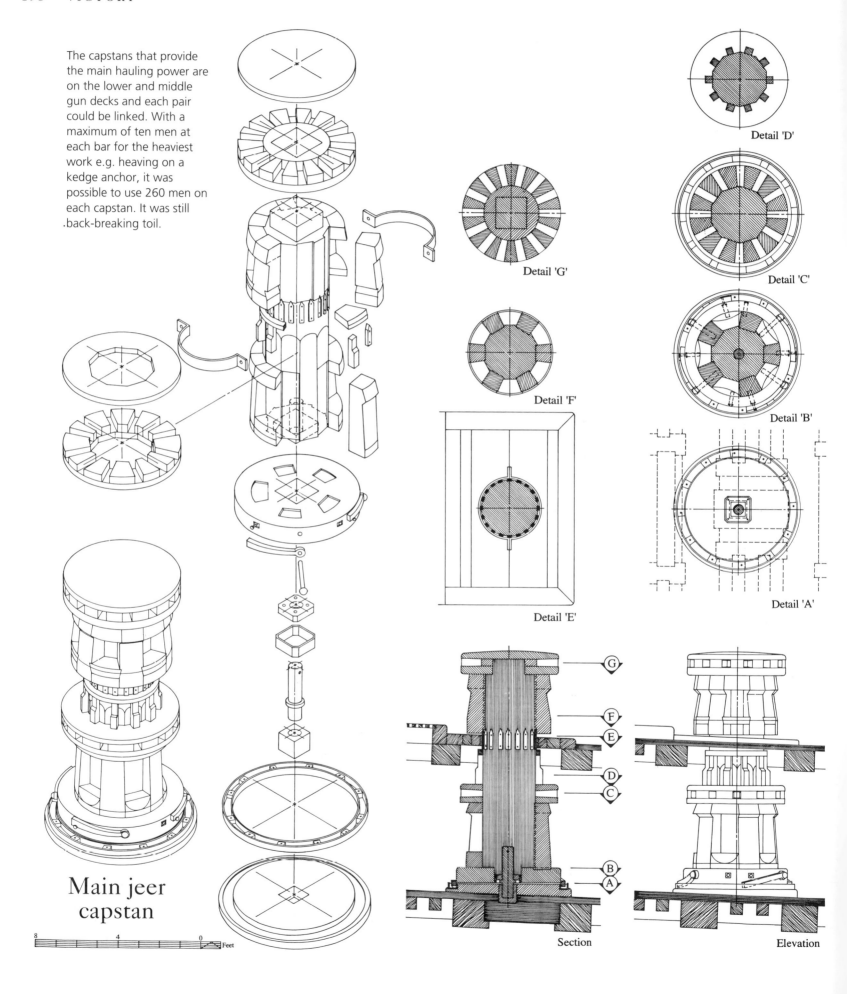

The capstans that provide the main hauling power are on the lower and middle gun decks and each pair could be linked. With a maximum of ten men at each bar for the heaviest work e.g. heaving on a kedge anchor, it was possible to use 260 men on each capstan. It was still back-breaking toil.

Detail 'D'

Detail 'G'

Detail 'C'

Detail 'F'

Detail 'B'

Detail 'E'

Detail 'A'

Main jeer capstan

8   4   0 Feet

Section

Elevation

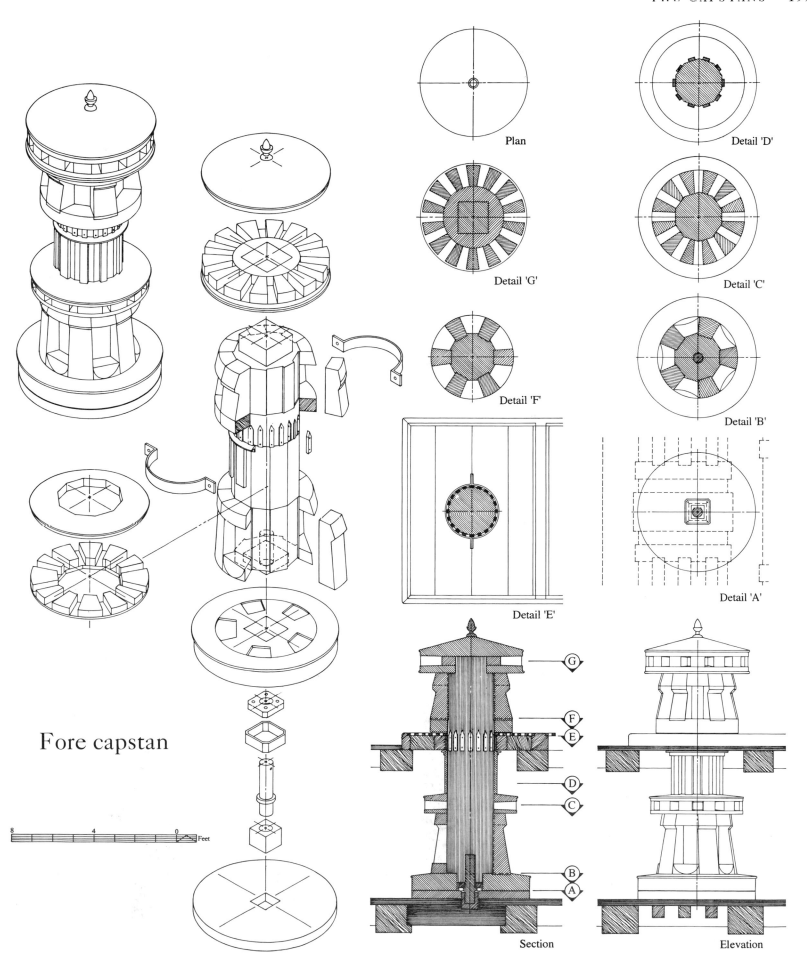

Plan

Detail 'D'

Detail 'G'

Detail 'C'

Detail 'F'

Detail 'B'

Detail 'E'

Detail 'A'

Fore capstan

G

F
E

D

C

B
A

Section

Elevation

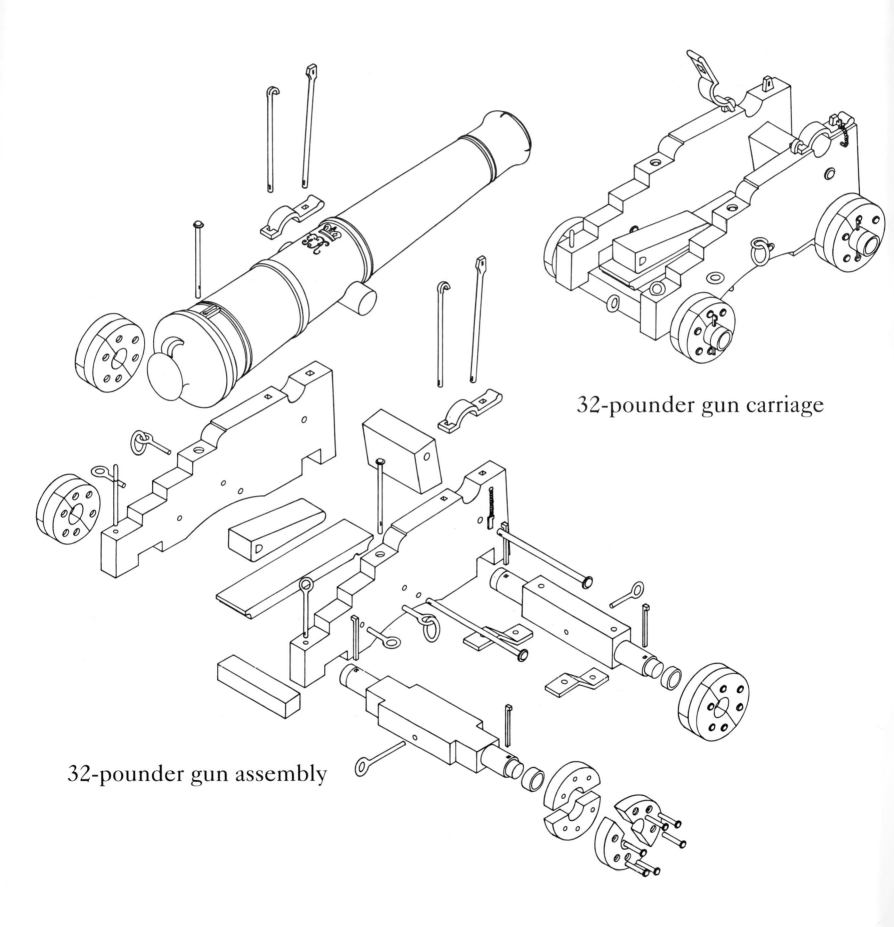

32-pounder gun carriage

32-pounder gun assembly

The 32pdr gun. Guns were provided by The Ordnance Board and each one was tested before being put into service. The sides of the carriages were of oak 5in or 6in thick. The elm trucks (wheels) were 6in wide, the front pair 18in in diameter, the rear pair 16in. The guns needed to be firmly secured for sea but could be made ready for action in seconds. The 32pdr was the heaviest gun on the ship at Trafalgar. All guns were similar in design, although some were given a longer barrel to increase their range, especially the two 'chase' guns that could be mounted in the bows.

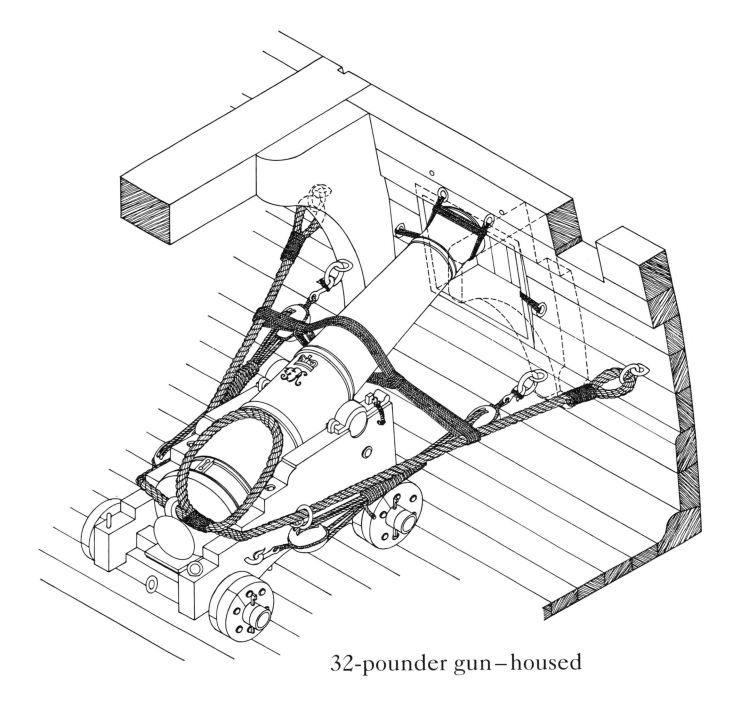

32-pounder gun – housed

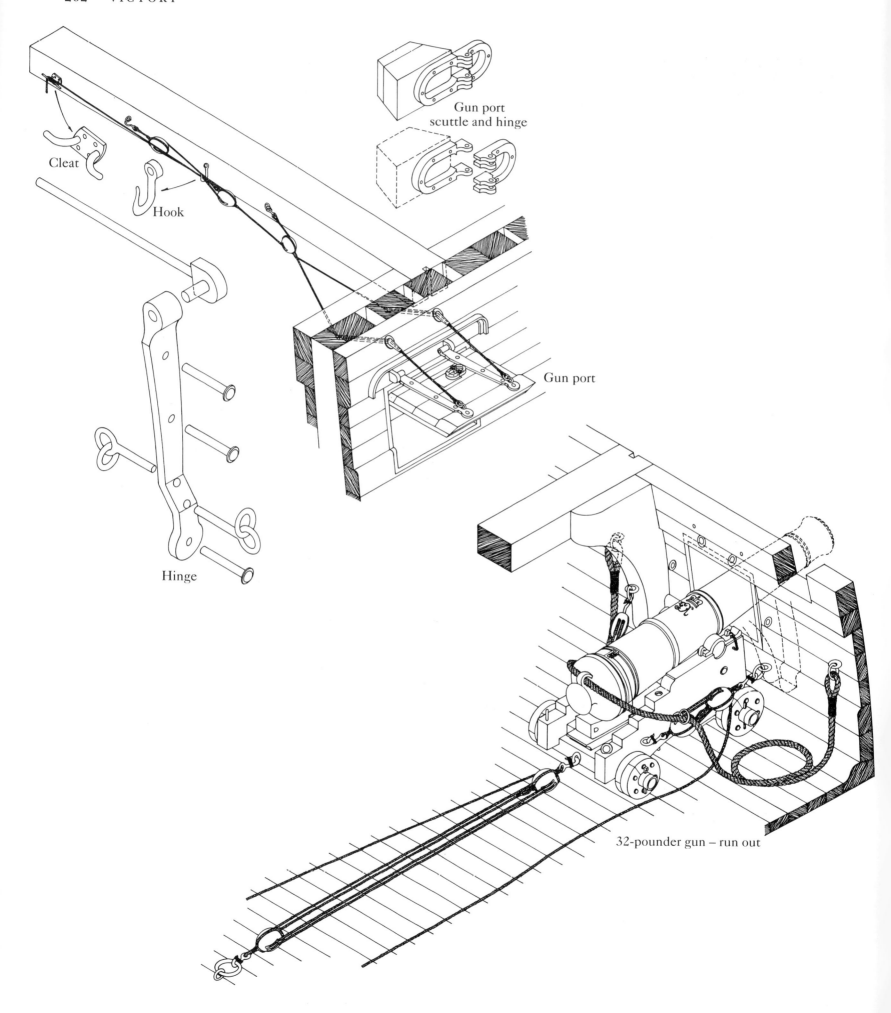

Cleat

Hook

Hinge

Gun port
scuttle and hinge

Gun port

32-pounder gun – run out

The guns and gun ports. Guns were run out (hauled out) to the firing position. The recoil, controlled by the breech rope and the tackles, was used to return it inboard for sponging out and reloading, after which it was run out again using the tackles. A well drilled gun crew could fire a 32pdr at a rate of a little over a minute for each round. The scuttle in the gun port lid allowed some fresh air on to the gun deck when the lids had to be closed

Handling guns

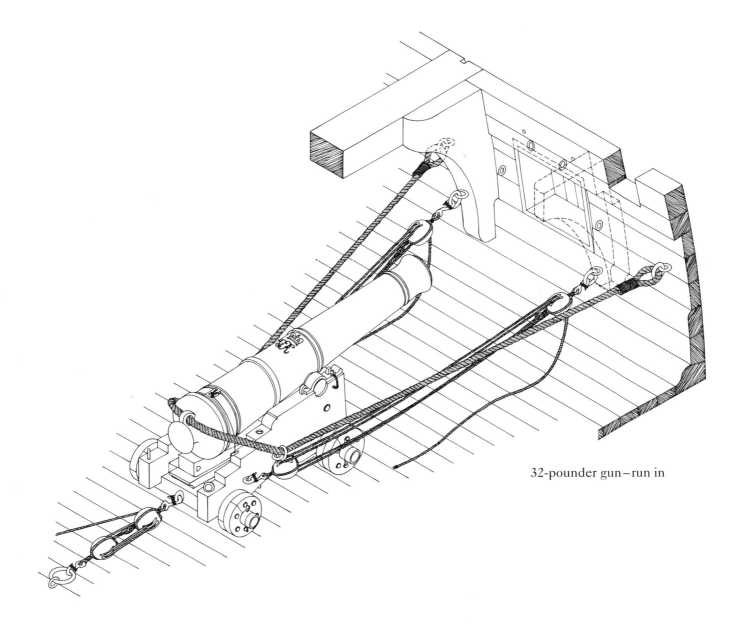

32-pounder gun – run in

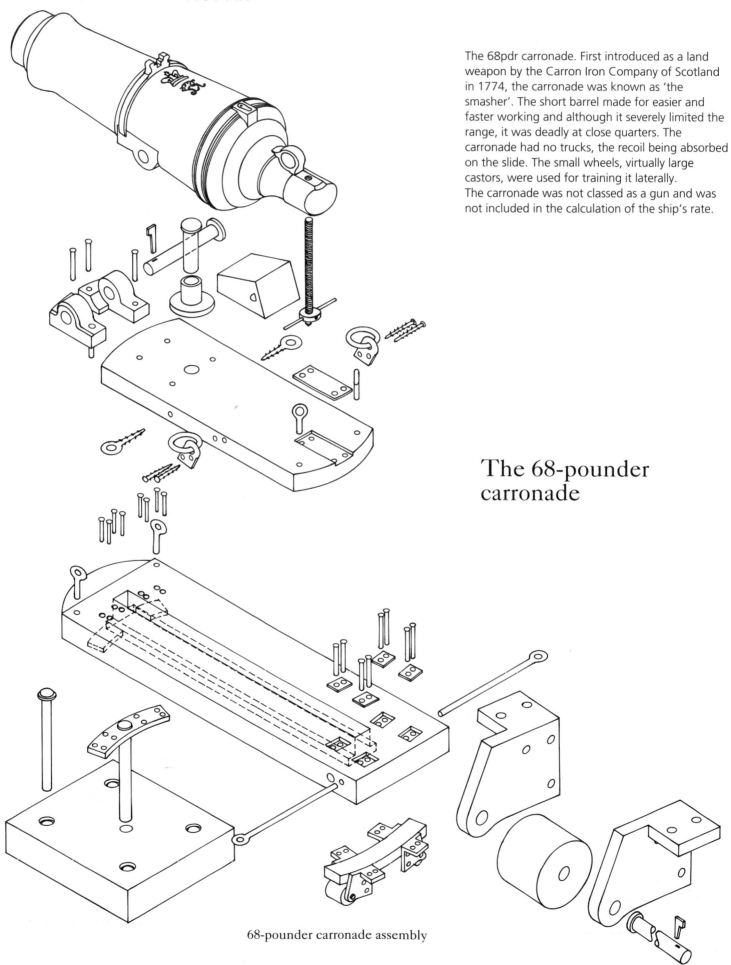

The 68pdr carronade. First introduced as a land weapon by the Carron Iron Company of Scotland in 1774, the carronade was known as 'the smasher'. The short barrel made for easier and faster working and although it severely limited the range, it was deadly at close quarters. The carronade had no trucks, the recoil being absorbed on the slide. The small wheels, virtually large castors, were used for training it laterally.
The carronade was not classed as a gun and was not included in the calculation of the ship's rate.

The 68-pounder carronade

68-pounder carronade assembly

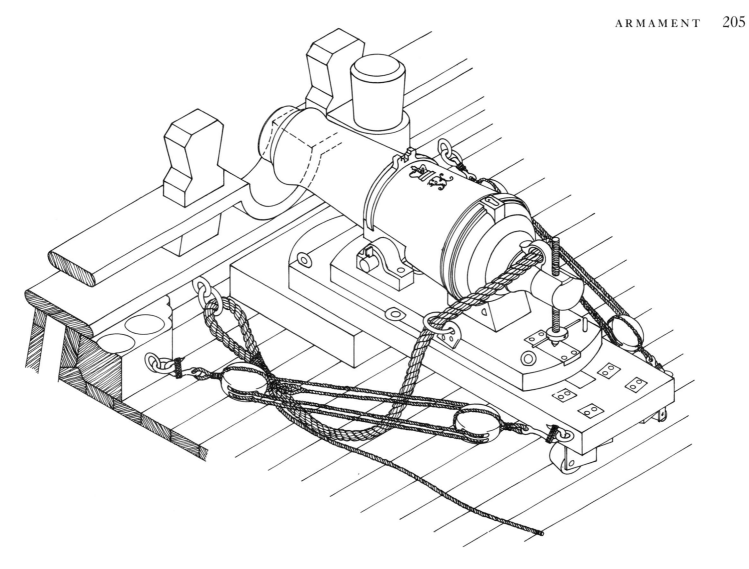

68-pounder carronade

GUN MONOGRAM
H.M.S. VICTORY

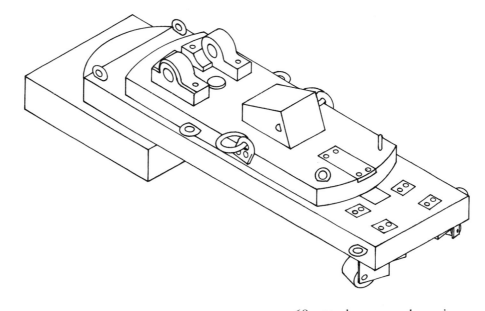

68-pounder carronade carriage

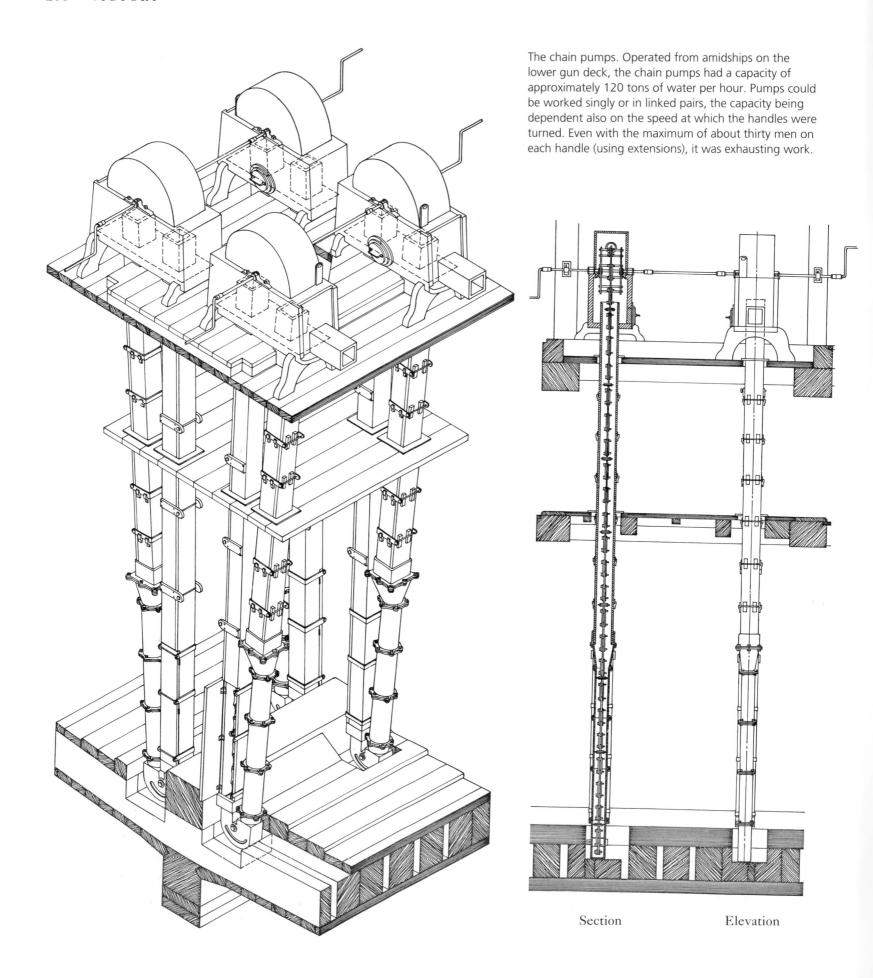

The chain pumps. Operated from amidships on the lower gun deck, the chain pumps had a capacity of approximately 120 tons of water per hour. Pumps could be worked singly or in linked pairs, the capacity being dependent also on the speed at which the handles were turned. Even with the maximum of about thirty men on each handle (using extensions), it was exhausting work.

Section   Elevation

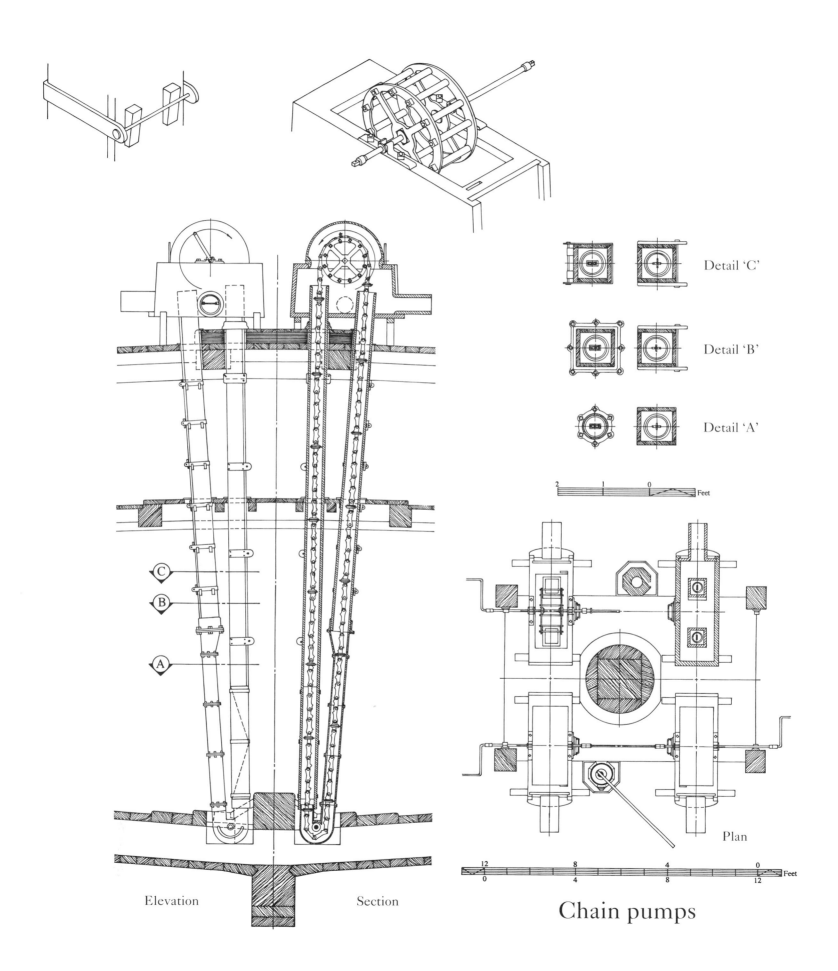

Detail 'C'

Detail 'B'

Detail 'A'

Elevation   Section

Plan

Chain pumps

Steering details. The binnacle, just forward of the wheel, contains two compasses illuminated by the lantern in the centre. The tiller sweeps in an arc just below the gunroom deckhead (see page 134).

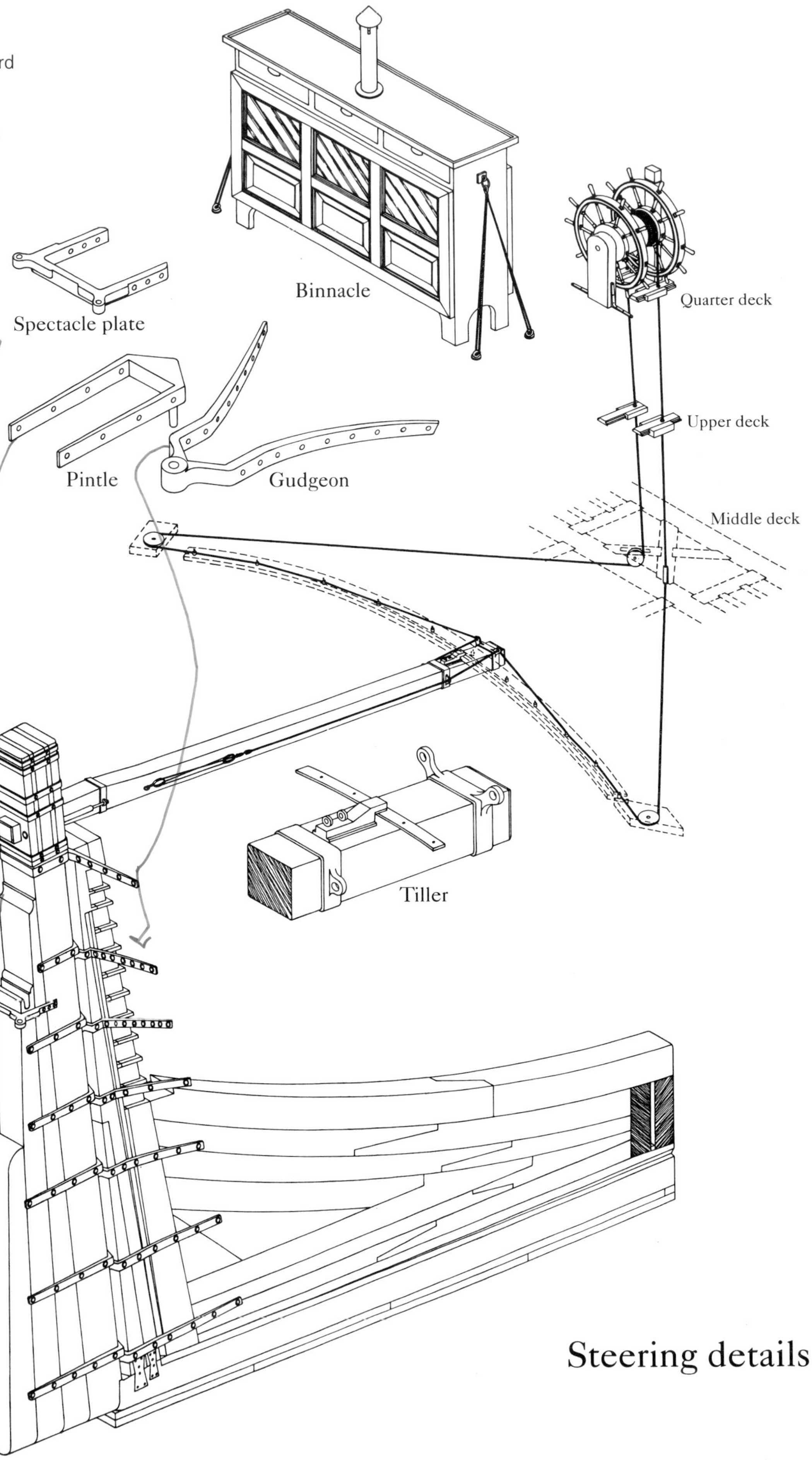

Binnacle

Spectacle plate

Quarter deck

Pintle

Gudgeon

Upper deck

Middle deck

Tiller

Steering details

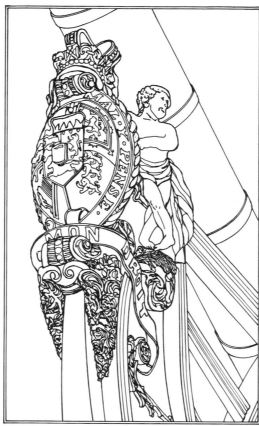

The bow and figurehead. The original double figurehead was huge and complex, 24 ft long, 18 ft wide and 12ft high. It depicted George III, supported by Britannia, triumphant over the four continents: Europe, America, Africa and Asia. It was replaced by a simpler single figurehead in 1803, which was renewed in 1815. This was replaced again in 1989.

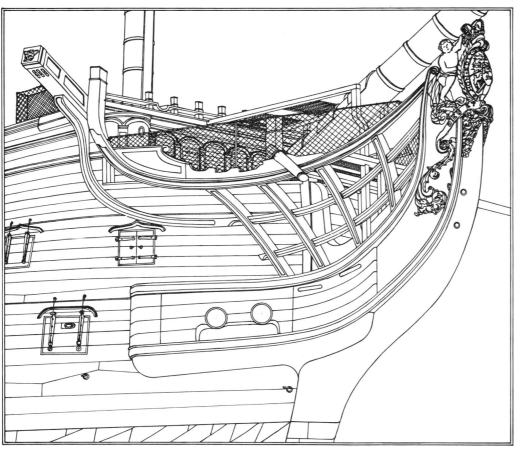

The Figurehead

Victory with the signal "England expects that every man will do his duty", Trafalgar Day 1964. (MoD (N))

GLOSSARY OF TERMS AND ABBREVIATIONS

abaft   behind *eg see* 'quarterdeck'.

Able Seaman   the rating of a fully trained seaman, 'able to hand, reef and steer'. As a general rule it took two years at sea to qualify.

apron   a curved timber fixed abaft the lower part of the stem.

battening   strips of wood from 1in to 3in wide used to delineate a curve or hold in position timber from which support has been removed.

baulk   properly, timber that has only been squared; colloquially used to mean any large piece of timber as a prop.

beak   that part of the ship forward of the forecastle.

beakhead   that part fitted to the forward face of the stem.

beam-end chock   a shaped wooden block fastened to the ship's side and fitted under the end of a beam to provide additional support.

beam shelf   a plank which receives the end of a beam; also called a stringer, shelf piece or clamp.

bearer   any timber that supports another.

bees   pieces of hardwood bolted to the bowsprit, through which the fore topmast stays are reeved; rings or hoops of metal.

bilge   that part of the floor that is nearer horizontal than vertical; the turn of the bilge is where the floor joins the second futtock and begins to turn upwards.

bolt rope   rope sewn to the edges of a sail or canvas to prevent tearing.

boundary   a batten secured to the deck marking the extent of a cabin.

breasthooks   large timbers, shaped like knees, fitted across the stem to strengthen it.

bulkhead   any timber partitioned within the ship, rising from a deck to the deckhead.

butt(s)   the joint where two planks meet end to end; butt end, the end of a plank.

cant frame   a frame or timber that is raised at an oblique angle to the keel.

carlings   square timbers lying fore and aft between the beams.

carpenters' walk   a passage way between the ship's side and cabins or store rooms on the orlop to allow access to the timbers of the hull for inspection or repair.

carronade   a short gun of relatively large calibre for use at close quarters; it takes its name from the Carron Iron Company which successfully developed and produced it.

cathead   a heavy timber projecting through the bow bulwark; its principal use is for raising or lowering the anchor while keeping it clear of the ship's side.

cat tail   the inboard end of the timber forming the cathead.

caulking   oakum or unpicked rope forced into the seams or joins of planks to prevent the ingress of water.

ceiling   planking laid on the floors, ie the timbers forming the bottom of the hold.

chains   an abbreviation of chainwales.

chainwales   heavy planks projecting from the ship's side abreast of, and slightly abaft the masts, bearing the chain plates which take the weight of the shrouds.

channels   a colloquial form of chainwales.

clamps   substantial strakes on which the beams rest.

clench bolts   bolts driven through a drilled hole and secured on the inside by a pin or ring or by the point expanded by hammering.

coaming   raised woodwork on a deck to prevent water entering a hatch or grating.

cockpit   the area on the orlop around the after hatch-way, the place out of the way in relative safety where the wounded were tended.

dead-eye   a circular block of wood, usually elm, fastened to the chain plate with its pair on the end of the relevant shroud. The lacing together of the dead-eyes by means of the laniard through the three holes in each creates a purchase to set up the shrouds. The term 'dead' probably refers to the fact that while it has a similar function to a block, a dead-eye has no sheave and therefore no moving part.

deadwood   the parts of the ship at each end of the keel formed by solid pieces of timber scarphed longitudinally on it.

dump   a short bolt or nail used to hold timber in place while the permanent fastenings are made.

Extraordinary   see Ordinary.

fairing   adjusting the line of plank or timber in order to achieve the desired curve or shape.

fife rail   the rail on each side of the poop and quarterdeck; the rail that encircles a mast and which holds the belaying pins.

fish   a length of hard wood, appropriately shaped and used to strengthen a spar that has sprung; best used in pairs.

floors   the ship's timbers that are set immediately across the keel, the futtocks being a continuation upwards of the floors.

forefoot   the foremost part of the keel, or a timber which terminates the keel at its forward end, forming a rest for the lower end of the stem.

forepeak   the narrowest part of the hold close to the bows.

frame timbers   the floor timbers, futtocks and top timbers which are fitted at right angles to the keel.

futtocks   the separate pieces of timber that make up a frame.

gammoning   a particular type of lashing used to bind the inboard section of the bowsprit to the stem.

hammock cranes   the metal stanchions supporting the hammock netting.

hogging   the arching upwards of the keel and keelson consequent upon their being strained.

hold   in a man of war the space below the orlop, used for the stowage of ballast and stores of all kinds.

hull   the body or shell of a ship.

inner lining   planking on the inboard side of the frames.

jalousie   a louvred panel admitting air but not rain.

keelson   an internal keel binding the floor timbers to the keel proper and acting as a strong back to it.

knee   a piece of timber that has grown so that the grain follows a right angle thus having greater strength than one so cut to shape. It is used as a bracket. A cast knee is one set at an angle; a hanging knee is set vertically; a lodging knee is set horizontally; a standard knee is inverted and fitted on top instead of below that which it supports.

knightheads   large timbers, one each side of the stem, supporting the bowsprit which is fixed between them.

knot   a knot is a nautical mile (6080 ft) per hour.

landsman   the lowest rating with little or no experience at sea.

ledges   timber used in framing the decks and let into the carlings athwartships.

limber holes   grooves cut through the floors on each side of the keelson allowing free passage of water to the pumps.

light-compartment   a light room; the space partitioned off from the magazine in which a lantern could safely be lighted giving light to the magazine through a double-glazed window.

maintenance book   the record of maintenance carried out.

maintenance schedule   the schedule of maintenance to be carried out regularly.

manger   small area on the lower gundeck in the bows, extending beyond the hawse holes on each side. The strong coaming surrounding it contains any water shipped through the hawse holes when the cables are bent on, or produced by scrubbing the cable as it comes aboard when weighing. The manger is drained by large scuppers.

marines' walk   the gangboard running from the top of the beakhead bulkhead to the bowsprit.

margin plank   the edge plank of any decking or platform.

mast coat   a conical canvas collar fitted over the wedges round the mast at deck level to prevent water running down the mast.

mast step   a large block of timber fixed upon the keelson in which the heel of the lower mast rests.

maul   a heavy hammer used by shipwrights; the head is faced at one end and pointed at the other. When the latter is specifically needed the hammer is sometimes referred to as a pin-maul.

Muntz metal   a soft alloy of copper and zinc.

oakum   used for caulking and obtained by untwisting and picking apart the strands and fibres of old rope.

Ordinary   a term originating in the accounts of the Treasurer of the Navy to indicate charges borne on the ordinary or normal expenses granted for all costs that remained constant, such as wages for permanent employees and the maintenance of buildings and dockyard installations and the provision of services to vessels in reserve. From the eighteenth century at least such ships were referred to as in 'Ordinary'. Their upper masts and rigging had been struck and laid in store and each major warship was in the hands of its standing officers: boatswain, gunner, carpenter, purser and cook. In the case of smaller vessels the standing officers were responsible for several of them. Sea-service – a much greater expense per vessel – was counted an Extra-ordinary charge.

Ordinary Seaman   a reasonably competent but not complete seaman. A landsman would normally be so rated after a year at sea. See also Able Seaman.

orlop   the lowest deck; immediately above the hold, it is below the water-line.

partners   a framework of thick plank fitted round the various holes in the decks through which capstans, and particularly masts, pass.

pay   to pour hot pitch on to a caulked seam to seal it.

plank   thick boards used to cover the outside and inside of the frames and for decking. Plank is properly at least 18ft long, 1½-4ins thick and 9-10ins broad. When of smaller dimensions it is called board or deal and is frequently fir or pine.

plank-sheer   the planking covering the heads of the top-timbers.

poop   the aftermost and highest deck.

Press   a body of seamen usually commanded by a lieutenant, empowered to take seamen and compel them to serve in the Navy.

quarterdeck   the upper deck abaft the mainmast.

quarter-gallery   balcony, often glazed, near the stern on each side of a major warship.

ratlines   cord lines running horizontally across the shrouds at 15in-16in intervals, forming a type of ladder up the mast.

rattan   a cane commonly carried by the boatswain, properly from the climbing palm *Calamus* of the East Indies.

rattling-down   to set the ratlines on the shrouds.

rase mark   figures or letters scored into timber with a rasing knife for purposes of indentification.

ribbands   long fir battens fastened temporarily on the outside of frame timbers to hold them in place.

Roberts bracket   a wrought-iron bracket introduced at the beginning of the nineteenth century; used to strengthen a joint.

scarph   the lengthways joining of two pieces of timber but maintaining the same thickness by sloping or stepping the overlap. A snaped scarph is bevelled.

scrieve the marking, by gouging, of the lines of the forward or after body of the ship on a specifically prepared board so that, for example, the outside shape of a futtock may be correctly worked.

scuttle an opening in the ship's side, bulkhead or deck (when it is a small hatchway), usually for ventilation.

Seraya a tropical hardwood.

sheer the longitudinal curve of a ship's deck or sides.

shores props.

shot garlands racks on the deck providing ready use shot near the guns; 'garlands' perhaps because in some cases they form the surround of hatches.

skid beams beams across the opening forward of the quarterdeck, on which the ship's boats rest.

snape the bevel or angle at the end of a timber to fay upon an inclined plane

sole a piece of timber attached, often as a sacrificial member as on the bottom of the rudder or the keel.

spirketting the inboard strakes of planking between the waterway and the lower sill of the gunports.

standards columns used to support the centre of a beam.

stations for ease of reference the frames are numbered from bow to stern.

stealers planks in which the butt nearest the rabbet is narrowed in strakes that end short of the stem or sternpost; they serve to reduce the number of strakes as the hull's girth becomes smaller.

stemson a heavy timber scarphed at its lower end into the keelson; fitted to the after side of the apron with which it forms a reinforcement to the stem as the keelson to the keel.

sternson a large knee, the lower arm scarphed into the after end of the keelson; the upper arm fitted into the throat of the transoms.

strake a continuous line of planking.

stringers inboard strakes on which the beam ends rest; also called shelf-pieces.

taffrail the rail or bulwark at the upper part of the stern.

timber a general term for large pieces of wood, but also a technical term, often in the plural, for a frame or frames.

transoms the heavy beams running athwartship, bolted to the sternpost.

treenails cylindrical hardwood pegs, usually of oak or beech used to join large timbers or fasten planks.

tuck the aftermost part of the hull where the ends of the bottom planks terminate at the tuck rail.

waist the upper deck between the fore and main hatchways.

wale a line of strong planks fastened to the timbers and extending along the outside of the hull; the main wale in a First Rate consisted of four strakes each 15in wide and 10in thick.

wardroom the officers' mess cabin at the after end of the main deck; in a First Rate, on the middle gundeck.

waterway the heavy planking forming the edge of deck next to the ship's side, hollowed to form a channel to carry away water.

woolding several turns of tightly wound rope round a made mast to strengthen it; replaced by wrought-iron bands following an Admiralty Order in 1800.

SOURCES

Primary

Public Record Office; ADM 1/27660; ADM 106/2507-9.

HM Naval Base, Portsmouth; HMS *Victory* Progress Reports 1955-1998.

National Maritime Museum; CAD/A13 f108b verso.

Royal Naval Museum; 14/84

Secondary

Abell W, *The Shipwright's Trade* (Cambridge, 1948)

Albion R G, *Forests and Sea Power*, Harvard Econ. Studies 29 (Cambridge, Mass. 1926)

Bennett Geoffrey, *The Battle of Trafalgar* (London, 1977)

Broadley H M and Bartelot R G, *Nelson's Hardy* (London, 1909)

Bugler A R, *HMS Victory, Building Restoration and Repair* (London, 1966)

Callender Geoffrey, *The Story of HMS Victory* (London, 1914)

Clowes W L *et al*, *The Royal Navy* vols 4–7 (London, 1899-1903)

Collingwood G L Newnham, *Correspondence and Memoirs of Vice Admiral Lord Collingwood* (London 1837)

Falconer R, *Marine Dictionary* (London, 1789)

Fenwick, Kenneth, *HMS Victory* (London, 1959)

Fincham J, *A History of Naval Architecture* (London, 1851)

Harland John, *Seamanship in the Age of Sail* (London, 1984)

Laughton L G Carr, 'HMS *Victory* Report for the VTC', *The Mariner's Mirror* vol 10 (London, 1924)

Lavery Brian, *The Ship of the Line*, 2 vols (London, 1983–84)

Lavery Brian, *Shipboard Life and Organisation 1731–1815*, Navy Records Society 138 (London 1998)

Lees, James, *The Masting and Rigging of English Ships of War 1626–1860* (London, 1979)

Lever, Darcy, *The Young Sea Officer's Sheet Anchor* (London 1808; reprinted Boston 1930)

Lewis Michael, *The Navy of Britain* (London, 1948)

McGowan Alan, *The Jacobean Commission of Enquiry 1608 and 1618*, Navy Records Society 116 (London, 1971)

McGowan Alan, *The Century Before Steam* (London 1980)

McGowan Alan, "Further Papers from the Commission of Enquiry 1608", *The Naval Miscellany*, NRS 125 (London, 1984)

McKay John, *The 100-gun Ship Victory* (London, 1987)

Munday John, *Naval Cannon* (London, 1987)

Roger N A M, *The Wooden World* (London, 1986)

Smyth W H, *The Sailor's Word Book* (London, 1867)

Steel David, *The Elements and Practice of Naval Architecture*, (London 1805; reprinted London 1977)

Steel David, *Rigging and Seamanship* 2 vols (London 1794; reprinted London 1978)

Whitlock Peter, "Jottings from HMS *Victory*" *The Mariner's Mirror* vol 62 (London, 1976)

INDEX